PUBLIC EDUCATION

D1570949

PUBLIC EDUCATION

THE "FINAL SOLUTION" IN THE CONQUEST OF AMERICA'S IDEALS

JEFFREY WICK

WinePressPublishing
Great Books, Defined.

WinePress Publishing (PO Box 428, Enumclaw, WA 98022) functions only as book publisher. As such, the ultimate design, content, editorial accuracy, and views expressed or implied in this work are those of the author.

ISBN 13: 978-1-4141-2032-4
ISBN 10: 1-4141-2032-X
Library of Congress Catalog Card Number: 2011921212

This book is dedicated to our nation's founders, chosen by God to do His service, and to those thereafter who have continued to fight and sacrifice their lives to preserve our freedom.

CONTENTS

ACKNOWLEDGMENTS

MANY PEOPLE DESERVE thanks for helping me complete this work:

Cathy Burke, an esteemed colleague and outstanding teacher—with whom I spent many hours debating and discussing education, faith, politics, and American culture—read my rough draft and provided helpful feedback.

Col. Robert "F" Pyner, a tremendous educator who offers motivation and encouragement, steady admiration for our awesome nation, and confidence in conservative ideals, provided feedback while reading the rough draft.

Pastor Kevin James of Salem Baptist Church, who provides guidance by being a strong example of living the Christian life, took time out of his busy schedule to read and respond to my rough draft.

Dr. Tony Dapena, an invaluable friend and consummate man of faith, spent the most time supporting my efforts in writing this book by proofreading, assisting with editing, and being an earpiece and source of guidance. Also special thanks for his instrumental role in my growing in the Christian faith, studying the Bible, and building my relationship with God and Christ.

I also thank Kory, Cricket, and Dwain Smith, Mike and Dorislyn Palmer, Karri Zellerino, David "Hooter" and Jennifer Burruss, Jessica Wick, Bobby Plaskett, Rob Mercer, and Glenda Rinaldi for their unwavering friendship and encouragement.

My parents, John and Barbara Wick, deserve immeasurable credit for their upbringing, support, encouragement, moral guidance, work ethic, sacrifice, and love they have shown throughout my life. Thanks to my brother, Jason, for demonstrating the will never to give up or quit in the pursuit of becoming a champion; and to my sister, Janine, for exhibiting the ability—and providing the inspiration—to overcome any obstacle one may confront.

Finally, I wish to thank our Father, the Creator, for His generous mercy, kindness, counsel, and patience; as well as the ability, family, and country with which He has blessed me; and His Son and our Savior Jesus Christ, for His free gift of salvation He offered by sacrificing His life for the world.

INTRODUCTION

A CONCERTED ATTACK on three cornerstones of American greatness has damaged the foundation of American culture and society. This attack began during the 1920s with the philosophy affecting the development of the modern public school system (led by John Dewey, known as the "Architect of Modern Education"), during the 1930s with Mr. Franklin Roosevelt's socialist New Deal program, and since the hippie revolution spawned during the 1960s. The goal of this assault is to annihilate these cornerstones and fundamentally transform our society. These attacks have been well planned, coordinated, aggressive, and effectively executed. Though the offensives have negatively impacted our awesome nation, they have thus far fallen short of completely destroying this triad and fully changing our culture.

Nevertheless, incessant attacks continue. The perpetrators obsessively strive toward their goal of morphing the United States into a socialist, dependency-based, religiously benign country controlled by a dictatorial, oppressive ruling party. Part of their objective is to promote an international governmental authority over U.S. sovereignty. Achieving this goal would be an important step toward allowing world leaders to create a one-world government that works cohesively to regulate people throughout the world.

The public education system is the mechanism through which socialist-leaning liberals can topple America's democracy and erect in its place a tyrannical government that controls its dependent populace, which is carefully trained to rely on government through this education system. Once America is conquered, the conditions are ideal for the aforementioned one-world government to control all people. Because the United States serves as the primary sower of freedom and democracy throughout the world, the dissolution of our form of government would be the first domino to fall and cause all other free nations to collapse.

Let us consider U.S. interests. When we review statements Supreme Court justices have made, we cannot help but be alarmed by those who encourage the United States to follow the lead of international legislative bodies instead of administering its own authority. Justice Ruth Bader Ginsburg, for example, complained that the United States Supreme Court fails to reference international law in its decisions frequently enough.[1] In 2003 Justice Anthony Kennedy promoted the European Court on Human Rights' protection of the rights of homosexuals—rights that counter our traditional Christian heritage and morals.[2]

In 2002 Justice Sandra Day O'Connor said the United States Supreme Court needs to learn from other jurisdictions (meaning other nations), look at decisions of foreign constitutional courts, and reference international law in executing its duties. "The international community should at times constitute pervasive authority in American courts," she said.[3] The word *pervasive* means spreading throughout every part; therefore, Justice O'Connor advocates the penetration of international law into every aspect of our culture. Liberals outside the judicial branch—from college professors to journalists, from politicians to presidents of the United States—cherish this attitude.

The greatness of the United States comes not from the failed, perverse principles of foreign nations, from which the millions who immigrated to America fled, but from the foundational principles established by the Founding Fathers and colonists who settled this awesome nation. Certain people throughout the world would like nothing better than for America to put asunder its principles of freedom based on Christianity and return to an aristocratic, restrictive, oppressive, dependent way of life.

Throughout this book I use several terms to describe participants in this bout against our American way of life, including relativist, secularist, statist, elitist, radical environmentalist, socialist-leaning liberal, socialist, and liberal. All these interchangeable terms describe those who are sickened by the principles that made America great, including, but not limited to, freedom, faith in Providence, rugged individualism (succeeding without governmental intervention; self-reliance), sacrifice, and the God-given unalienable rights of "Life, Liberty, and the pursuit of Happiness." Due to their abhorrence of these precepts, they have declared and engaged in a war against them, and they will not rest until they have won. This victory will occur when America is transformed into a socialist nation with a small, powerful government that lords over its dependent subjects. Again, the public school system encourages this dependency, and in the following chapters we will discuss its contribution in detail.

CHAPTER 1

THREE AMERICAN CORNERSTONES BESIEGED

CHRISTIAN FAITH

ONE OF THE three cornerstones against which this concurrent offensive is being waged is religious faith in general and the Christian faith in particular. To establish a sense of dependency on government, one must first discredit religion and God's authority over others—in the process revising our nation's Christian foundation. Patrick Henry eloquently stated, "It cannot be emphasized too strongly or too often that this great nation was founded, not by religionists, but by Christians, not on religions, but on the Gospel of Jesus Christ!"[1] Citizens can serve only one master. If they are communing with God, attending church, reading the Bible, and engaging in religious activities to receive counsel, encouragement, and strength, they are not leaning on government for aid or guidance. Since liberals do not believe in moral absolutes, a topic we will discuss later in this book, they must reject an authoritarian, righteous God who expects people to behave in a certain and proper way.

In the mind of statists (those who believe in the supremacy of the state over the individual), only they can provide for the needs of the pathetic, helpless commoner. This is their perception of the common citizen—he is weak, poor, helpless, and stupid. Thus citizens cannot survive without the assistance, generosity, direction, and wisdom the messianic statists provide. Since relativists worship themselves and the environment—Mother Earth—in which they live, they see themselves as omnipotent and omniscient; they are your saviors. They just need to convince you of this truth so you will only open your eyes and see them in such a light. Therefore, they must attack your faith, criticize it, disparage God as a figment of your imagination, parody your faith, and portray it as foolishness. Once the statists succeed in this endeavor, they, as gods, slip into the resultant void left behind.

God and faith have always been questioned in all generations and cultures. This is nothing new, nor do many consider such questioning inappropriate. Yet it is one thing to question faith; it is quite another to intentionally seek to invalidate faith and extricate it from society.

America's Christian Foundation

When we focus on America, we notice that it was founded on Christian principles from its birth, and many examples illustrate this truth. When Jamestown was founded in 1607, one of the colony's goals was to propagate Christianity in the New World.[2] In 1620 the Pilgrims established Plymouth after signing the Mayflower Compact. Part of this agreement stipulated the Pilgrims' service to God the Almighty by doing His will. The Compact begins with, "In the name of God, Amen." It continues, "Having undertaken for the Glory of God, and Advancement of the Christian Faith." The Founding Fathers mentioned our unalienable, God-given rights and referred to Providence in the Declaration of Independence and other writings.

Numerous references to faith in "God," "Almighty God," "Providence," "Divine Providence," "Sovereign Ruler of the Universe," "Great Legislator of the Universe," "Jesus Christ," "the Creator," and other Christian references appear in numerous state and federal documents dating back to the establishment of the colonies and the United States of America. The Declaration of Independence includes four references: "God," "Creator," "Supreme Judge," and "Divine Providence." The U.S. Constitution mentions "the Lord" once in reference to its ratification by the states[3] and, in honoring the Sabbath, refers to not counting Sundays in the ten-day limit for the president to veto a bill after he receives it from Congress.[4] Moreover, all fifty state constitutions mention their dedication to God, Providence, or the Lord. The God to which they refer is the God of the Bible, the Christian God. Most newspapers in the colonial era were explicitly Christian, and 75 percent maintained that status in 1830, according to one poll.[5]

Furthermore, many immigrants migrated to this country for religious liberty, which meant the freedom to choose their religion without government compulsion. For a large majority of these people, the choice in their native countries was between a form of Protestantism and Catholicism—Christian religions.

For more about the endless examples of documents that indicate the nation's founding upon Christian precepts, please read *Original Intent* by David Barton, *America's Providential History* by Mark Beliles and Stephen McDowell, and primary sources such as the Virginia Charters (1606, 1609, 1612), the Mayflower Compact (1620), the First Thanksgiving Proclamation (1676), the Declaration of Independence (1776), and so forth.

In his first inaugural address on April 30, 1789, President George Washington summed up the importance of the Christian faith to the survival of democracy. "It would be peculiarly improper to omit, in this first official act, my fervent supplications to that Almighty Being who rules over the universe....The propitious smiles of Heaven can never be expected on a nation that disregards the eternal rules of order and right which Heaven itself has ordained."[6]

1960s Rebellion

Along with the hippie rebellion against authority, tradition, and morals in the 1960s came the more aggressive assault on faith. No authority figure, including parents, teachers, pastors, priests, and police, was exempt from the hippies' disaffection. In a nutshell, they dismissed standards, restrictions, and boundaries on behavior in exchange for free love, drug use, and the elimination of inhibitions. The consequences of this trade in values continue to plague our society today. We can see them in the acceptance of behavior once considered deviant, the actions of teenagers, promiscuity, sexually transmitted diseases, the number of children born out of wedlock, and the crude content of popular entertainment.

The hippies especially targeted the Christian faith and church due to what they perceived as "oppressive" regulations against human nature that prevented others from feeling good and enjoying life. They perceived those commandments as old-fashioned restrictions that had outlived their usefulness; they were the previous generations' way of doing things. Now times were changing, and the rules of personal conduct had to change with them; those decrees stifled creativity, self-expression, self-actualization (reaching self-fulfillment or full potential), personal enjoyment, instant gratification, and true freedom.

Notice that these terms all focus on self. People are perceived as their own individual, god, and center of their unique universe; therefore, they worship themselves as they strive to attain peace, happiness, and success. These three goals, the means to arriving there, and the definition of right and wrong are open to individual interpretation and definition; thus moral relativism supplants absolute right and wrong as a person's guide in his journey through life. Their value system is individualistic, subjective, and ever changing. The convenience of this philosophy is that one can change his mind and morals at any time. No circumstance or consequence is problematic because people can alter their values to suit themselves regardless of the effect their actions have on others.

This leads us to another side effect of the hippie revolution: the belief that the consequences of one's actions are neither the person's fault nor his responsibility to bear. For example, let's say someone contracts a sexually transmitted disease. It would become the government's responsibility—and thus the taxpayers' burden—to fund research to find a cure or provide medication so the individual could be healed or comfortably live with the disease. Then the person continues to negligently engage in the behavior that caused the problem. In addition, schools and other agencies should provide contraceptives to save these rebels from their own recklessness and lack of self-control. Notice that this last term, self-control, is absent from the previous list of words that focus on self, as are the terms self-discipline, self-reliance, self-sacrifice, and selflessness. This is not an oversight by the proponents of the rebellion. After all, they would say we are all humans with natural instincts no one can expect us to control.

The state of culture has declined to the point that cities provide clean needles to drug users in an attempt to prevent them from contracting HIV or hepatitis through the sharing of contaminated needles. Somehow this service is supposed to help people, but one cannot extinguish immoral behavior by providing tools that promote it. Is it possible that those who institute such programs do not consider the behavior undesirable? After all, an addict is often in a state of dependence.

The incidence of HIV or any other disease will not decline because clean needles are provided to drug users. This brand of charity encourages others to engage in such behavior; at some point clean needles will not be available, and the addict will seek his fix regardless of the risk. Has offering condoms in schools reduced the teen pregnancy rate? Has the right to an abortion lowered the number of women who unintentionally become pregnant? Does inventing medications that suppress the effects of an STD discourage people from participating in risky behavior or decrease the number contracting such disease? These questions are rhetorical, for the answer to them is obvious.

Government Grows

What we see here is the moral confusion that results from rejecting Christian principles and replacing them with relativism and self-worship. We also see how the government gains increased control and influence over its populace. If people cannot discipline themselves and regulate their own behavior, the government will finance their needs or provide for them through products, research, or services. At some point, what the government offers becomes restrictive, such as services through a government-run health care system. The government's cost becomes overwhelming, so the government must enact repressive laws or regulations to try to control the people it is allegedly assisting. Such restrictions lead to rationed health care, which will occur under Obamacare.

We live in a licentious society; eventually the government will be forced to pass stringent legislation to restrict behavior and manage its citizens. This is happening already. For example, the government forces us to wear seatbelts, has reduced the DUI level from .10 to .08, has proposed regulations to require green standards in home construction, and has required consumers to install certain light bulbs in homes.

Automaker Audi's commercial with the "green police" is more creepy than funny. In this ad, the "green police" confront people about excessive hot water temperature settings and the use of incandescent light bulbs, plastic bags, batteries, and foam cups, among other things. The ad reminds us of those who disguise their true opinions through "humor." Some of these initiatives sound altruistic on the surface, but the federal government's role is not to care for people or supervise them in an oppressive fashion. Eventually others expect this behavior from government; they become more dependent on it, and in small increments the government assumes greater power over time.

Statists have promoted and capitalized on this rebellion against God and church authority since at least the 1960s. Through the public and higher education systems, they have excluded, criticized, and satirized faith while encouraging moral relativism. Once God has been excluded from the equation, someone or something else must take His place. The Supreme Court banned prayer in public schools in *Engel v. Vitale* (1962) though Bible study and Christian education had been part of the system since the nation's founding.

Though some individuals worship themselves as deities, they are incapable of caring for themselves in all circumstances. Recall the above discussion about the treatment of STDs. The statist government ultimately steps in and fills the void created by the abandonment of religious faith; it is the all-powerful government that becomes society's savior. With God eliminated from culture, the government inefficiently and incapably attempts to become god for its citizens, vainly and tirelessly trying to provide for their every circumstance. Schools become "little brother" in the government's scheme, providing every possible service to keep the populace depending on it. But the relativistic statists actually believe they have the skills, abilities, and wisdom to accomplish this goal. Hippies should add two additional terms to those regarding self from the 1960s revolution: conceited and self-deluded.

Unfortunately, liberals who have assumed government positions have been seduced into believing that they are God (but they are really god) and that they can provide for the needs of their citizens. It is sad for them and the populace that they believe this delusion.

Since they embrace this belief, they continue to indoctrinate citizens aggressively and without shame, beginning in elementary school, continuing in high school, and finishing in institutions of higher learning. The media are their strong ally in spreading their messianic message while discrediting the Christian faith and religion. With the passing of each successive generation, the statists' worldview gains a stronger foothold in society at the expense of America's Christian foundation.

FAMILY

The second cornerstone the liberal statist has pilloried is the family. The Puritans correctly believed that the family is the instrumental ingredient to a stable society.[7] If the family is stable, it bequeaths its strength to the community, the state, and the nation. The socialist also recognizes the importance of strong families in a country. The problem is, loyalty to the family means less dependence on the government and its influence. Does it then make sense that statists want weak families? Probably not, unless one is obsessed with the accumulation of power and influence.

How do weak families benefit socialist-leaning liberals? The answer is simple: if people lack parents or family members in whom they can rely, the government has more emptiness to fill. Gangs or other criminal groups sometimes fill this space, but the void also provides an opportunity for the government to increase power, which is manifested in the public school system. Moreover, if families teach values to children, they can pass on a value system counter to that of secularists.

Promiscuity

Another negative consequence of the 1960s hippie revolution is the family's breakdown. As many grew in their desire to experience free love, unplanned pregnancies multiplied and led to an increase in single-parent families. Furthermore, the value of marriage began to decline. Divorce and remarriage occur more frequently today than ever before. In 1890 one out of every seventeen marriages (6 percent) ended in divorce;[8] by 1990 the divorce rate had risen to 50 percent, where it has remained according to 2008 preliminary data.[9]

One negative result of the high divorce ratio is the raising of children in single-parent households or in homes with a stepparent. Though not all of these situations are bad, they certainly are not ideal. Many children are raised successfully by a single parent, stepparent, or grandparent; however, this isn't always the case. Many single parents struggle to raise their children. Many grandparents rear their grandchildren due to the parents' negligence. In many circumstances, a single mother raises several children, sometimes from different fathers.

Also, when a teenager bears a daughter out of wedlock, her child regularly repeats the cycle of teen parenthood. Boys suffer most when they lack a positive male role model at home and often become the next generation of absentee fathers, sometimes fathering multiple children to different mothers. This is the proud legacy of the free love movement. My purpose is not necessarily to denigrate those in this situation but to explain the consequences of the free love mentality.

Stating that premarital sex and unwanted pregnancies occurred before the 1960s shouldn't be necessary here, but if I do not, liberals across the fruited plain will accuse me of making that insinuation. The point is, since the free love of the sixties, this problem has only increased. When I graduated from high school in 1985, a few girls from my school became teenage mothers. Before the explosion of promiscuity in the 1960s, such an occurrence was rare. Between 1962 and 2001, births to unmarried teenagers increased from 15.7 to 78.9 percent.[10] In addition, the percent of all births to unmarried women rose from 5.9 percent (1962) to 33.5 percent (2001), and births per one thousand unmarried women between the ages of fifteen and forty-four increased from 21.9 to 45 during the same years.[11] Is it coincidental that this explosion occurred after the 1962 *Engel* decision that banned prayer in public schools (not to overlook *Roe v. Wade* in 1973)?

Unless we are liberals, we know that single-parent families are not the best environments for raising children. We also know that unwed teens becoming parents is far from ideal. Of course, a number of single parents, largely mothers, do an outstanding job in this endeavor. But both mothers and fathers have unique roles to fill in the multiple facets of their children's development; children acquire positive traits from both their mother and father. The fact that fathers and mothers bestow important characteristics the other parent is incapable of passing along cannot be understated. For example, it is beneficial for girls to see their fathers model how to treat a woman; it is also important for boys to learn how to be strong from their father.

Sure, some parents are abusive, controlling, or neglectful, but this problem does not justify the disparaging of the family. One should not project exceptions on a population to generalize experiences, yet this is the "reality" liberals often create to advance their agenda; they dwell in what I dub the "valley of exceptions." Overall, a man and woman who fulfill their proper roles allow children to develop emotionally, intellectually, physically, and morally. The connection between broken families and crime, drug use, alcohol consumption, promiscuity, gang activity, and the high school dropout rate is well documented.

We cannot overlook the prevalence of divorce in this equation. The rate of divorce at 50 percent has contributed significantly to single-parent or unstable families. Though children may visit the parent (usually the father) with whom they do not reside, the ideal family life is broken. Ask any parents who see their child on weekends if they believe the separation has a detrimental effect on their child and their ability to parent; most likely the answer will be yes. Even if the child lives in a two-parent household with a parent and stepparent, valid concerns arise about divergent values being taught or about parents playing children against each other. Again, in some arrangements, dilemmas like this are absent, but in many cases, the problem affects children psychologically. Moreover, stepparents or live-in partners often impact a child's psyche and development. This scenario regularly leads to the child's future promiscuity and begins the process of the child repeating a broken home later in his life.

Even when an intact, two-parent marriage is in place, parents regularly rely on day care, babysitters, or nannies to nurture their children while they work or pursue recreational activities. As a result, parental influence on children lessens, and children form their values, morals, philosophy of life, and so on from a hodgepodge of sources, including pop culture, friends, maybe gangs, and even the curriculum learned in the education system.

Public School Role

Probably one of the biggest influences on the breakdown of the family is the public school system. From ages five to seventeen, most students spend the bulk of their time at school, with many beginning school in prekindergarten or day care. The average school day is seven hours long, excluding after-school activities such as tutoring, sports, and clubs. Students spend a minimum of thirty-five hours a week at school. If they play a sport like basketball, for example, they easily spend fifty-four hours a week at school when we factor in three nights a week for practice and two nights for games. Practice averages two hours per night, while games can constitute up to seven hours of time when we factor in junior varsity and varsity games each night, with games beginning at six o'clock and ending at nine. If a game is somewhere other than the child's school, more time must be added for travel.

At the least, then, students attend school thirty-five hours per week for thirteen of the most formative years of their lives (excluding preschool). During that time, students often receive instruction with a liberal emphasis on topics that sharply contrast with what their parents believe. These topics can include environmentalism, sex education (including promiscuity, homosexuality, and abortion), diversity, revisionist history, and secularism (atheism, relativism, and evolution). American ideals are also attacked, such as prayer in school, the right to bear arms, and patriotism.

Of course, when teachers present the theory of evolution, they omit alternate and prohibited viewpoints such as creationism or intelligent design. But this practice is true with all topics. Case in point: when they teach about climate change, they present only the alarmist, man-made global warming indoctrination. If they mention the opposing viewpoint, they do so only in a critical manner. When they teach liberalism in general, they often present current events only from the liberal point of view; this presentation includes the use of liberal political cartoons to illustrate a point. These cartoons either promote the liberal opinion or criticize the conservative one. In addition, teachers use curriculum written from the liberal stance, so these activities simply support the curriculum.

Real Example of Indoctrination

Another example from environmentalism highlights this propensity. When indoctrinating students in the environmentalist agenda, teachers say that too many trees have been cut down and that few are left. As a result, we must recycle, constrict the lumber industry, and halt deforestation. In 2000 *Forest Voice*, an extremely liberal, earth-worshiping periodical that promotes the radical environmentalist agenda, was distributed to several teachers, including me. This particular issue included maps that purportedly indicated the number of trees in America during certain periods of our history. Shading on the maps allegedly showed the number of trees in the United States in 1620, 1850, and 1999.

As you can guess, the shading decreased as the dates progressed. According to the 1999 map, no trees existed in over 95 percent of the Appalachian Mountains. States such as Virginia and Pennsylvania contained very few or no trees. Furthermore, the 1620 map indicated that up to that time no trees had been cleared in the eastern half of the United States.[12] Of course, the information conveniently omitted the fact that Plymouth had been built on cleared land, which may have been the site of an Indian village years earlier.[13] And we know that hundreds of tribes and villages existed in America during colonization, as is often emphasized in public school and university classrooms across the fruited plain.

Anyone observing the local environment in which he lives should easily dismiss the *Forest Voice* and the assertion that it makes; unfortunately, many teachers subscribe to such foolishness and teach it to their students. As a matter of fact, many citizens ingest whatever information they are given without questioning it to any degree.

Since I was a sensible, intelligent teacher, I guided my students through the analysis of these maps. I asked them what the maps showed, and they stated the number of trees in America. I then asked them to think about what the 1999 map was showing and to compare it to the community in which they lived. At this point in the discussion, they were a little slow, so I asked if any of them lived near A. P. Hill, a military base in the county. A couple of pupils said yes. I asked them if trees were there. They said yes. I asked by a show of hands how many were hunters and asked if they hunted in their county; they said yes.

Then the lightbulbs illuminated, and they shined brilliantly. The students noticed that the map showed no trees in Virginia; they noticed that though A. P. Hill military base comprises about 25 percent of the county, mostly woods, no trees appeared on the map. They recognized that the 1999 map showed few trees in the Shenandoah Valley, even though voluminous acres of forests exist there. They noticed the same discrepancy when they examined the Rockies and other places in the United States with which they were familiar. After that discussion, I showed pictures of forests in Pennsylvania that had been farmland forty years before. I explained that the forests had retaken the fields and pastures. I showed them pictures of trees lining both sides of Interstates 80 and 76 in Pennsylvania for miles; none of these trees had appeared on the *Forest Voice's* map.

My students learned the lesson that you cannot trust a printed source just because it says something. They learned that they must closely examine any information given to them and compare what they are told with what they experience and observe on a daily basis. They learned that they cannot trust education because the goal of some educators is to intentionally mislead them. They learned to think analytically and rationally. Regrettably, educators rarely teach these lessons and skills in the education system as they indoctrinate students in liberalism. Let me remind you that such "education" is not confined to the public school system. It is probably more rampant in institutes of higher education—or should I say "higher indoctrination"?

Let me repeat. As the family is depreciated, the school system ("little brother") steps in to fill that role. In the process it transmits its values, including the religion of environmentalism, to children.

Scores of other resources, including textbooks, advance the radical, environmentalist, and liberal agenda but usually in a more subtle fashion. It is unfortunate that most teachers have succumbed to this philosophy, lack the ability to think through issues critically, and thus impart these beliefs onto children. The sadder fact is that many of these children grow up and go on to college, where the indoctrination continues more aggressively and with less restraint. In public schools, parents can be involved, can be heard, and can have some influence. In higher education, however, children are separated from their parents. It is an accepted fact that parents are not involved in their child's higher education other than giving them money and advising them to go to class, study, and get good grades. The saddest fact is that these effectively indoctrinated graduates enter the workforce, many as teachers, and believe, pass on, and promote this brainwashing.

Government Grows

Therefore, the cycle continues, the impact in the following generation deepens, and secularists more easily advance their agenda. Once the old guard of teachers retires—those not exposed to such miseducation and pressure to accept a certain agenda—a well-trained, loyal corps of indoctrinated, liberal, environmentalist cadets replaces it. Fortunately, not all students are gullible and thus consumed by this indoctrination; however, they are an ever-shrinking minority.

As the years pass by, statists call to extend the school day and school year as well as to lower the school age. Just after I started writing this book, President Obama announced his plans to do just that. If any of these changes occur—the lower school age is already common though not mandated—they will translate into more time children spend away from their parents (and their value systems) and in the liberal school system, "educated" according to its precepts.

The school system supplants parents and the family. The liberal asserts that because programs such as Head Start benefit children, all children should start school early. The statist says that American students need more time in school so they can compete with their international counterparts. To rationalize school day extensions, the socialist presents data showing our academic inferiority compared to students from other nations. Also, as time goes by, students are brainwashed into believing the supremacy of the state over God and family. They believe government should determine the solution to all problems, struggles, or hardships. They learn that reliance on the statist ruling class is good. They exchange God-given freedoms, upon which our nation was founded, with self-gratifying freedoms that erode personal responsibility and increase dependence on the state, thus leading to tyranny.

The unstated goal is to decrease the time children spend with their parents so the state can indoctrinate them and make them dependent on it through "little brother." This is not the ambition of teachers; rather, they are steered by the whims of those who determine the philosophy of education. Education leaders often say that the school is the most important thing in a child's life. That's strange because I was raised to believe that God and family were the most valuable things in life. These so-called leaders may deny that they want to train a state-dependent populace, but if you pay close attention to what they say and do, their words and actions betray them.

Citizens have made choices that have allowed liberals to advance this agenda and thus increase our problems. Many parents have chosen to work two jobs for material gain at the expense of their children's upbringing and welfare. They have relegated the rearing of their children to strangers so they can have multiple cars, electronic devices, vacations, country club memberships, oversized houses, and so on. I must say that owning possessions is okay as long as people are spending within their means and not sacrificing their children in the process.

This is not to say that parents should withdraw their children from public schools. As long as a parent is home when a child returns from school, mothers and fathers monitor what their child is learning, families eat dinner together, parents stay involved in their child's life through college, and parents impart their morals and values to their children, then the family will be fine. As a public school educator, I have seen a number of parents take those steps and raise morally strong children, whom "little brother" has not decapitated. But keeping the school system at bay is a battle that requires a concerted effort, high parental involvement, and a strong spirit of discernment.

The outcry in opposition to vouchers or school choice has nothing to do with what is best for students. Instead, the challengers wish to maintain power and control over the education of students. The teachers' unions, public school officials, developers of teacher education programs in colleges and universities, and statists in government know that many families would prefer school choice as an alternate route to the public schools. But this choice would undermine the liberal's goal of indoctrination by offering undesirable competition in the education of students. The only way to influence a whole society is to force it into your modality of education. Though they abhor the situation, relativists can tolerate those currently educated at home or in non-statist private schools, but they would not survive the mass exodus that could occur under a voucher or school choice program.

One educational leader expressed his disagreement with charter schools. He once said that a politician supporting the measure had control of the money and that more charter schools or school choice would give him and his supporters additional money, control, and power. This leader was unable to grasp that his reason for opposing school choice was the same as his reason for preserving the current public school system—money. The current public school system holds the money and thus maintains control and power it has held for a long time.

In summary, liberals have weakened the family through the free love movement of the 1960s and the ever-expanding, influential education system. The phenomenon of the sixties helped increase the number of single-parent families and divorces, leading to an unforeseen acceptance of the belief that the importance of the two-parent family is exaggerated. At the same time, the breakdown of the family opened a portal for the government to become more influential through the public school system. This expansion of power is justified to "help" and "benefit" children. Moreover, the public school system and institutes of higher learning attack the importance of family.

The weakening of the family and the supplanting of family values, many of which were Christian, with relativistic ones have allowed the statist via the education system to gradually replace parents as the guiding force and authority figure in the lives of children. I have dedicated more space to the education system later in this book.

PATRIOTISM

The final cornerstone to be attacked and destroyed is patriotism or pride in the United States of America. Many list nationalism, a synonym for patriotism, along with European rivalries, militarism, and alliances, as one of the causes of the world wars. Simply, nationalism is devotion to national interests, unity, and independence, especially of one nation above all others. In other words, nationalism is pride in one's country and culture. Liberals generally frown on patriotism because being proud of America and promoting our interests create dissension and hurt feelings, which cause conflict and lead to war. How dare we say we are better than any other nation? How dare a liberal assert that his philosophy is superior to that of a conservative? Ah, the hypocrisy evident in all things liberal.

Textbooks began teaching nationalism with a negative connotation, at some point attacking American patriotism. Unlike their assault against the previous two cornerstones, socialist-leaning liberals often masquerade as American patriots when they talk about America's prestige or about returning America to her greatness. Their goal, however, is to destroy traditional America and transform it into a socialist, secular, relativistic nation. The actions of statists reveal their intentions despite their dialogue to the contrary. Statists continue to trample on the Constitution and the founding principles of our nation, of which our Founding Fathers so eloquently wrote and conveyed. Liberals continue to harp about a "living Constitution," legislate from the Supreme Court instead of through the legislative branch, disregard votes on referendums, and increase federal government power in defiance of the principles of federalism. Federalism is defined as the division of power between the states and federal government.

Examples of the Supreme Court legislating from the bench include the following:

- Allowing Congress to regulate intrastate commerce (a state right), which is "closely related" to interstate commerce (*NLRB v. Jones and Laughlin Steel Corporation, 1937; Wickard v. Filburn, 1942*; and *Maryland v. Wirtz, 1968*)[14]
- Applying the First Amendment to state and local governments and invoking the manufactured "wall of separation" phrase (*Everson v. Board of Education, 1947*)[15]
- Creating the allegedly constitutional "right to privacy" in cases involving contraceptives for married couples (Connecticut, *Griswold v. Connecticut, 1965*)[16] and unmarried individuals (Massachusetts, *Eisenstadt v. Baird, 1972*)[17]
- Legalizing abortion (*Roe v. Wade, 1973*)[18]
- Overturning state laws that prohibit partial-birth murder (*Stenberg v. Carhart, 2000*)[19]
- Granting to foreign enemies of the United States what is supposed to be a citizen's right to a fair trial (*Rasul v. Bush, 2004*).[20]

Some may agree with an adult's right to use contraception, but the federal government's duty is not to grant such a right or to fabricate one in the Constitution, where it does not exist. Issues such as these are local or state concerns, which the local or state government should appropriately handle. If you would like to read more about the Supreme Court's seizure of power, I highly recommend Mark Levin's *Men in Black*. Also, to read about the statists' continuous grab for power in contravention to our Constitution's precepts, I strongly recommend *Liberty and Tyranny*, also by Mr. Levin.

Why Criticize Patriotism?

Why the attack on American patriotism? I have identified three reasons for this assault. First, as mentioned, statists believe patriotism is evil because love of country promotes too much self-centered pride in one's own nation. This pride then creates conflict with other countries and causes wars.

Second, relativists are really anti-American. Socialists at heart, they believe they have been ordained with wisdom and knowledge their subjects are unable to attain or comprehend. The American ideals of democracy and government by the people threaten their beliefs in aristocracy, dictatorship, and even monarchy. In their minds the American people are too stupid to govern themselves and will not survive unless supreme leaders save them from their own idiocy. If socialist-leaning liberals made public statements to this effect, a large part of the electorate would reject them—with the exception of those who either support socialism or do not understand the breadth of its ideology.

How much responsibility does the education system bear for those who lack the ability to think analytically? The liberal-leaning education system has misinformed and poorly educated many. In addition to schools, the media have falsely reported on a variety of issues, and numerous citizens are too lazy or disinterested to seek the truth.

Third, statists undertake this strategy to destroy the United States of America, the only nation that can protect, preserve, and advance democracy and liberty. Once they have achieved their objective, they will reestablish the old order of aristocracy throughout the globe under a one-world government. Here, a small group of "wise" rulers will care for the incompetent "serfs" of the world; if you doubt this, observe the actions of the United Nations. Therefore, socialists are duplicitous elitists. They make deceptive statements to the general public about loving America while simultaneously cringing at such sentiments as they gradually, intentionally, and methodically dismantle our founding precepts.

America's Principles Despised

From the moment the Founding Fathers presented the Declaration of Independence to King George III of England, the battle against democracy and liberty was born. This battle ensued due to the Declaration's bold statements about the social compact between citizens and their rulers as well as the law (or laws) of nature. The social compact (sometimes referred to as the "social contract") states that "men…unite into a community for… peaceable living…in a secure enjoyment of their properties."[21] The Declaration of Independence states, "Governments are instituted among Men, deriving their just powers from the consent of the governed." The social compact also endorses revolution as a last resort to change corrupt government. Again I quote the Declaration: "That whenever any Form of Government becomes destructive of these ends, it is the Right of the People to alter or to abolish it."

The law of nature or natural rights states, "The Law of Nature stands as an eternal rule to all men.…Laws human must be made according to the general laws of Nature, and…Scripture."[22] The

Founding Fathers first mention the laws of nature in the Declaration of Independence by asserting that people can assume "the separate and equal station to which the Laws of Nature and Nature's God entitle them." They then wrote that "all men...are endowed by their Creator with certain unalienable Rights, that among these are Life, Liberty and the pursuit of Happiness." So these are natural, God-given rights as opposed to ones stipulated by allegedly God-chosen kings or aristocrats.

Although the likes of John Locke, Sir William Blackstone, Richard Hooker, and Thomas Hobbes discussed these doctrines, many considered it outlandish that a bunch of insubordinate rabble rousers would not only issue such a proclamation but also deliver it to the greatest nation and king on earth at the time, genuinely believing they could establish a government without a monarch. Protesting taxation without representation, having a tea party, or engaging in a minor massacre was one thing, but creating a brand-new form of government was completely different. It was intolerable and unimaginable.

As we know, the colonists won the War of Independence and thus founded the United States of America with thirteen original states. Of course, none of the world powers at the time—England, France, Spain, Denmark, the Netherlands, or Russia—believed this experiment in self-government would succeed. Those nations lacked the wisdom to recognize that God was on America's side as He helped it defeat the strongest army in the world—but that is a different story to be dissected later.

After the Revolutionary War, Europe patiently waited for this experiment in representative government to fail. Several glimpses of hope came with the Whiskey Rebellion (1794), the election of 1800, the second engagement with Britain in the War of 1812, the Mexican War (1846–48), and the Civil War (1861–65). But the young country held its own, and the European hope of dividing the nascent American nation after its anticipated self-destruction never materialized. (I will examine these events in greater detail in a later chapter.)

America has endured for over 235 years since its founding, but the threats against liberty persist. Especially since President Franklin Delano Roosevelt and his New Deal program of the 1930s, the federal government has been expanding its power not only in defiance of our Constitution's precepts but also to the detriment of American citizens. Today, the more people statists can convince that America is evil, greedy, imperialistic, and selfish, the more quickly they can create their dominant, oppressive, controlling central government. Once they have annihilated American democratic principles, they can restore aristocratic ideals. Attacking patriotism since at least the 1960s in schools and later in the media and popular culture has allowed elitists to erode American pride as they bolster their power and influence. Or has it?

Patriotism Thrives

Despite innumerable efforts over forty years to thwart Americans' pride in their country and delegitimize faith in God through anti-American and anti-Christian propaganda, socialist-leaning, secular statists have failed to change the hearts of the majority of Americans in these matters.

One must simply look at the reactions of U.S. citizens to the horrific terrorist acts of September 11, 2001. It would be impossible to estimate the number of expressions of patriotism and faith throughout the country after that day. American flags appeared everywhere and on everything imaginable (and still do)—yards, windows, cars, T-shirts, jackets, towels, bathing suits, lapel pins, team uniforms, hats, dresses, ties, magnets, and more. People sang the national anthem with an increased sense of pride, zeal, and fervor as giant American flags were unfurled at stadiums of college and professional teams. Phrases honoring the greatness of the United States appeared on marquees of schools, businesses, and churches. Moreover, people prayed and referred to prayer, displayed "God Bless America" slogans, expressed their faith in God in a multitude of venues, and followed the national anthem with a rendition of "God Bless America" or "America the Beautiful" at sporting events and other functions.

Liberals had spent at least four decades forcing anti-American propaganda and revisionist history down people's throats with little resistance or the provision of equal time to the opposing point of view. For more than forty years socialists had berated faith in God, especially Christianity, under the manufactured guise of separation of church and state. Statists had labored forty-plus years with near monopoly status in the media and education systems to indoctrinate our citizens and youth to hate America and abandon their "childish" Christian or religious beliefs. Despite their efforts, elitists witnessed after 9/11 that the fruits of their incessant labors were paltry, rotted, and rancid. Secularists observed that over four decades of constant, relentless, well-orchestrated indoctrination were a dismal failure. They realized that blatant dishonesty, revisionism, misreporting, miseducation, and criticism had not taken deep root in the American psyche. And they loathed it! So they amped up their offensives to a new level of intensity. Such disappointment may explain their desire to advance their agenda through the "people-less" judicial branch, as previously discussed.

After more than forty years of indoctrination to the contrary, bountiful expressions of patriotism and faith were unfathomable in their minds. Such sentiments were beyond the socialists' comprehension. You could hear it in their voices, see it on their faces, and read it in their articles. A certain sarcasm, contempt, and cynicism were evident when they reported on acts of patriotism and expressions of faith. How could this be? They spent almost a half-century breaking down American pride and its Christian foundation just as a cult leader might break the spirit of his followers until they exchange their values for his leadership. Yet how could this outpouring of patriotism and faith be the return on their investment?

Not unlike the Japanese military in World War II or Osama bin Laden on September 11, I believe they underestimated the traditions and principles upon which our great nation is constructed—freedom, family, Christianity, hard work, as well as "Life, Liberty and the pursuit of Happiness." Only statists, who detest these ideals, could miscalculate the importance of their influence and imprint on the American spirit. They continue to fight, and they are making headway, but they realized after that terrible day that they had miscalculated their degree of advancement.

CHAPTER 2

ATTACK OF THE PUBLIC SCHOOL SYSTEM

S EVERAL TIMES UP to this point, I have alluded to an important vessel through which secular, socialist statists have pushed their agenda on the American people. This is the education system, including both the public school system and higher education. I stated earlier that public school students spend a minimum of thirty-five hours per week in school, beginning at the age of five. This statistic does not include the time children spend in preschool beginning at an earlier age (or day care programs). This involvement adds up to a great deal of time students are separated from the nurture, influence, and overall upbringing of their parents.

Back in the day, school values mirrored those of the family; today the values of the two often clash with each other, and the education system spends a great deal of time clarifying values for its customers. Then a large number of teenagers enroll in colleges or universities, and most spend all their time away from family, excluding weekends and holiday visits. When students graduate from college with a four-year degree at the age of twenty-one, they have been under the tutelage of strangers, many with value systems different from their parents, for sixteen years or 76 percent of their lives. I focus on the public school system because that is where children engage in the first battle for their minds, lives, and souls.

School Expectations

The number one concern of public schools is expectations or standards. All people, from education leaders to parents, community and business interests, and teachers, talk about establishing and maintaining high expectations. Despite all the hyperbole in this regard, can we really say that schools demand excellence from the students they serve? Many say yes if their philosophy of education and life is based on affective or emotional learning. Many who demand genuine excellence say no based on the dumbing down of curriculum and the poor achievement of many public school students. Many assert that low achievement is the result of following an outdated school calendar and teaching methods. They lobby for longer school days and years as well as more creative ways of reaching students.

The problem, however, is that expectations are low, curriculum has been simplified, and academic rigor has been reduced. As the National Center for Education Statistics has reported, many states have decreased expectations, failing to challenge students or allow them to develop complex knowledge and skills.[1] Parents and students bear the brunt of the responsibility for these results based on their poor attitudes and low value placed on education; however, schools pander to this mentality by lowering standards instead of maintaining high expectations to improve student development through a rigorous curriculum.

Measuring Performance and NCLB

Along with the recent call for higher standards has come what has been dubbed high-stakes testing. This scenario dictates that students are tested at or near the end of the school year. States have adopted different methods by which to measure these standards. As a rule, students are required to pass a certain number of tests to meet graduation requirements. The pass rates determine if students are learning the respective subject areas the tests measure. Minimum pass rates in all tested subjects—70 percent, for example—allow schools to be accredited by their respective state.

Additionally, these pass rates allow states to meet standards as required by federal No Child Left Behind (NCLB) legislation. According to NCLB, individual schools and school districts must meet Adequate Yearly Progress (AYP) benchmarks in math and reading as set by the federal government to be considered an adequately performing school. However, state accreditation and federal AYP requirements can be different.

State of Virginia and AYP

During the 2008–2009 school year, the AYP benchmark in Virginia was 81 percent in reading and 79 percent in math (accreditation was 70 or 75 percent, depending on grade level). Those numbers increased during 2009–2010 to 85 and 83 percent, respectively. In 2004–2005, the pass rates for reading and math were 65 and 63 percent, respectively.[2] Moreover, this percentage of students passing applies to the total student population in the school as well as to a variety of subgroups, including white, black, Hispanic, Native American, Asian/Pacific islander, Limited English Proficient (LEP), economically disadvantaged students, and students with disabilities.

So if during the 2008–2009 school year 81 percent of a school's overall population plus the separate subgroups listed above passed the reading test but only 60 percent of special needs students did, the school did not meet AYP. The original goal set by NCLB is that 100 percent of students pass these exams by the year 2014. Much debate has focused on whether or how to amend this mandate by either reducing the percentage or extending the mandate beyond that year. Early in his presidency, Barack Obama hinted at implementing such a change.

REACTION TO NCLB

The question is whether schools are meeting these standards. Some are, and some are not. Some schools meet the standards in certain years but fail to do so in others. Immediately after the passage of the NCLB Act, many argued that expecting 100 percent of students to pass a test was unrealistic. Though it is an idealistic goal, too many variables affect a student's ability, desire, or both to pass these tests and work toward academic achievement. These include family life, the value of education a child possesses or which is instilled in him, motivation to learn or do well in school, maturity, peer pressure, and the list goes on.

The National Education Association's (NEA) initial reaction to NCLB was intriguing. NEA representatives and members are considered experts in their professions. What was their response to the implementation of NCLB? What alternative plan did they devise? How did these educational masters draw on their expertise to produce a counter proposal for improving education? After all, NCLB was drafted in response to the disappointing performance levels of American students, and one would think the teachers' union would have a proposal to correct its own incompetence. In short, these educators had no constructive reaction. Instead, the NEA filed a lawsuit, claiming the new mandates were underfunded. You read that right; the NEA and its proud members, the experts in education, sued the federal government. This response reveals much about the so-called education leaders in our nation.

At the same time, many have become proponents of the legislation and its intention, which is to create a consistent curriculum that is completely and effectively taught to all students in the country (though states possess flexibility in creating their own curriculum and choosing assessment tools). In doing so, accountability for schools and teachers increases as the results of administered exams are used to monitor teaching and learning as well as analyzed to spark improvement in weak areas. Supporters also want to see more realistic goals established. Nevertheless, schools are making progress toward improving their pass rates and meeting steadily increasing AYP benchmarks.

LOWERING STANDARDS

How are schools achieving these standards? The following is based on my experience in the Virginia public schools as a teacher and administrator. During the twelve years I spent in a school system, I witnessed my colleagues strive to improve their teaching and student learning. They expended a great deal of hard work and effort to improve the school so they could not only meet state and federal expectations but also exceed them. These efforts produced a number of positive changes and results. By pointing out the weaknesses in the system, my goal is not simply to criticize. I am an educator; therefore, my objective is to educate people, help them understand, and guide them toward genuine school improvement and student achievement.

Decreased Rigor

As a high school social studies teacher, I saw that schools across the state were struggling to reach the 70 percent pass rate required to meet accreditation for those subjects. In 2000 students needed to get thirty-nine and thirty-eight correct questions out of sixty to pass the VA-U.S. History and World History exams, respectively. In 2002 these "cut scores" were lowered to thirty-four and thirty-two, respectively. As expected, the pass rates for those subjects skyrocketed, and the Virginia Department of Education proudly announced that social studies scores improved throughout the state. Concurrently, the "resource guide" for those subjects, which is the written, taught, and tested curriculum, was reduced by approximately one-fourth. Although this was probably a fair adjustment due to the large volume of material previously taught, this fact was rarely if ever publicized.

Moreover, in 2004 the cut score for both tests was further decreased to thirty correct answers out of sixty questions. Once again the state experienced an increase in social studies pass rates, and it did not restrict its celebration of this success despite keeping the lower expectation buried from the public.

What we see here is a situation where the cut score for the tests was lowered and the volume of material in the curriculum reduced. Experts would argue that these changes were reasonable based on standard deviations and other explanations of data, but in the end the standards were still lowered. If you were to speak with a math teacher who works in the system, he would tell you that math standards have also been lowered and that once-common math concepts have been omitted altogether. For example, concepts once taught in Algebra I are now reserved for Algebra III classes. The only way to reach a 100 percent pass rate is to continue to water down curriculum, decrease minimum cut scores for passing tests, and compose easier tests. In all fairness, the state of Virginia implemented procedures to meet federal requirements.

Alternate Tests

Virginia also developed alternate testing for students with disabilities who cannot pass the regular end-of-course exams: the Virginia Grade Level Alternative (VGLA) for elementary and middle school students, the Virginia Alternate Assessment Program (VAAP) for special needs students at all levels, and the Virginia Substitute Evaluation Program (VSEP) for high school students who have a learning disability. The only students eligible to take these types of assessments are those with individualized education plans (IEPs) or 504 plans, which are written for students who have a physical, intellectual, or emotional encumbrance that impairs their ability either to learn or to perform well on tests. Even in these cases, before they are eligible to take an alternate option, the school must show that the student's disability precludes him from being successful on traditional assessments.

In theory, most schools try to limit the number of students taking these assessments, and the state limits VAAP tests to 1 percent of a district's population. These assessments require teachers to compile a portfolio of work, completed by the student, that demonstrates the student's proficiency in various components of the particular subject being tested. These "authentic assessments" can include worksheets, graphic organizers, photographs of students working, DVDs, CDs, and projects students have completed under teacher supervision. A committee scores these assessments using a rubric. Though students can pass or fail them, the large majority earns a passing score on these tests. If students fail, they retake only the portions of the assessment where they were unsuccessful. Therefore, these assessments are a lower standard. At the high school level, the VSEP allows a student to pass an end-of-course test, earn a verified credit, and qualify upon graduation to receive the same diploma awarded to students who pass more rigorous tests.

The VGLA, VAAP, and VSEP exams also count toward the accreditation and AYP standards for a school and district. If state and federal governments believe certain students legitimately need alternate tests, the results should be counted separately from accreditation and AYP percentages. Including alternate assessment results in accreditation and AYP numbers gives the impression that achievement is higher than it is, especially for schools that administer large numbers of VGLA or VSEP assessments. Since the administration of alternate tests has constituted a large percentage of the total tests administered by some school systems, the federal government and hence states have recently called for a reduction in the number of substitute tests being given.

Other problems accompany the use of alternate tests. First, they allow students and their parents to feel good about their achievement in school, but the student in this situation is less equipped to compete in the real world once he leaves the public school. Second, if pupils use an alternate path to graduation, they should receive a diploma that is different from the one their classmates earn. However, such a practice would irreparably damage the self-esteem of those students; schools have a goal to make students feel good about themselves and have a positive self-image, even if students do not realize genuine or equal achievement. All students must receive equal praise and honor regardless of the level of success they attain.

It would better serve these children to place them in a different program that meets their abilities, allows them to take needed courses, exempts them from needless assessments that do not measure their ability to learn in a rigorous academic setting, and permits them to graduate with an alternate diploma. This difference need not be advertised in school or at graduation, just as students who receive advanced diplomas, standard diplomas, modified standard diplomas, or IEP diplomas are not disclosed at graduation ceremonies. After high school, these young adults can still pursue career goals consistent with their abilities. This step would spare everyone from the circus that provides short-term good feelings.

Graduation Requirements and Verified Credits

Let me clarify the graduation requirements in the state of Virginia. Students must earn twenty-two credits and six verified credits to graduate with a standard diploma, and they need twenty-four credits and nine verified credits to graduate with an advanced diploma. Students receive a credit for passing a class, and the school awards a verified credit when students pass a class and its associated end-of-course (EOC) test. Not all classes require end-of-course tests. To receive a standard diploma, students earn their six verified credits by passing one math test, one social studies test, one science test, two English tests, and one test of their choosing from the first three subject areas. They must pass an additional math test, social studies test, and science test to earn an advanced diploma.

Are verified credits a strong measure of student achievement? Students are required to take a minimum of three courses in each subject area, but they must pass only one of the EOC tests in that subject area. The exception is English; all students take four years of English and must pass both a reading test and writing test.

A practice that occurs in some school divisions, though it did not happen in my district, is removing an excess of students from classes in which they are struggling and placing them in courses that do not offer an EOC exam. This step is taken to prevent failing scores that would lower the school's pass rate and hamper its ability to meet accreditation and AYP requirements. The Virginia Department of Education addressed this practice in March 2008, which was a follow-up to a June 2001 directive. It stated that "students…in courses…for which there are end-of-course tests are expected to take the tests" and "avoid giving the impression that the requirements of the assessment and accountability programs are being circumvented."[3] The only reason for such a memo to be published is the prevalence of the practice in certain school divisions. When this practice occurs, students are often placed in worthless classes such as Russian and sign language; these students may struggle with reading English, but at least they are learning Russian. Students earn elective credits in these classes, but they do not take EOC tests or earn verified credits.

Schools also misrepresent achievement by placing students into tracks. For example, low-achieving pupils may be placed in an earth science class to earn their verified credit in science, but in subsequent school years, they are put into non-EOC classes such as Ecology, Environmental Science, or a low-level class such as Principles of Biology. Though students can and do learn in these classes, testing does not occur, and the quality of education being administered is suspect. In fairness to teachers, the large majority who teach such classes provide high quality instruction to their students. However, one can also see that pass rates alone on end-of-course tests are not necessarily a viable measurement of educational quality or academic achievement.

Learning Styles and Differentiated Instruction

In addition to the debacles associated with testing, other philosophies weaken the education system. Another way weakness has been instilled in the public school system is through the idea of learning styles. The essential premise here is that all students have a preferred or innate way of learning, so following their learning styles allows them to achieve success based on their strengths. Teachers sometimes assess students at an early age to identify their predominant learning style, whether visual (seeing or writing), auditory (hearing), or kinesthetic/tactile (doing or touching). Many, if not all, students learn in a variety of ways, but again, the identified learning style is the child's preferred way of learning. The notion that children learn best via a particular method is then hammered into their heads until they believe they can learn only in that particular fashion.

It is frustrating to hear students or adults comment on their respective learning styles, as if they are otherwise incapable of learning or remembering information. This diagnosis becomes an excuse for failure. For example, students can say they are struggling in a class because they are visual learners and the teacher mostly lectures. Students can claim they learn through hands-on activities, which the teacher rarely implements. Both parents and students resort to this excuse when the opportunity presents itself. It occurs when a class is too challenging and the student wants to drop it or when a personality conflict exists between the teacher and student. Perhaps a teacher has high demands and expectations the student does not want to fulfill. Maybe the student is lazy and puts forth low effort, or perhaps he wants to change classes to be with friends. Of course, the real reason for the problem is never expressed; that is, students use the learning style excuse to camouflage the actual reasons for failure or to change teachers.

Students, parents, and educators have bought into this farce. It is especially problematic when administrators persecute teachers who employ traditional but effective techniques. Sometimes they demand that teachers change their teaching styles to suit modern children. Otherwise they are recommended for non-renewal, if not encouraged to resign or retire.

This is not to say that teachers shouldn't incorporate "differentiated instruction" (varied activities, assessments, and methods of teaching) into classroom lessons that focus on different ways of learning. When feasible, teachers should use a variety of activities, methods, and assessments. However, teaching students that they have an innate style of learning and can only learn that way is dangerous. Such thinking allows them to fail when that style is not offered. This problem has reached the point that some adults who forget to fulfill job responsibilities or are incapable of following policies and procedures use the excuse that "I'm a visual learner, so I didn't understand what we were told to do."

Addressing different ways of learning and instituting a variety of teaching methods should keep the classroom interesting and avoid boredom, but teachers should not promote them due to the false belief that people can succeed only when the teacher has addressed their unique way of learning. In addition, teachers should not convince students at an early age that they learn a specific way, thus stunting their growth and providing an excuse for failure.

An effect of "differentiated instruction" in the attempt to address various learning styles is a school in which the teacher is completely responsible for a student's learning via the means described above. The student is dependent on the teacher to present information in several ways, which consume instructional time. In this system the teacher presents concepts in three or four ways to cover all the learning styles and to impart material in "fun" and "interesting" ways. For many students, studying is an antiquated notion. Since teachers present material in so many forms, the students do not need to study at home. Then they pass a basic test at the end of the school year, and everyone celebrates the achievement realized in the public school system.

Basic activities are included in lessons that allow students to become successful, so to speak, but they do not challenge students to become stronger academically. On the contrary, they make learning easy and give the impression that our children are achieving at higher levels than they really are. At least this is true until SAT results are published and one examines college dropout rates and remediation courses offered to the incoming college freshman class. Then we wonder why experts and politicians propose to extend the school day and year. They do so not because Americans are incapable of learning during the 180-day school year but because much time is wasted, the curriculum is watered down, and students are not challenged through rigorous academics. Even most "homework" is completed in class.

A second detrimental consequence of differentiated teaching at the high school level is that students are poorly prepared for a college-level education. Stronger students cruise through their high school careers and then hit a wall in college they may or may not be able to traverse. On the other hand, average or weak students may not develop the skills to be successful in college. I believe many students drop out of college primarily due to the poor preparation they received in high school. Sure, some strong students are focused, take advanced classes, work hard, and succeed in high school and at institutions of higher learning. But many could become stronger students and be successful in college if schools provided proper modes of preparation.

Many "strong" students struggle in college because they easily managed the high school curriculum but were never truly challenged and afforded the opportunity to develop. I venture to say that students who are not at the top of their class but work hard are better prepared for college because they have developed skills to succeed in high school, skills and a work ethic that transfer to the demands of a post-secondary education. I told many parents of bright students, who struggled in my college-level classes, that I was genuinely challenging their child for the first time and that he would reap the benefits in college—and so it came to pass. Too often, parents and students accustomed to easy courses want to drop a demanding class, thus hampering their academic and intellectual development as well as their ability to acclimate to increased rigor at the higher education level.

Many colleges have also modified their courses and offer remedial classes to more and more enrollees to pander to a weaker clientele. In 2003 the state universities in California offered remedial English and math courses to 48 and 37 percent of their incoming freshmen, respectively, while such courses were taken by 53 percent of freshmen nationwide.[4] A partial explanation may be inflated grades. Due to a preponderance of graded assignments in classes, an overabundance of extra credit, "weighted" classes that increase students' grade point averages, and a diluted curriculum, high student achievement in many cases is an illusion. Also in California, 2008 test scores in reading, writing, science, and math ranked forty-seventh nationwide.[5]

Let's look at test scores in the nation as a whole. In 2003 state assessment results in fourth-grade reading lagged far behind those of the federal National Assessment of Education Progress (NAEP), which publishes *The Nation's Report Card*. Of the forty-eight states with comparable data as well as the District of Columbia, all but one experienced lower proficiency on the NAEP test, with the average deficiency falling between 20 and 50 percentage points. Only Missouri's state results were equal to NAEP's, and one state had a deficit of sixty-nine points.[6] NAEP results are similar in its *2008 Report Card*, which uses 2007 test data. In that year, forty-eight states had reportable data. Every state fell below NAEP's proficiency range in reading for grades four and eight. One state (Massachusetts) reached the NAEP range in fourth-grade math, and two states (Massachusetts and South Carolina) did so in eighth-grade math.[7]

When I was a young tot in elementary school, teachers didn't instruct me based on my learning style; my classmates weren't instructed that way either. As a matter of fact, when I was teaching tenth graders while completing my student teaching assignment in 1999, I was surprised to hear them talking about their learning styles. This discussion was something new to me because the concept hadn't existed in the schools I attended as a youngster (if it did, it was not openly discussed). Regardless, neither my teachers nor my parents would accept the assertion that students had innate learning styles. I was taught at a high standard in all subject areas. When teachers identified an area of weakness, they didn't minimize it and replace it with an area of strength so I could achieve something and feel good about myself. That area of weakness became the focus of instruction so I could do better in that area and become a well-rounded student.

At the elementary level, the school implemented a variety of activities that offered students a wide array of learning opportunities. Unlike today, as I rose through the grades, teachers replaced basic, elementary-level activities with more arduous, challenging ones. At the high school level, teachers rarely used simple activities and games in favor of more meticulous and challenging assignments that promoted independent learning and development. This workload more effectively prepared students for the demands of a college education and participation in the real world.

Although I was not as strong academically as I could have been when I entered college, I had a firm foundation and base upon which to grow and build my academic abilities. Furthermore, my college professors probably thought my peers and I were weaker coming out of high school than they had been—and they were probably right. I can say the same about high school graduates today compared to when I left high school.

A huge difference exists between the education I received in the 1970s to the early '80s and the one provided today. In the '70s, when teachers identified one's strengths and weaknesses, the weaknesses became the focus of attention to create a stronger overall student. Today, although teachers often mention educating the whole child, many rarely practice this philosophy. Today's schools emphasize strengths and minimize weaknesses; therefore, they prohibit children from developing into academically stronger, well-rounded individuals.

We find a comparison in athletics. Since I played baseball, I use that sport in my illustration. Many baseball players are capable of hitting fastballs but often struggle with off-speed pitches, such as the curveball. As a result, coaches often instruct players to practice hitting the latter pitch instead of the one in which they demonstrate proficiency. Having players work on their strengths would not produce better athletes; such a strategy would limit players' development and make them and their team mediocre at best. Imagine players on a baseball team who could hit only fastballs. It would not take much for opponents to defeat that team.

The same rationale applies to schools. For students to reach their full potential, schools must give them the opportunity to improve by giving more attention to their areas of weakness than their areas of strength; proficient areas would still be addressed, but they would not be the focus of instruction. So if a student were a strong visual learner (as most are), the teacher should give him more instruction via lecture. If students are good at taking multiple-choice tests, the teacher should emphasize essay tests. If students can recite facts but are unable to synthesize information, teachers should stress the latter. In the end teachers should make the curriculum more rigorous as students progress through the grades.

Let me return to my baseball illustration. Eight-year-olds learn the basics, such as how to grip a bat, but instruction becomes more complex as they age. In many schools, however, we are stuck on teaching students how to hold the bat.

Some may present a specialization argument here by asserting that people excel at their highest when they specialize in areas in which they best perform or most enjoy. For example, secondary teachers focus on a subject such as English, doctors practice a specific type of medicine such as orthopedics, professional athletes concentrate on a single sport and a specific position within that sport. It is true that at some point specialization is necessary, but an orthopedic doctor studies all aspects of his trade, an English teacher studies various subjects and can teach a variety of English courses within his profession, and a world-class athlete plays a variety of positions in several sports before becoming a pitcher on a professional baseball team.

Therefore, students must work to perfect all ways of learning to the best of their ability. Perfection may not be the result of these efforts, but well-rounded individuals will. By the time students finish high school, their specialization is determined by the subjects in which they are more skilled or interested. For example, some students have a knack at computing numbers and thus do well in math. Others have a tendency to understand vocabulary and therefore perform highly in English. Others enjoy reading about wars and are strong in history. Yet others are proficient in all these areas and choose a career that may or may not be related to their strongest academic subject.

Some students may have a strong tendency to learn a certain way, but others may have no such tendency. Regardless, we should not identify a child's learning style and use it to restrict him; on the contrary, if we discover strengths, we should deemphasize them while prioritizing weaknesses to afford the child the opportunity to reach his full potential in all facets of learning. The goal is not to make children feel good about themselves; it is to allow students to grow and develop, even if that means hardship, struggle, challenge, disappointment, and even failure along the way. Martin Luther King Jr. said, "They must make mistakes and learn from them, make more mistakes and learn anew. They must taste defeat as well as success, and discover how to live with each. Time and action are the teachers."[8]

Entertaining Students

Another destructive philosophy permeating education insists that students must be entertained to learn. The justification for this delusion is the fact that students live in a world inundated with videogames, fast-paced television programs, and access to the Internet. These media impact their lives every day. One cannot omit multifunctional cell phones, text messaging, and iPods from this equation. Continuous entertainment and contact with others are instantaneous with the press of a button.

The logic of educational leaders is that students must be entertained in the classroom, thereby sparking interest and keeping their attention spans. Only a noneducator would assert that videos, computers, Internet access, and games have no place in classrooms. Educational benefits definitely arise from these media. However, emphasizing entertainment as the primary mode by which children should be educated is erroneous; moreover, one should rarely employ the use of these media in high school.

At the high school level, coddling and handholding must end. Teachers must instill in students the realization that education and learning require hard work, effort, and personal responsibility. Actually, the process of instilling this mentality should begin at the elementary level and be ingrained in students' minds by the time they enter high school. Learning and academic development require studying, reading, writing, and memorization—therefore, hard work and effort by individual students. Students cannot accomplish learning through a myriad of games, group work, and entertaining activities. Teachers will help, guide, and encourage, but students must begin to develop skills that will allow them to succeed in college, think analytically even if they do not attend college, and become independent citizens who can comprehend issues and discern between sources of conflicting information.

Cultural tendencies or fads should not dominate the classroom, weakening the education promoted there. The fact that we exist in a faster-paced, technologically saturated society that offers a large number of electronic entertainment sources doesn't mean these sources should inundate the education system. Around the turn of the century, education leaders insisted that computers were necessary to effectively educate children, but such an assertion is far from the truth. If pupils learn how to think, they can transfer that ability to the use of technology; conversely, learning how to use computers does not equate to honing thinking skills. Public schools have poured millions of dollars into technology, but such expenditures do not necessarily produce better learners.

Teachers are supposed to be educators, not entertainers. Students should be learners, not members of an audience. The most effective method of transferring knowledge is by lecture, and the most effective way to learn that knowledge is through study. When educators attend a conference, colleagues share information primarily via the lecture method. The reason for this is simple: presenters can effectively dispense large amounts of knowledge, and learners can review the material independently to comprehend and master it. Teachers should supplement studying and rigorous teaching with videos and games, but they should rarely utilize such activities.

As a teacher, I incorporated a few excellent games that helped students learn material and concepts, but they were a special privilege. The infrequency of those activities increased their value to students, magnifying their effectiveness and learning benefits.

Another drawback of entertainment is the increased time required to complete tasks, which translates into a need to decrease the amount of material one can teach during a school year. As previously stated, some propose extending the school calendar. Proponents of an extended school year point to low American academic achievement compared to that of foreign nations, an outdated calendar based on an agrarian society, and the loss of knowledge during summer vacation to justify their opinion. If schools genuinely challenged students, the above problems would disappear. Instead of extending the school day and year, schools should readjust the curriculum to reflect the same level of demands in place several decades ago, not forgetting the more stringent academic and behavioral expectations in foreign countries.

Furthermore, when students enroll in a college or university, they will discover that the primary mode of teaching is the lecture, while students bear the responsibility to study and learn the material. Lectures from my college history professors ignited in me the fire of enthusiasm for the subject. Because they deeply probed into the details, intricacies, nuances, and complexities of history, their courses were interesting, exciting, and challenging. To earn a good grade, one was required to attend class regularly, pay attention, take good notes, and study hard. Those conditions provided an excellent learning environment and allowed me to become more knowledgeable and academically stronger. The foundation for such achievement, laid during my Catholic and public school years, allowed me to be successful in this demanding atmosphere.

Also, a significant reason for the high dropout rate at institutions of higher learning is the inability of many students to adjust to these increased standards after spending thirteen years in the undemanding public school system. I do not overlook the lack of self-discipline, indulgence in the freedoms associated with college enrollment, lack of time management skills, or other reasons that lead to failure in college, but poor preparation is a major factor in this setting. For example, in the City University of New York (CUNY) system, only 10 percent of the 2009 freshman class could solve a simple algebra problem, and only 33 percent could convert a fraction into a decimal. As a result of these statistics, professors estimate that many of these students will struggle, fail, or drop out.[9] High school graduation rates are high, but students are unable to demonstrate basic skills that will permit them to improve their lots in life. This is an ideal scenario for the statist who wants to engineer an incompetent and therefore dependent populace.

Affective Learning

Another detrimental philosophy of the modern education system that has negative implications for our nation is the focus on affective learning, which emphasizes feelings and emotions to ensure that students have a high self-esteem. Who does not want children to have a positive self-image? People normally want others to feel good about themselves. The problem here is that the education system lowers standards to promote a feel-good mentality.

As already stated, rewarding low achievement so students can feel good about themselves harms everyone in society. If students choose not to study, they can play games or complete simple assignments to raise their grades and feel good about themselves. In the high school where I worked, teachers were required to offer a minimum of eighteen graded assignments per nine-week grading period. Many teachers greatly exceeded that number. When I was a student in high school, classes offered three to five grades per nine weeks, and few had more than seven or eight.

The problem with the two-grades-per-week policy is that many assignments, often referred to as "authentic assessments," are composed of charts, graphs, worksheets, and other simple work. Though some authentic assessments are challenging, many are used to provide a so-called realistic assessment because many students are considered poor test takers. (Similar to learning styles, many students and parents have been convinced that they are poor test takers and often employ this excuse when they cannot pass exams. Although this problem may be valid for a few learners, it has become a crutch for many.)

Even better, students can complete an almost-endless amount of extra credit to improve their grades. These tasks include such achievements as bringing in canned food for a food drive or old eyeglasses for the poor, quietly testing one's locker combination at the beginning of the year, holding the door open during a fire drill, bringing in soda can tabs for a fundraiser, and the list goes on.

Even better than that, students never have homework, complete "homework" in class, or cannot receive a zero for failing to complete their homework. Concerning the latter, a "brilliant" concept states that students should have unlimited time to submit homework or make up missed assignments due to absence or for simply refusing to complete them in the first place; or they receive half credit (50) for each assignment they choose not to complete. As long as no one's feelings are hurt and failure is not an option, everyone is happy.

Social Promotion

More shocking than that, believe it or not, teachers can pass students to the next grade for doing absolutely nothing and failing every subject in their current grade. Teachers do not want students to feel bad about who they are because they fall behind the grade level of peers their age. After all, according to education experts, if students are retained, they will drop out of school anyway.

According to a 1975 study by Gregg Jackson, "There is no reliable body of evidence to indicate that grade retention is more beneficial to grade promotion for students with serious academic or adjustment difficulties."[10] Studies in 1984 and 1989 also reveal that the retention of students has more negative effects than positive ones.[11] Moreover, students retained in elementary school are more likely to drop out of high school, 78 percent of dropouts have been retained at least once, and retention increases the dropout risk between 20 and 50 percent.[12] In cities with the highest dropout rates, 40 percent of freshmen repeat the ninth grade, and 25 to 30 percent of repeaters drop out of high school.[13]

No one wants that to happen. It is much better for high school graduates to read at an elementary school level, isn't it? It is far more appropriate for students to receive a worthless diploma without possessing reading or math skills or the ability to think intelligently than it is for them to drop out at the age of sixteen, isn't it? It is beneficial to society to have a high graduation rate and for students to possess a high self-esteem by graduating with their friends in return for low achievement, isn't it? What's more important—learning math, reading, history, science, and thinking skills or feeling good about yourself and having proper socio-emotional adjustment?

Therefore, incapable students who may be multiple grade levels behind their peers are socially promoted so they can feel good about themselves. At some point these youth reach high school and have no chance to succeed. They will still drop out or be given a diploma after several years of social promotion, ill prepared to positively contribute to society. This is not their fault.

Also, the high school will be held responsible for providing alternate services to these students (so they can succeed and feel good about their accomplishments) so it will meet minimum graduation requirements. In this case the system is its own enemy because the elementary and middle schools socially promoted the pupils in an alleged attempt to help them. Now the high school is burdened with putting these students in a situation where they can graduate, and the poor students are stuck between a rock and a hard place—either not graduating by dropping out or receiving a diploma for below-average work, which will make them feel good for accomplishing nothing. As a result, thousands of students graduate from high schools every year with a diploma that makes them little more accomplished than their peers who have dropped out. Deep inside, I think, many of these students realize they are being rewarded for mediocrity.

If a student is smart enough to earn a GED or needs more than four years of high school to graduate, the state or federal government punishes the school because it does not have enough students graduating with a diploma or finishing school on time. Yet these are two legitimate alternatives (acquiring a GED or graduating in more than four years) to on-time graduation that allow motivated students to achieve and become equipped for gainful employment.

A number of consequences result from social promotion. First, students are not prepared to be productive citizens because they earned passing grades and a diploma for poor effort. Second, students expect future rewards for the same low initiative and achievement because a pathetic reward system conditioned them. Third, young adults now expect some type of intervention so they can keep a job and earn a salary in the employment sector. Fourth, students are cognizant of the fact that they are being rewarded for nothing. This thinking causes them to mock and further con the system, thus stunting them as learners, achievers, and producers. Or this awareness creates the opposite of the intended effect, giving them low self-worth because they realize they are merely being pushed through the system. Fifth, society suffers because schools produce a work force unequipped to positively or effectively contribute to society; moreover, these citizens do not possess the mental capacity to make wise decisions at the ballot box—which is a mockery of Mr. Thomas Jefferson and other Founding Fathers' purpose for a compulsory education system.

This should come as no surprise since socialist-leaning liberals mock every principle upon which our nation was founded. Citizens have not developed the ability to think rationally, logically, or analytically; they have been conditioned to expect government intervention for their inadequacy, and a biased media deceives them, causing them to make poor voting decisions detrimental to the United States of America.

INCREASING EXPECTATIONS

At what point should schools expect students to learn at a higher level? When should teachers ratchet up education a notch or two to make learning more rigorous and challenging? Based on my experiences in education, beginning at the high school level (ninth grade) teachers should deemphasize and minimize the simplified methods of teaching I have described. At this juncture teachers should train students to listen, take notes, study on their own time, and memorize information. Lecture should be the primary teaching method (many educators may cringe and possibly require resuscitation after reading this statement), along with reading and writing activities that compare, contrast, analyze, summarize, and interpret the taught information. This strategy places the burden for learning on the student as opposed to the teacher—which is how schools used to operate and explains why students were once stronger, more capable, and better educated.

I again draw from my experiences as a teacher. I had the pleasure of teaching college-level history classes in a high school. Through these classes, students earned credit from the local community college. Unlike my predecessors, I taught the classes at their intended level. These challenging classes forced students to rise to a new level of dedication, determination, work ethic, and effort to earn the grade they were accustomed to receiving.

Students who took these courses had habitually earned straight As in their other classes with little thought and minimal effort. Some students were stellar in my classes from day one, but the majority had to make major adjustments in their academic habits to be successful. After taking their first test a few weeks into the course, students panicked and talked about dropping the class if they earned a C, D, or F, which neither they nor their parents were comfortable seeing on their report card. From my viewpoint, dropping this class was not an option; I didn't permit students to drop the class unless they were failing at the end of the first semester. Students were enrolled in two separate U.S. history classes, one during each semester, so they had to drop the second class if they failed the first (since the school had paid the students' tuition to the community college, it dropped them from the second class if they failed the first).

I would not allow these students to drop the class when they experienced initial failure. However, I also provided motivation, encouragement, guidance, and instruction on note taking and study skills. I built up these students and told them they could succeed if they changed their habits, challenged themselves, and truly put their abilities to the test. I explained that they would take courses of this magnitude in college and that their continuation and improvement in my course would aid their adjustment to college.

I also counseled their parents since they were concerned about the effect of a low grade on their child's grade point average, a key determinant of college acceptance.

These students took pride in their education and performance, and they believed they could improve and succeed. Through the teacher's efforts, the students' perseverance, and the patience of the parents, these young adults became stronger, prouder, more refined, better equipped, and intellectually improved. They realized they could reach high levels of expectation through hard work, dedication, and desire. They also believed they would succeed in college as a result.

I taught these courses for four years, which included a combined total of approximately 180 to 200 students. I cannot recall how many students and parents thanked me for challenging them or their children in preparing them for college. Many informed me that my classes (as well as a couple of others my colleagues taught) helped their transition into college as freshmen, in contrast to their poorly prepared peers. Many students, if poorly prepared for college, are placed on academic probation or drop out altogether. The high demands of the classes I taught, however, were instrumental in allowing many of these students to successfully transition into higher education. Of course, some would have done so without my classes.

Finally, the students deserve a commendation for not quitting, for buckling down, for striving to improve, for persevering through hardships, for assuming responsibility for their success, for sacrificing leisure opportunities to study, and for working hard to experience true achievement. All they needed was someone to inspire them to do so. The parents also deserve credit for placing their trust in me as an educator, especially when they heard something foreign to them. Dedication, perseverance, personal responsibility, sacrifice, hard work—these are terms we do not see often enough in today's education system or society.

Thomas Jefferson's purpose for a compulsory public school system was to create an informed electorate that would make wise decisions and therefore preserve democracy.[14] If he witnessed the low expectations, the emphasis on entertainment, and the foolish initiatives such as schools teaching students how to write in the lingo of text messages instead of learning how to properly write a five-sentence paragraph, he would probably have the proverbial conniption.

Many teachers would like to teach their classes as I did. A basic curriculum guide that stipulates the material instructors must teach so students can pass an end-of-course test does not restrict college-level courses. At one time, teaching to the test was frowned upon; today, it is encouraged and celebrated as proper teaching. Many instructors would teach more rigorous classes if they could. Many do the best they can, considering the circumstances of education in our day. Hopefully, we will return to a more demanding education system in the future.

How many more students would have an easier time adjusting to college if all high school courses demanded higher expectations? How many students would be stronger even if they were disinterested in attending college? Schools would produce stronger citizens across the board, regardless of interests, goals, or abilities. As they say, a rising tide affects all ships. All courses do not need to be college-level classes to increase standards, so the bar can be raised a great deal. Sure, some may struggle. But weakening the system as a whole to make children feel good about themselves is damaging society in its entirety. Lowering standards and simplifying the curriculum do not create strong students. On the contrary, increased demands that may cause some students to struggle would better serve our nation than the current low expectations that reward low achievement, allow students to feel good about little accomplishment, turn out poorly educated graduates, and produce poorly trained citizens.

Once educators, parents, and students recognize that standards have been raised, many stragglers will eventually rise to the occasion as well. Students often put forth the minimum effort that will allow them to succeed. If expectations were raised, however, effort for most pupils would naturally increase so they could be as successful as they want to be. A key word here is *want*. A teacher can encourage, motivate, counsel, and demand all day long, but some students will choose mediocrity, if not less. Not everyone will pass the class, not everyone will pass the test, and not everyone will graduate. The latter may be hard for some to swallow, but the fact that some students are given high school diplomas today is a farce. I intentionally use the word *given* because a number of students pass through the system and do not *earn* a diploma. Instituting genuinely high expectations, challenging standards, rigorous demands, and an excellent education for those who choose to acquire it is far more valuable than offering an "education" to students to make them feel good for low achievement and distributing diplomas that are not worth the paper on which they are printed.

Today's teacher is forced to entertain students, make learning fun, and provide simple activities and assessments so children can be "successful." It is okay to implement fun activities, but they must be the exception as opposed to the focus of learning.

The good news is that some students realize soon after graduation that the real world is vastly different from the public school system; unfortunately, some do not learn this lesson or, as mentioned, are poorly prepared to do anything about it if they do. Other students, whose parents possess the high value of education and instill in them a solid work ethic, realize genuine accomplishments and contribute to their community at a high level of productivity. How much potential is lost in students who do not get the wake-up call until after the feel-good public school system ambushes them, if they receive that call at all?

CHAPTER 3

EDUCATION AND SOCIALISM

GOVERNMENTAL CONTROL AND influence in education is the next topic of discussion. What I mean by that statement is the control of citizens by promoting dependence on the government. One can infer from that statement that liberals are promoting socialism through the American education system. This phenomenon occurs in several ways, but most, including those who work there, do not connect the actions of schools with this destructive philosophy. Of course, state departments of education dictate actions of schools, with federal mandates, interests of teachers' unions, and other special interest groups often influencing their actions.

In the first chapter, I wrote significantly about the intentional, strategic breakdown of the family that gives the government increased control over that precious unit. The simplest way for the government to gain influence and thus indoctrinate children is through public education because all students between the ages of five and seventeen are required to attend school. This is another reason to be wary of federal calls to increase the amount of time students spend in school. If that change occurs, children will spend even less time with their families, thereby increasing the hours they spend in the governmental indoctrination center.

SOCIALISM EXPANDS

As I stated at the beginning of this book, the expansion of socialism has been gradual. With each passing generation, however, this destructive force claims more and more people. I believe it has expanded exponentially over the last twenty years. Current students are so accustomed to being pandered to that government will easily expand its power when they join the electorate. They are so accustomed to being served that they will vote for any promise of a government entitlement that is "free" and alleges to make their lives easier. This may be the motivation of those who call for lowering the voting age to eighteen years old. Not only have these students been thoroughly indoctrinated; they've had limited life experiences by which to make wise decisions that will impact a nation. The same could be said about a growing number of twenty-one-year-olds.

For the liberal statist, the education system is the perfect way to gradually impose socialism on a country that has a heritage based on the values of freedom, hard work, and personal responsibility. It is difficult to introduce the principles of socialism into a society where the nation's traditions and foundational precepts naturally oppose and reject them. If socialist-leaning liberals were to openly discuss their ambitions, they would face outright rejection; so they must find another way to inject their ideals into the society they want to transform in order to create the world order to which they have pledged their loyalties. They must devise a surreptitious method by which to execute their plan. Through the education system they can reach the multitudes and do so without alarming the passive public that perceives the education system as a vital necessity for self-improvement, gaining empowering knowledge, and getting ahead in life.

Through altruistic, benevolent-sounding initiatives elitists have gradually expanded government power, taken away parental authority, and established a sense of dependence on the local government, which is the school system. Their allies are the media, which uplift the relativists' ideals while chastising the opposition's viewpoints. Over time, the socialist shapes a mindset in the populace that more readily accepts the notion that the government is responsible for its care. This population begins to tolerate the liberals' value system to the detriment of its own. The cycle continues until the socialist wins and the citizens of the nation choose to sacrifice their God-given liberties to a tyrannical government.

Local Schools and Socialism

You may contemplate how the local school system and local government can advance socialism at the federal level. This is simple. Decisions your local school district has made are based on a socialist philosophy that benefits the federal government, and many of those decisions are based on federal mandates. Dependence cannot be assigned only to the local level; once it is ingrained in the psyche, it affects all facets of society. Once citizens become acclimated to receiving government assistance from one level, they expect it from all levels; once they willingly seek and accept help in one area of their lives, they expect it in all areas of their lives. When students are conditioned to receive a mediocre education at the elementary level, they have the same expectation at the high school level, which is where the buck stops in regard to meeting graduation requirements. Once the government fuses into students' minds an entitlement mindset while they attend the public school and higher education systems, a dependent mentality grows in the electorate while accumulation of power increases for those in authority. Both results are the desired outcome for the liberal, socialist statist.

Many education leaders buy into the notion that the school system should provide for students and families. In addition, many in state government conform to this philosophy. Furthermore, those who formulate teacher education programs are adherents of this set of ideals, and they include the teachers' unions and other special interest groups. Moreover, federal regulations and mandates force states and local schools to adopt policies that promote these values, often with the threat of forfeiting federal monies if they fail to enact federal initiatives. Schools receive greater sums of money by aggressively adhering to federal guidelines; for example, more students listed on free and reduced lunch rolls translates into increased allocations from the federal government for the "economically disadvantaged" population. The socialist philosophy trickles down from the federal level, the universities, and the state to the local school systems, which institute the socialist program that, through association, benefits the federal government. The idea comes from above, the action occurs below, and the grassroots effort ("little brother") benefits those who possess power and influence ("big brother") over the masses.

SCHOOLS BECOME PARENTS

What are some ways the government wrests control from parents, allowing it to influence and indoctrinate children? One way is through various school policies such as an attendance policy, for example. Through such policies, students typically fail the grading period, semester, or school year after they have been absent from school for a specified number of days. Many affirm that this policy is good because it encourages students to attend school; it requires their attendance and promises a consequence for neglecting to follow the rules. The problem with attendance policies is the notification systems, which vary from one district to another. I must say that some school systems place the bulk of the responsibility for attendance on students and parents. Many, however, do not. This essay references those school systems that assume responsibility for compliance in areas of attendance and other policies, thus creating in parents and students a mentality of dependence on the system, the local government, to keep them in line.

How is the local government involved? The local board of supervisors approves the school budgets and spends local, state, and federal tax revenue to fund its schools. Since tax dollars fund schools, schools are tools of the local government. As mentioned earlier, many school policies are based on regulations enacted by both the state and federal governments.

Some actions school systems take to monitor attendance include the following: multiple notifications mailed by teachers, administrators, and attendance clerks; phone contacts by teachers, administrators, and truancy officers; conferences involving school personnel, parents, and students; attendance contracts signed by all or some of the above-listed persons; and appeal hearings initiated by school personnel, the school board office, or the school board. In limited quantities, these interventions are necessary and acceptable. The prevailing logic has become that students with poor attendance have incompetent parents; therefore, the school system must invoke a number of interventions to solve the problem and help children. This area is where the line is crossed between parents raising their children versus the schools, or the government, assuming this role.

As I mentioned, a limited number of interventions are appropriate, but excessive amounts undermine parenting and promote dependence on the school. When the school takes on this role, parents become conditioned to expect the school to take the initiative regarding their child instead of them doing so. Once this process begins and spreads via word of mouth, the number of parents and students expecting the school to assume this responsibility increases; more importantly, students who experience such school involvement expect and more easily accept such services when they have their own children. Therefore, dependence grows, and this generation becomes more government reliant than the previous one.

If, in parents' opinions, the school fails to take adequate action, students must be exonerated from the consequences of breaking school policy. Adequate action often reflects the measures listed above, which the local school board establishes. The board often formulates policy according to the superintendent's desires or based on the trends seen in other school districts. If adequate action is not taken, district administrators blame and reprimand school personnel for not abiding by school board policy. These administrators acquit the parent and student of wrongdoing and reward them for neglecting personal responsibility. This practice then expands the cycle of families growing increasingly dependent on the local government (the school system) and of government in general assuming more responsibility in citizens' lives.

Low Grades

This mode of operation, not confined to attendance policies, is repeated in abundant situations in school systems. Say that a student has failing grades on his first-quarter report card. A typical parental reaction is that they were not aware of their child's low grades; parents feel that teachers were derelict in their duties by not informing them. Therefore, the student should be given a passing grade or the opportunity to make up missed work, and parents fail to acknowledge that they neglected their parental duties.

The following is a list of actions schools undertake to advertise their schedules so parents can be involved in their child's education: They schedule an open house the week before school begins. After school starts they schedule a back-to-school night so parents can follow their child's class schedule and speak to every teacher. They communicate important information through websites, student agendas, newsletters, calendars that reflect important dates (such as the beginning and end of grading periods), interim reports that indicate student grades halfway through the quarter, and parent-teacher conferences scheduled several times throughout the school year. Despite all this, they insist that their child should be given a reprieve if they do not receive a phone call from a teacher about a poor grade.

High school students have been in the school system for a minimum of ten years upon their entry into ninth grade; therefore, by then parents should know how the school operates. Yet they still claim ignorance, and many school administrators support the parents. Despite all the tools available to parents, they have become dependent on the school to raise their children. If parents were not so dependent, they would take steps to be aware of their student's level of success, know when their student was not doing well, and at least accept responsibility for not knowing.

I need to state here that many parents do take an active role in their child's life and do not expect the school to assume parental responsibility, but this number is lessening. When I attended school, parents did not expect teachers to call them. My parents were involved in my education, asked me about school almost daily, monitored when I was or was not doing homework, and knew when report cards were issued. If I received an F, they didn't mention the teacher or the school in the discussion; the subjects of the conversation were my poor effort and my responsibility to earn acceptable grades regardless of the teacher or his teaching methods. Ah, the good old days of high parental involvement and individual responsibility!

Tutoring

Tutoring is another avenue through which the government nudges control away from parents. As a rule, after-school tutoring is a good thing. Students who struggle in a class or with a particular concept can receive attention in small groups or one-on-one to help them master the particular area of need. A problem arises when schools promote after-school tutoring to give students a place to hang out. In a number of cases, students stay after school to socialize with friends and pass time as opposed to working to improve their academic proficiency. Therefore, the school becomes a babysitter for students, who can purchase snacks and drinks from vending machines to tide them over until they ride home on the school-provided activity bus, another service the school system and taxpayer pay for. God forbid a student is a little hungry before he gets home after 5:00. Educators say students need to eat so they can concentrate, and then the same educators turn around and complain about obesity in the current generation.

Some argue that it is better for students to stay in a supervised location while their parents are at work than to linger in an unsupervised home, where they can get hurt or engage in illicit activities. But the school's purpose is to educate, not to babysit, yet some parents place their children in after-school tutoring for this very reason. It is the parents' job to provide supervision for their children or to arrange it in their absence. It is not the local government's duty to provide day care services.

Another form of tutoring comes through Saturday school. Certain school systems typically offer or mandate this for students who receive disciplinary referrals for violating the code of conduct. Sometimes the requirement to attend Saturday school replaces out-of-school suspension (OSS), and sometimes schools use it to make up for time missed from school due to OSS. Once again, the school provides day care services, this time for those who refuse to behave properly.

Most students who attend Saturday school are repeat offenders who have committed a long list of offenses in school. The cost for providing this service includes paying a teacher, administrator, or both to babysit these students for a few hours. Heat or air-conditioning must be turned up when the building is occupied, and sometimes the school provides a small snack so the poor children do not suffer from hunger or malnourishment. After all, many of these students come from "economically disadvantaged" households that may not be able to afford breakfast, if any meal. Yet many of these children come to school wearing $125 jerseys, $100 pairs of shoes, and brand names such as Timberland, Tommy Hilfiger, and Polo. They own cell phones, iPods, and multiple video game systems. Parents purchase expensive gifts for their children to exchange with friends for Christmas, Valentine's Day, and birthdays, yet they do not have the means to provide a meal at home.

Based on the number of overweight children in America, we know that most are eating their fill and then some. Although some students are impoverished, they are the exception rather than the rule. Unfortunately, our nation's tendency is to use the minority that experiences a certain circumstance to change the way of life for everyone. George Washington warned, "If the laws are to be trampled upon with impunity, and a minority (a small one too) is to dictate to the majority, there is an end put, at one stroke, to republican government."[1] This is an admonition against residing in the aforementioned valley of exceptions.

In the end, this is yet another area through which schools are the substitute for parents by bearing the responsibility for the supervision of children. Furthermore, some schools provide counseling services such as anger management, career counseling, good decision-making skills, and so on. This counseling thus perpetuates the indoctrination of students in socialist ideals through the government care center for misguided and misunderstood youth. Some often ask, "What can the school do to serve the children?" We should interpret this question as, "What can the government do to help kids and, by association, instill in them and their parents a sense of dependency on the state?" Despite clarion calls to be proactive, no one in public education has pondered what this generation will demand from the local, socialist government when it has its own children.

Dress Code

Clothing provides another opportunity for the local school to assume responsibility for people's actions and foster dependence on government, thereby supplanting individual and parental self-regulation. In the twenty-first century, it is not uncommon to see people of all types wearing inappropriate attire, including sagging pants that reveal one's undergarments; extremely short miniskirts and shorts; tight shorts and pants; and blouses that reveal the midriff, cleavage, or both. How can parents not teach their children how to dress properly? Why do parents purchase such clothing for their children? What type of value system is being taught that encourages children to disrespect themselves and any code of decency? Some parents allow their scantily clad daughters to frolic in public without restraint, then complain when they are sexually promiscuous, if not already pregnant or raising a child as a teenager. Suddenly, their child is a victim who had no control over her circumstances.

Why are schools not viewed as sacred places where learning is valued while improper, distracting attire is considered inappropriate? Some students and parents do have this view and are repulsed by improper dress, but they are forced to tolerate those who respect neither themselves nor the system. Why should public schools (those that choose to do so) bear the responsibility of teaching proper dress to children and enforcing dress codes within its confines? Of course, schools should have proper dress expectations, but they shouldn't find it necessary to publish extensive dress codes delineating inappropriate clothing.

Moral Relativism

When I attended high school, a dress code was unnecessary; everyone knew the expectations and dressed accordingly. Today, dozens of confrontations occur daily in most schools as teachers try to create a proper learning atmosphere. In some schools, however, teachers don't confront anything since improper dress is accepted and tolerated under the guise of diversity. In some schools, the magnitude of the problem leads to tolerance because the battle becomes counterproductive and not worth fighting, or the attitude of diversity prohibits the establishment of a standard. Again, where are parents in this situation? Again, values have eroded, and it is up to the local government to solve its citizens' problems. Again, parental authority lessens, government influence expands, and dependence of parents and students broadens.

This byproduct of moral relativism, in which all options are acceptable, has ruled our culture since the rebellious sixties. Those who disagree with any unsuitable behavior are told they must tolerate the dissolution of our values. This state of affairs is reminiscent of Pandora's box; now that the box has been opened, innumerable and unpredictable behaviors, attitudes, opinions, actions, and feelings have flooded our culture.

According to the tale, the gods of Olympus, upon Zeus's orders, created Pandora to rain down affliction upon mankind, including trouble, sickness, and misfortune.[2] These ailments are no different from what mankind has experienced beginning with Adam and Eve. However, in contrast to Pandora's jar, the original container Pandora held, today's social ills have been placed on humans due to their own ignorance, foolishness, intemperance, licentiousness, and acceptance of any notion conceived in their minds. What we are experiencing today far exceeds the ills released from Pandora's jar, making her afflictions seem small and insignificant by comparison.

No one can comprehend the detrimental consequences of this phenomenon on our society. Who could have predicted the fad called "embedding," in which teens embed various items in their bodies, such as nails, crayons, glass, and other items? I will refrain from listing many other disturbing behaviors, but I know a number crossed your mind when you read the last sentence. What will the next fad be? What will "troubled" teens do next with justification by pop psychologists as a legitimate reaction to some type of oppression? What next popular fad teenagers or young adults engage in will adults and parents adopt? When will adults reclaim their duty to train the next generation instead of letting their children's values influence them? Based on their behavior, how will today's youth be able to properly train their children? They won't, and that's exactly where socialist-leaning liberals want our culture to be.

Proponents of relativism don't care about consequences because they believe no one has the right to tell anyone else how to live (unless he works in government). And when consequences do come, the government will provide answers, research, medicine, excuses, or whatever is needed to allow citizens to continue engaging in destructive behavior, just as long as they are happy, feel good, and experience instant gratification. Who cares about the negative impact on those who abstain from such behaviors or disagree with them? They can obtain from the government the same medicine or solutions that irresponsible, shameless relativists receive. However, if you disagree with valueless relativists, who claim that all opinions carry equal validity, they will accuse you of being wrong. That's right; you will be told you are wrong. Relativists make such an accusation without realizing that their philosophy does not permit the concept of wrong, which makes their sentiment void and moot. Moral relativism, therefore, lacks a valid or solid foundation upon which to stand.

Nevertheless, this relativistic attitude has spawned an overabundance of noxious byproducts on our great nation, and inappropriate dress is only one of them. Therefore, the school, as described above, must author an exhaustive dress code stipulating what can and cannot be worn in school.

The sad reality is that parents have become incompetent in this area (among others). Students have no sense of what they should wear because of both their parents' incompetence and the pop culture's promotion of the relativistic agenda. In addition, society has become tolerant and avoids accusations of being fascist, racist, prudish, insensitive, or intolerant of the new generation—X, Y, Z^2, or whatever it is dubbed. The sadder reality is that the socialist government must intervene to save citizens from their own absurdity; the local school system must establish a dress code, repeatedly enforce the code, and counsel parents and students on proper dress through mailings, fashion shows, and parent-student conferences. The saddest reality is that when schools confront parents and students about inappropriate dress, a growing number do not understand why an outfit is inappropriate or express outrage at the violation of their civil right to dress however they want.

SOCIALISM BECOMES INGRAINED

The point should be clear. The socialist local government, the school system, steps in to "help" parents and students understand what is acceptable. Consider the following results: The "beneficiaries" of this process become better inhabitants of their community and citizens of their nation. The socialist local government takes pride in "improving" people and society. The "benefactors" of this activism become more dependent on the local, socialist government as they gratefully look forward to receiving future assistance. The local, socialist government then seeks ways to further "assist" its constituents and thus create a better planet. The dichotomy between offering provision and receiving assistance continues and gradually increases in intensity, slowly and surely ensconcing socialism in America.

Through this process the federal government ("big brother"), with its secular, socialist ideology, benefits most. Essentially, the public school system ("little brother") is the vehicle by which socialism has been propagated in our nation. A large majority of Americans do not realize this atrocious act has occurred because proponents have brought it on surreptitiously and in slow, gradual increments.

Parents Cede Authority

How many parents have ceded their authority to the public school system just because that is where children are supposed to be? How many expect the school to raise their children? How many have lowered their guards because they know the school will intervene, if needed? How many parents know what textbooks teach their children? How many community members, who support their school system with their taxes, realize what is included in a state or school's curriculum? If they are aware, how many perceive the curriculum as harmless or something that will fade away with time (such as instruction in environmentalism)? How many parents accept school policies and procedures without reviewing or understanding them? How many parents are so uninvolved in school that they do not realize their children are taught that their parents' values are not applicable to their lives? Children therefore reject those values and formulate their own utilitarian ones, while parents do not recognize this threat to their moral code, authority, or influence. How many care?

This undermining of parental values has occurred every day in schools for at least the last several decades. The final result is a gradually expanding acceptance of socialism due to steady, intentional, and calculated indoctrination toward that end. As parents and students become accustomed to the school addressing their concerns, and as they become comfortable with the school's value system, they in turn become increasingly dependent on the local government. This dependent thinking takes deeper root as they accept the notion that the school is the center of the community and as they get used to reminders, services, initiatives, and actions the school takes on their behalf. Dependence on the school then translates into dependence on government in general. As students who have experienced the charitable education system enter the workforce, they expect similar care as adults from the government. Such thinking permits the federal government to increase power, influence, and control over its populace, effectively instituting socialism in our nation and tyranny over its people. And yes—government achieves it all through the "safe," "caring," "supervised" public school system.

The list of programs and services schools offer includes the following:

- Breakfast
- After-school programs that allow both parents to work
- Character education introduced due to problems created by lax rules and the removal of prayer
- Incentives and rewards for proper behavior and academic performance
- Tips on diet (including how to eat, how much to eat, and reminders to drink water instead of sugary soda), proper dress, text messaging, hygiene, and hand washing (yes, this occurs at the high school level)
- Steps to treat swine flu, bird flu, MRSA (skin infection), or other exaggerated afflictions
- Flu vaccinations
- Hearing and vision tests
- Sex education that can include instruction on abortion, masturbation, condom use, and acceptance of the gay or lesbian lifestyle

- Multiple opportunities to make up missed work and pass end-of-course tests
- Various remediation opportunities
- Numerous reminders to sign up for tests, attend tutoring, take tests, apply for college scholarships, pay fees, and fulfill graduation requirements
- School personnel setting up parent conferences and scheduling appeal hearings
- Transportation home from after-school activities
- Teachers calling home about grades, attendance, mood swings, behavior, socialization problems, or personality changes
- Multiple interventions for disabilities, laziness, disobedience, bad parenting, poor attendance, and a variety of excuses
- Counseling on organization skills, honesty, bullying, and so on
- Continual extension of deadlines for negligent students
- Multiple letters and phone calls home concerning possible failure
- And the list goes on and on.

Many items on this list sound benign and harmless and may appear to be helpful and appropriate. But through small steps such as these the local, socialist government seizes power from parents and advances socialism on the country through the development of a dependent mindset.

If you are over forty, how many of these services do you remember the school providing to you as a parent or student? What if you are between thirty and forty? Between twenty and thirty? Students graduating from schools today view these and other school services as normal, necessary, appropriate, and deserved. Parents and pupils become more amenable to such services, the government widens it breadth of service provision, and both service provider and customer continue to move in their respective directions. Again, the end result is the slow increase of dependence on government that promotes the steady escalation of government power and the advancement of socialism in America.

School Breakfast

I discuss school breakfast to illustrate this point. When the economy at the beginning of 2009 worsened, Virginia's Department of Education issued a memo to schools, summarizing the difference between the number of lunches and the number of breakfasts served in Virginia schools; breakfasts lagged far behind lunches. The objective was for schools to promote breakfast to students during National School Breakfast Week.

Encouraging students to eat breakfast sounds like an honorable effort. Studies show the benefits of beginning the day with a healthy breakfast in areas such as energy, attention span, concentration, and achievement. The memo stated that schools should encourage more students to eat breakfast in their cafeteria. Because the struggling economy may have negatively impacted parents, the state of Virginia suggested that requesting children to eat breakfast at school was more economical for parents. The memo said, "As finances become tighter for families and schools, eating breakfast at school is a great bargain economically and nutritionally."[3] Sounds benevolent, does it not? The compassionate government offered to help parents by providing a low-cost, nutritious breakfast to their children; at the same time, the government entity would benefit economically.

The problem comes when the socialist state government requests schools to encourage families to become more dependent on the schools, the local socialist government. Instead of providing for their families, parents can trust the government to do it for them. The memo further promoted this idea as "an important step in improving the health of Virginia's students."[4] Notice that the language emphasizes the improvement of the state's children, not the parents' children.

State governments do not monopolize such paternalism. During the swine flu "crisis" in fall 2009, Ms. Kathleen Sebelius, secretary of the Department of Health and Human Services for the Obama administration, stated on October 20, "Public health officials weigh toward keeping schools open if there's enough personnel to do that. It's dangerous for kids often to not be in school, to not have a safe place to go, to not get fed on a regular basis."[5] Again, the socialist government's duty is to feed children and keep them safe, not to mention to keep them corralled in the institutions of indoctrination. Once the government initiates such a process, it is difficult to restrict it. Look at welfare and its expansion since President Franklin Delano Roosevelt's "benevolent" New Deal legislation encouraged citizens to go on the dole and become reliant on government assistance.

Failure of the Village

Contrary to popular opinion, the United States is not a "village." The village mantra perverts individual contributions, the family, and the team concept, while promoting the communist ideology, in which all share to the benefit of the state and the detriment of individuals. Of course, such an arrangement requires supervision by a small group of privileged, "wise" leaders (this is discussed in more detail in chapter 6). The village or commune is a dismal failure. The Plymouth plantation was on the verge of self-destruction due to a communal mindset until William Bradford instituted the policy of private property for families. This forced the people to work for their own survival, thus allowing the colony to survive. Jamestown was in the midst of collapse when John Smith exhorted its citizens that "he who shall not work shall not eat." Like Plymouth, coercing people to work for their own subsistence benefitted the entire community.

What the education system intentionally fails to teach in its mission to revise our Christian history is that Captain Smith's decree was biblical. Second Thessalonians 3:10 says, "If anyone will not work, neither shall he eat." Furthermore, as I highlighted in chapter 1, Plymouth was dedicated to advancing the Christian faith. In both localities, people were waiting for others to work and complete tasks, but the colonies flourished only when individual responsibility was required.

Under the foolishness of "It takes a village," individuals become complacent when they wait for others to be productive. The spirit of a nation flounders when a growing multitude relies on its fellow citizens or the government to solve its problems and offer provision for its needs. As a result, families become inefficient entities when they become dependent on government infiltration and train their children to be the same. At the same time, the socialist-leaning education system indoctrinates students in government supremacy and nurtures a dependent mindset in its consumers. In the process, it emphasizes "teamwork." Unfortunately for many, this is another slang term that relates to the "village." People proudly assert that "there is no 'I' in team." At one time that phrase built camaraderie and unity among team members by discouraging selfishness. Today a large majority sits idly by or expends minimal effort as a small percentage of its "teammates" perform the large proportion of work, reminding us of the mentality that nearly capsized the Jamestown and Plymouth colonies.

As a school leader, I taught my employees that if you rearrange the letters in the word *team*, you find "me" in there. It takes every individual working hard, sacrificing, fulfilling responsibilities, executing duties, completing commitments, and overcoming adversity for an organization to be effective and excellent—a true champion. Teamwork is the only way. This is true for a school, a business, a family, and a nation. Hiding under the new definition of "team" or "village" produces mediocrity at best and allows for the growth and expansion of an oppressive, aristocratic government to fill the resultant void left by a lazy, incompetent, weak, dependent populace.

Although some families may require assistance during tough economic times, it is not the role of the school system to provide that assistance or to encourage others to accept it. A responsibility of relatives, churches, local groups, or private sector organizations is to help their fellow citizens in time of need. "Honor widows who are really widows. But if any widow has children or grandchildren, let them first learn to…repay their parents….If anyone does not provide for his own, and especially for those of his household, he has denied the faith and is worse than an unbeliever" (1 Tim. 5:3–4, 8).

Even better, we must learn to adjust our spending habits and lifestyles during difficult times so we can help ourselves and care for our own family without burdening others. The best strategy is for citizens to adopt a lifestyle that allows them to survive difficult times without the necessity of adjusting from a profligate routine. One of the teacher regulations in 1872 New Mexico stated, "Each teacher should lay aside from each pay a goodly sum of his earnings for his declining years, so that he will not become a burden to society."[6] This is wise advice for people of all vocations. Again, to avoid an attack by liberals, a percentage of people may need help, but they are the exception. Someone who has strong discernment can differentiate between those who need assistance and those who do not. But during a time of hardship, the government cashes in by manipulating a "crisis" to promote dependence on it while confiscating the power of the people.

Dependence on Government Increases

How does this situation translate into increased dependence on the federal government? After being provided with babysitting services for most of their lives, graduates, who are now adults, transfer the expectation of such services to the federal government, state government, or both. They do so by demanding the following entitlements:

- Unemployment compensation
- Health care through Medicare, Medicaid, or a government-run health care system
- Social security
- Disability benefits
- Free college education
- Cash-for-clunkers type programs
- Affirmative action
- Bankruptcy during a time of hardship, even when large amounts of credit were irresponsibly charged for conspicuous reasons
- Tax payment forgiveness
- Child credit for having multiple children out of wedlock
- Government-funded abortions
- Complimentary needles and condoms
- Free counseling for obesity, smoking, or contracting HIV
- And the list goes on and on.

Also remember that local schools follow state and federal guidelines and regulations; therefore, many programs in schools are initiated at one of those levels. If a state or school does not want to participate, it may lose government funding; therefore, it is basically bribed into abiding by the wishes of the central government. In other words, "big brother" uses "little brother" to achieve its ends.

Even worse, if a local or state government elects not to participate, its constituents condemn it for not accepting "free" money. Too many education leaders at the local level have succumbed to the socialist ideology through the indoctrination they received while studying for their advanced degrees, so they are often anxious to implement another program that "serves" their clientele.

In addition, teachers have an inherent desire to genuinely help students, explaining why the large majority chose education as their profession. Unfortunately, many of today's attempts to help students and families are more destructive than beneficial. Many teachers want to help students and not hurt them or society, but they are caught in a tsunami-like wave they can neither control nor swim free of; on the other hand, some support socialist ideals and are doing all they can to advance a socialist agenda. An old adage says that evil begets evil; in this case, dependence begets dependence and births socialism as a populace becomes too weak, lazy, negligent, incapable, or irresponsible to provide for itself. In the end, therefore, evil does beget evil.

CHAPTER 4

PROPAGATING RELIGION IN THE EDUCATION SYSTEM

A NYONE WHO HAS read the U.S. Constitution knows that it does not contain a single provision requiring the separation of church and state. Rather, it stipulates the following in the First Amendment: "Congress shall make no law respecting an establishment of religion, or prohibiting the free exercise thereof." The first statement, referred to as the Establishment Clause, means the government cannot establish a national church supported by all citizens. The second statement, called the Free Exercise Clause, means that government cannot restrict free religious expression. Through the Supreme Court case *Everson v. Board of Education (1947)*, Justice Hugo Black invoked the separation of church and state clause by writing, "The First Amendment has erected a wall between church and state,"[1] which has been used ever since to continually restrict public expressions of faith, primarily the Christian faith.

SUPREME COURT ABUSES POWER

A more sinister motive exists here. The Bill of Rights was intended to restrict the federal government; in this case, Justice

Black applied the First Amendment to state and local jurisdictions. This is an inappropriate application of the First Amendment and abuse of power by a Supreme Court justice; it is one example of the Supreme Court grabbing power, overstepping its boundaries, legislating from the bench, and violating the separation of powers clause of the Constitution. In addition, through the judicial branch the federal government now regularly prohibits the free exercise of the Christian faith.

For schools, Bible reading and prayer are prohibited unless they are student initiated or led, and as long as they do not disrupt the learning environment of other students. Therefore, if students read the Bible during study hall, at lunch, or in another nonacademic setting, they are permitted to do so. Preaching to students against their will or causing a distraction by praying loudly is considered a disruption the school can restrict.

An abundance of lawsuits have been filed against schools regarding prayer or Bible references in school and at graduation ceremonies, sporting events, baccalaureate, and other school functions.

- The ability to engage in voluntary, nonsectarian prayer in New York schools was outlawed via *Engle v. Vitale (1962)*.
- Invocations and benedictions were prohibited at Rhode Island graduation ceremonies through *Lee v. Weisman (1992)*.
- In Illinois, *McCollum v. Board of Education (1948)* banned religious classes that were voluntary, elective, and required written parental permission.
- *School District of Abington Township v. Schempp (1963)* prohibited the reading of Scriptures in Pennsylvania schools.
- *Stone v. Graham (1980)* declared the posting of the Ten Commandments in Kentucky unconstitutional.

- Because of *Wallace v. Jaffree (1985),* Alabama schools could not institute a one-minute moment of silence due to its alleged purpose of promoting voluntary prayer.

In most, if not all, of these cases, a single person filed a complaint, and an overly exuberant Supreme Court restricted the rights of the large majority as a result (recall the George Washington quote in chapter 3, which warned against a small minority trampling upon laws). Often the complainant's own children either do not object to the activity or enthusiastically participate in it (*Schempp* case). More importantly, in such cases the Supreme Court has interfered in state or local jurisdictions or both.

Furthermore, students of faith have been discriminated against regarding school clubs, T-shirt slogans, essays, and class projects that have emphasized their faith. Again, the large majority of these examples involved the Christian faith. Students have been reprimanded, suspended, criticized, and given penalties or failing grades because of their expressions of faith. Interestingly, the NCAA enacted a rule change beginning with the 2010 college football season concerning eye black players place under their eyes. The new rule prohibits writing any words, logos, numbers, or other symbols on the eye black, although doing so has been a common practice for some years. Is it coincidental that this rule was written in response to the Bible verses former University of Florida quarterback Tim Tebow wrote on his eye black and because of the conversation they spawned? I think not.

On a positive note, the courts have often supported student and families' First Amendment right in these incidents, to the derision of some school personnel and other antireligious, secular, or atheistic interests. But such court support does not occur until the intervention of a Christian organization, such as the American Center for Law and Justice, forces litigation or frightens a school system into retreat.

Let me repeat: the First Amendment (and Bill of Rights) was written to restrict federal government power and is not applicable to state and local governments. Furthermore, the Supreme Court has amassed power the founders never intended it to have, thus broadening our federal government's authority while effectively reducing the power of the people. Thomas Jefferson warned of this possibility when he wrote, "The Constitution...is a mere thing of wax in the hands of the judiciary which they may twist and shape into any form they please."[2] Mr. Jefferson, a strict interpreter of the Constitution, believed it should be stringently followed according to the authors' intentions, so he did not approve of this possibility.

Most importantly, restricting the expression of faith was not the Founding Fathers' intent; instead, they understood the importance of practicing Christianity for the health and survival of the nation. John Hancock stated, "Sensible of the importance of Christian piety and virtue to the order and happiness of a state, I cannot but earnestly commend to you every measure for their support and encouragement....The very existence of the republics...depend much upon the public institutions of religion."[3] Benjamin Franklin noted, "We have been assured, Sir, in the Sacred Writings that except the Lord build the house, they labor in vain that build it. I firmly believe this; and I also believe that without His concurring aid, we shall succeed in this political building no better than the builders of Babel."[4] According to Daniel Webster, "The Christian religion—its general principles—must ever be regarded among us as the foundation of civil society."[5] These are only three among literally hundreds, if not thousands, of quotes by numerous founders that relate to the important contribution of the Christian faith, the Bible, God, and prayer to the maintenance of a civil, moral, lasting nation.

CHURCH AND STATE ARE INSEPARABLE

Can separation of church and state really exist in public schools or in any institution for that matter? The answer is a resounding and confident no! No matter what you do in life or where you live, faith of some sort will guide your decisions, actions, words, and efforts. Faith, therefore religion, cannot be amputated from life.

If this assertion is true, then what is happening in public schools regarding faith? Is Christianity being taught? No. What about other religions, such as Judaism, Islam, or Hinduism? Not in most cases, unless a teacher presents their basic principles along with Christianity through a world history, world geography, or world cultures class. Based on the premise that we cannot disconnect faith from life, I ask another crucial question: what faith is being taught in the public school and higher education systems?

As a believing, born-again Christian living in a Christian nation, I use Christianity as my reference point in this discussion. I also want to reinforce my support of our Constitution's precepts about the free exercise of religion. Of course, readers need to understand why the First Amendment, which includes freedom of religion, was written. Various violations of free worship occurred under European monarchs, and conflict grew during the Protestant Reformation, when subjects were ordered to worship according to the official state religion. The founders wanted to ensure that no Christian denomination would become the national religion. Therefore, through the First Amendment they handicapped the federal government from establishing a state religion.

Although they were opposed to dictating a state religion, our founders fervently practiced and promoted Christianity. Declaration signer Charles Carroll wrote, "Observing the Christian religion divided into many sects, I founded the hope that no one would be so predominant as to become the religion of the State."[6] Preventing the establishment of a state religion does not preclude the promotion or worship of Christianity.

As a Christian nation, America offers the freedom and security to worship any denomination of Christianity, any other religion, or no religion at all. But religion and faith cannot be separated from each other; one who claims no religious affiliation still has faith in one or more things, and that faith can be interpreted as his religion. Those who deny the Founding Fathers' Christian faith should note that fifty-one out of fifty-five representatives (93 percent) at the Constitutional Convention pledged service to a Christian denomination.[7]

THE FAITH OF THE EDUCATION SYSTEM

Christians believe in the Trinity, which comprises the Father, Son, and Holy Spirit. Socialist-leaning statists also believe in a trinity composed of environmentalism, relativism, and self.

Environmentalism

Socialist-leaning liberals worship the environment and aggressively proliferate their faith in high schools, colleges, mainstream news networks, the media, and pop culture. The United Nations Population Fund (UNFPA) stated in a report that universal access to abortion, which it called "reproductive health," will "help reduce green-house gas emissions in the long run."[8] There you have it—murdering unborn babies will help save the planet. In schools environmentalists have embedded their agenda in all subjects: history, English, science, foreign languages, career and technical education, and health. I cannot speak for math because I have not recently enjoyed the pleasure of reviewing word problems, but if it's possible, the message is in there too.

These curricula highlight man-made global warming, deforestation, recycling, animal rights, alternate energy sources, and evolution, though the latter does not fall under the environmentalism umbrella. I must include a qualifying statement: certain ideas such as recycling are good. Conservation and proper management of resources are important; worshipping the environment, however, is a disparate concept altogether. Furthermore, liberals do not possess a monopoly on conservation or concern for the environment; on the contrary, the root word of *conservation* and *conservative* is the same—*conserve*. This fact makes the conservative a natural ally of common-sense conservation while intelligently using the world's resources.

Not all initiatives to preserve the environment are misguided; rather, what I reference is the radical, earth-worshipping wing of this movement. Unfortunately, its ideology has infiltrated all facets of society, brainwashing people into believing alarmist rhetoric and engaging in impractical measures to "save" the "doomed" planet. The only idea crazier than that man is destroying the planet is one that alludes to space aliens traveling here either to annihilate earth-disrespecting humans or to help us save our motherly planet.

How many times have you heard someone say something along the lines of, "How many trees were killed making those copies?" Or, "Do you know how many trees died for this?" These people are serious; they have been indoctrinated in radical environmentalism to the point that they fail to comprehend or refuse to acknowledge that trees are a renewable resource, that America has more trees today than it did one hundred years ago, and that man exists on the planet to use and manage its resources. Remember the discussion in chapter 1 about the Native Forest Council? Through its publication, *Forest Voice,* it intentionally published and distributed misleading propaganda in schools about the number of trees in America.

Man-Made Global Warming

One "crisis" the environmentalist movement has perpetuated and used to indoctrinate students is the fantasy dubbed "man-made global warming." The deluge of misinformation dispatched in schools about this topic never provides evidence to contradict this fallacy. That fact alone should be enough to cause a large majority of Americans to question and reject this daydream. I guess when one is never provided with another viewpoint, he is unaware that it even exists. Schools should share all information from both sides of an issue, but they don't. The education system egregiously omits facts that effectively question the man-made global warming theory while presenting opinions, falsehoods, and manufactured "facts" from proponents of this "transgression" upon society. This one-sided agenda includes showing Al Gore's mythological movie, *An Inconvenient Truth*, without offering the factual rebuttal, *The Great Global Warming Swindle*. How many Americans are aware that the latter movie even exists?

The key to understanding and effectively dismissing any environmentalist claim is by simply comparing various sources on a topic, analyzing the acquired information, discerning fact (truth) from myth (lies environmentalists want you to believe), and most importantly, observing the world around you. Liberals can insert propaganda into schools, magazines, and television programs to portray an issue in a certain light, but they cannot alter personal observation.

For example, one need not be a scientist or possess a PhD from a liberal university to determine that temperatures in many regions of the United States have been lower than normal over the last twelve to eighteen months (as of October 2009). Some argue that a year and a half is an insufficient period of analysis to conclude that the planet is cooling. They assert that such data is an anomaly and perhaps not indicative of a cooling trend. True. But these same "experts" should also recognize that a twenty-year period is insufficient to prove their man-made global warming theory when they consider that miniscule span in the context of a nation that is 235 years old, a continent (Europe) where Christianity is two thousand years old, a planet with a climate record of at least ten thousand years, or a planet that, according to evolutionists, is millions of years old.

Meanwhile these self-proclaimed environmental "experts" conveniently forget and purge from the record that in the 1970s they accused man of precipitating not only global cooling but also the next ice age due to the same activities that allegedly cause global warming. The rage in the 1990s (which has since been forgotten) was the "ozone hole," a naturally occurring gap in the Antarctic's stratospheric ozone layer that appears annually near the end of the Antarctic winter. First discovered in 1956, it repairs itself in three to five weeks and is not caused by man-made pollutants.[9]

The hallucination has changed in the minds of relativistic, socialist-leaning statists, but their enemy is the same—man's progress through the tools of liberty, democracy, and the free market. Their unchanged goal is to promulgate a socialist society that depends on government, in which a small group controls wealth, exercises authority over the populace, and exorcises freedom, moral absolutes, strong families, faith in God, rugged individualism, and patriotism from its spirit. Statists cannot allow any of these ideals to interfere with their agenda; they must pulverize them to force their scheme on their subordinates. By manufacturing a dire cause, such as climate change, proponents of big government advance socialism by increasing regulation and governmental authority. They restrict freedom and advancement through the democratic free market and assault the three cornerstones of American exceptionalism in the process.

By observing the daily highs and lows, you can determine whether your locality is experiencing an overall increase or decrease in average temperature. But let's place in the forum of public thinking some facts the average person may not have considered.

Egypt was a prosperous nation due to the fertility of the soil surrounding the Nile River. During the reign of one of the Ramses pharaohs, however, the prosperity of Egypt shrank to the point that Ramses conducted conquests to gain favor in his subjects' eyes by defeating other nations and acquiring their wealth. A drought had caused Egypt's recession. As the arid conditions persisted, the Nile receded, the soil lost fertility, and prosperity was lost. Guess how long the drought in Egypt lasted. Was it five years, a decade, or fifteen years? The answer is one hundred years. That's correct; a drought plagued Egypt for an entire century.

Did man-made global warming cause this misfortune? Did man's prosperity, innovation, and improvement of culture induce it? Did the Egyptians multiply too quickly and consume too much water for crops and personal use? Did they cut down too many trees, erect an excessive number of pyramids, or burn too many fires in their fire pits and at their barbecues? Did the flatulence of sheep, goats, and oxen cause this phenomenon? No. Droughts, weather, and climate patterns occur naturally, change without warning, and change again without indication, making scientific or computer-model predictions futile.

If retro-hippie environmentalists were living over two thousand years ago, they may have uttered such assertions. If today they could return to past eras via a time machine, I am confident they would search for and discover "evidence" leading to such conclusions. I can imagine the following headlines being broadcast throughout the world upon their return: "Egyptians Spurn Prosperity by Disrespecting Environment," "Egyptians Were First Culture to Cause Global Warming," "Narcissistic Pyramids Cause Global Catastrophe," or even "White European Adventurers at Root of Egypt's Drought."

Arctic Ice Cap

Another "crisis" the earth-worshipping environmentalists hype is the receding ice sheet surrounding the Arctic Circle. Most of us have heard sad fables about drowning polar bears, distressed whales, and other tales environmentalists weave for the public. As is the norm for these extremists, their ignorance of facts and history conveniently bolsters this fairy tale. Here are a few things to think about.

Around 15,000 BC, the North American ice sheet extended from the Arctic Circle, encompassed Canada in its entirety, and continued into the United States. In doing so, it reached as far south as the middle of the states of Indiana, Illinois, and Ohio; northeastern Pennsylvania through Maine to the east; and part of Iowa, most of Minnesota, and portions of South Dakota, North Dakota, Montana, and Idaho to the west.[10] Also around 10,000 BC, the ice sheet began to slowly shrink, an event known as "deglaciation," until it reached the general location where it is today.

What precipitated the retreat of the ice sheet? What acts forced the ice to recede over an estimated four million square miles? Were Indians in the United States and South America cutting down too many trees and burning too many campfires? Did pollution perpetrated by man against Mother Earth induce the ice to scale back to the safety of the Arctic Circle? Absolutely not! How do man-made global warming theorists explain this phenomenon? They cannot. The fact is, no one—no scientist, PhD, environmentalist, or pseudo messiah—can stipulate what the ideal or proper size of this ice sheet should be, if there even is an ideal or proper size.

The receding ice cap at the Arctic Circle has also been listed among the casualties of man-made global warming. In 2007 the Arctic ice sheet receded to a record low size, but ice in the Antarctic was at or higher than the highest levels ever recorded.[11] In 2008 Arctic ice had expanded by 13.2 percent or two hundred seventy thousand square miles.[12] One explanation the idolatrous earth worshippers would deride and dismiss is that God is in control. He planned the development of North America. He commanded the ice sheet to recede so the land of milk and honey could be revealed for that purpose. He sets the dimensions of the ice sheet as He sees fit and when He sees fit. "Indeed with My rebuke I dry up the sea, I make the rivers a wilderness" (Isa. 50:2).

Radical environmentalists try in vain to understand the idiosyncrasies of our planet, to determine the causes and effects of climate changes, and to set the course of human activity. We see their failed predictions on how long the earth will last; a number of predictions of doom by celebrities, including Ted Danson and Al Gore, have long expired. We also see their failed predictions on continued temperature increases caused by man; a cooling trend has occurred in the United States since 1998, while a more modest global temperature drop has continued since 2000.[13] When we keep these errors in mind along with their failed predictions on precipitation amounts as well as hurricane numbers and intensity, we see that they are the ones we can dismiss as incompetent, foolish, fanatical, and clueless. Americans need to wake up and choose not to fall for this bamboozlement any longer. Again, we do not require excessive scientific research to reach these conclusions. All we need is simple, individual observation, attention to current events, and knowledge of history.

Carbon Dioxide and Global Temperature

In the realm of global temperature, we must first note that while some areas of the world are warming, others are cooling.[14] One can see evidence of this disparity by observing weather patterns in the United States alone; while some areas of the country may have a warmer-than-normal summer, others may be at or below normal. The same occurs in winter. Various parts of the country typically experience normal, warmer, or cooler weather during that season. The winter of 2009–2010 may be the exception; most of the nation seemed to experience a colder-than-normal winter. The same can be said about summer 2009 in many locales. In addition, a timeline of the last four thousand years reveals a cyclical climate pattern that fluctuates between warm and cool periods.[15]

Over the last twenty years or so, society has been browbeaten with the "fact" that rising carbon dioxide (CO_2) levels have caused global warming and that, if not curbed, they will destroy the planet with droughts, famines, hurricanes, rising sea levels, floods, species extinctions, and so on. Even contradictions (floods and droughts) do not dissuade the environmentalist militants, and they suppress and ignore information contrary to what they spew. Case in point: as carbon dioxide levels have risen over the last decade, global temperatures have stabilized[16] or slowly declined.[17] At the same time, most of the warming during the last century occurred before 1940, while most carbon dioxide was emitted into the atmosphere after that date. Emissions soared from industrial growth after World War II, but temperatures cooled until the mid-1970s.[18] From 1920 to 1940, temperatures warmed while carbon dioxide was low; from 1940 to 1970, however, temperatures cooled as carbon dioxide increased.[19] I can still remember relatives talking about the "next ice age" when I was a child in the early to mid-70s.

Consider these additional facts about global temperature:

- During the 1930s, the United States experienced three of its warmest five years on record.
- One hundred twenty-five thousand years ago, no summer ice existed at the North Pole, and the sea level was fifteen feet higher than it is today.
- A few thousand years ago, Georges Bank near Cape Cod was part of the mainland, but today it is sixty miles offshore.[20]
- In 2007 global temperature dropped .7 degrees Celsius (1.26 degrees Fahrenheit), which, the fastest drop on record, set temperatures back to 1930 levels.

- In 2007 snow fell on Baghdad for the first time in hundreds of years, China endured a bitter winter, and Antarctica experienced its greatest ice levels since 1770.
- In 2008 Alaska experienced its third-coldest summer on record.[21]

Sunspot Activity

Environment worshippers refuse to acknowledge sunspot activity as a potential primary ingredient that causes global cooling or warming. It is common knowledge—or it should be—that the sun was predominantly in a period of high sunspot activity for about the last two decades. As of April 2009, the previous eighteen months revealed the lowest amount of sunspot activity in nearly a century.[22] Over the last century, temperature change has not matched carbon dioxide levels, but it has coincided with sunspot activity.[23]

Minima, periods of low sunspot activity, correspond with cooler world temperatures.[24] In essence, a lower number of sunspots = lower energy transferred to the earth = decreased ocean temperatures = decreased evaporation of water into vapor = decreased planet temperatures.[25] Carbon dioxide pales in comparison to water vapor as a greenhouse gas, while some believe carbon dioxide is a cooling gas.[26] Overall, carbon dioxide is responsible for only 3.6 percent of the greenhouse effect, while 97 percent of atmospheric carbon dioxide comes from natural, as opposed to human, sources.[27]

Therefore, sunspot activity plays a much larger role in the earth's temperature than do carbon dioxide levels. We recall from this discussion that the biggest increases in temperature during the twentieth century occurred when carbon dioxide levels were low (1920–1940). On the other hand, temperatures dropped while carbon dioxide levels were rising (1940–1970). Also, during the last decade, we have seen steady or declining temperatures while man-made carbon dioxide production has expanded.

How do we know that sunspot activity correlates with global temperatures? In 1610 Galileo was the first to observe sunspot activity, and continuous daily observation began in 1849 at the Zurich Observatory.[28] Important minima (low sunspot activity) include the Sporer Minimum (1460–1550), Maunder Minimum (1645–1715), and Dalton Minimum (1790–1830).

The Maunder Minimum is also known as "The Little Ice Age," during which practically no sunspot activity occurred.[29] During this period, the world experienced a sharp temperature drop, bitterly cold winters, and cool summers.[30] Rivers that were typically free of ice froze over, and snowfields occurred year-round at lower latitudes.[31] During the Dalton Minimum, the world's temperature dropped 2 degrees Celsius (3.6 degrees Fahrenheit) over twenty years, and the year without a summer occurred in 1816. During the years of the Sporer Minimum, temperatures were also colder than average. Although sunspots were not observed during this time in history, an analysis of the proportion of carbon 14 in tree rings, which strongly correlates with solar activity, provides this information.[32]

In conclusion, the sun was unusually active during the twentieth century, and five of the ten most intense solar cycles occurred over the last fifty years.[33] Even Mars is experiencing planetary warming. NASA reported in 2005 that images from the Red Planet indicated that its polar ice caps were dramatically shrinking.[34]

As one can see, man-made global warming is a reach at best or a delusion at worst. Too many factors impact the world's climate and temperature. No one can say that man-emitted carbon dioxide levels correspond with increased temperatures. No one can proclaim that man-made global warming has led to a reduced Arctic ice sheet. No one can assert that he knows the causes of climate change or its solutions. No one can prove whether carbon dioxide acts as a warming or cooling agent. No one at this time has possessed or demonstrated the capability to decipher the complex riddle of the climate, and hopefully extreme environmentalists can be stopped from causing incalculable damage to the planet and its people as a result of their foolish, inane, and poorly intended interventions. What Plato intended to be a charade, I think these people actually believe in their hearts. Plato wrote, "They were…formed…in the womb of the earth, [and]…the earth, their mother, sent them up; and so, their country being their mother…they are bound to advise for her good, and to defend her against attacks."[35]

Idolatry

A number of idols are embedded in environmentalism. These include animals, fish, birds, the sun, the moon, the stars, trees and other plants, water, and Mother Earth herself. Deuteronomy 4:15–19 admonishes,

> Take careful heed to yourselves…lest you act corruptly and make for yourselves a carved image in the form of any figure: the likeness of…any animal that is on the earth or the likeness of any winged bird that flies in the air, the likeness of anything that creeps on the ground or the likeness of any fish that is in the water beneath the earth. And take heed, lest you lift your eyes to heaven, and when you see the sun, the moon, and the stars, all the host of heaven, you feel driven to worship them and serve them, which the Lord your God has given to all the peoples under the whole heaven as a heritage.

After visiting Sea World in summer 2008 and witnessing idol worship to Shamu, the killer whale, via a chant and a dance, I vowed never to go there again. What most parents perceive as innocent fun is the subtle indoctrination of their children in environmentalism.

RELATIVISM

The second prong of the secular statists' trinity is relativism. In essence, they believe all things are relative; therefore, absolutes are nonexistent. How convenient is this philosophy? Since all things are relative, one can change his mind at any time on any issue without experiencing the repercussions of consequences, hypocrisy, dishonesty, lack of integrity, or a guilty conscience. In this view of the world, lies do not exist. Of course, it is okay for people to genuinely change their minds or to adopt a new opinion when they acquire new information, but for the relativist liberal, changing one's mind is a convenience based on whatever benefits the person at the time; therefore, people can change their minds to get votes, to respond to an opinion poll and be popular, to avoid trouble with the law, to shun responsibility for their behavior, to engage in an argument, or whatever the convenience may be.

You certainly must be wary of leaders who take stances based on opinion polls. Sure, leaders, especially elected officials, should represent their constituents, but they must also lead by honestly expressing their beliefs without worrying about the ramifications for doing so. Today a stance on an issue is wrong, tomorrow it's right, and next month it's wrong again. This is the thought pattern of a relativist.

Relativism Defined

In simple terms, relativism means that all points of view are considered equally valid. A more complex definition says that a particular instance exists only in combination with, or as a byproduct of, a particular framework or viewpoint. No framework or viewpoint is uniquely privileged over all others. Therefore, someone who believes marriage is a bond that lasts forever does so because of the culture or circumstance he is in. If someone does not hold to the same belief because of his situation, that doesn't mean one belief is better than the other. Also, if someone believes lying is wrong based on the teachings of his religion, but someone else, who does not subscribe to those religious beliefs and is not constrained by their restrictions, thinks lying is acceptable, the former person's value system is not superior to that of the latter person. Even if one declares the second definition of relativism explained above, he is really saying that all points of view are equally valid. In other words, the more complex wording of the second definition boils down to the simplicity of the first.

All Moral Codes Are Equal

Therefore, since no viewpoint is superior over another, all viewpoints are no more or less valuable than others. All things are relative, meaning that all thoughts, actions, behaviors, attitudes, and beliefs are equally valid. This equality of individual morals permits any behavior in which one "feels" the desire to engage. If one decides to change, that is okay too because all things are relative.

A marriage is sacred until one "feels" that it is constrictive or inhibits his development as a person. Then he can commit adultery or divorce and remarry on a whim. If someone commits adultery, that is a permissible practice because all behavior is acceptable in a relativistic society. If his wife wasn't such a nag, a man reasons, he would not be forced to cheat on her. Promiscuity within a marriage is appropriate as long as both partners "feel" the same way or until one develops strong feelings for another partner. Then tensions rise, people are abused, spouses are hurt, and sometimes someone is killed due to jealousy and hatred. But I guess that is okay too.

So then, retro-hippie relativists believe any thought, behavior, and moral code carries equal value. But to them this equality applies only as long as behaviors are nontraditional, push against societal norms, promote rebellion and deviance (another word that has disappeared from our culture), and encourage perversion and immorality. When those who possess traditional ideals charge relativists with being wrong, relativists rebuke the traditionalists and inform them that they are the ones in the wrong. This practice, of course, contradicts the whole basis of relativism, which states that all attitudes carry equal value; therefore, all things are right, and nothing is wrong. Yet when they accuse a conservative of being wrong, they destroy the foundational premise of relativism in the process, making it an invalid and illegitimate philosophy.

Absolutism Reigns

It is not unusual for people to say, "All things are relative," while listeners passively accept their premise. To the contrary, I postulate that all things are absolute, with absolutism encompassing relativism. Some absolutes include gravity, the boiling point, the freezing point, the revolution of the earth around the sun, the sun rising in the east and setting in the west, photosynthesis, heat capacity, decomposition, and a plethora of laws of physics and science.

But one may rebut by stating that people are vastly different—from height to weight, to skin color and tone, to hair color and type, to athletic and intellectual ability, to health, and so on. People look different because of their varying DNA. As the result of an absolute formula, you and I look the way we do. If someone has brown hair, olive skin, big feet, small ears, bony fingers, and a hairy body; stands sixty-eight inches tall; weighs 180 pounds; runs the sixty-yard dash in 8.2 seconds; has a disability or deformity; naturally bench-presses 250 pounds; or has an IQ of 120, an absolute formula is connected to such traits. If one could replicate the precise prescription, he would have two people who are exactly alike, which is the goal (yet unachieved) of cloning.

Furthermore, certain intangibles cannot be replicated via cloning, such as the soul, spirit, and nonliteral heart of a person.

Though one can clone DNA, these intangibles do not transfer, so an exact replica is not created. Immeasurable intangibles explain why some people, who possess strong athletic ability, do or do not reach the college or professional ranks, while less-skilled athletes excel over their "superior" peers. Their level of achievement is often the result of the desire, sacrifice, and work ethic they bring to the arena. These qualities come from the athlete's heart and spirit. The same is true for academic achievement, job accomplishments, marital success, and a host of other activities.

Here's another way to look at it. Let's say you intentionally drop two eggs. One egg breaks while the other remains intact. Several variables influence the outcome of this trial. Did you drop both eggs from the same height or on a surface with the same hardness? Did you hard-boil one egg but not the other? Did the eggs have different shell thicknesses? Though the result is relative, it is one we can explain according to an absolute formula.

Most declarations of relativism refer to income and material possessions, but this is absolutism enveloping relativism. One must confirm that such economic diversity is real; however, the differences some emphasize to justify relativism are the result of absolutes. Consequently, relativism is the resultant feature of absolute principles and laws. Many opine that all things are relative because everyone spends his whole paycheck despite the volume of one's salary. But if this were true, it is an absolute. The assertion that all people spend their entire paychecks is an absolute statement. The sum of money may be different and therefore relative, but this fact does not make the behavior relative.

Let us accept the notion that some do and others do not spend their total monthly salary. This would be a relative statement because some people engage in this behavior while others do not. But for those who do, that they choose to do so is an absolute. Divergent, and therefore relative, reasons may exist for engaging in such behavior, but the behavior itself is not relative. The same holds true for those who abstain from expending their entire wages. In the end the absolute envelops the relative because absolute reasons explain why people do or do not spend all their money. Relativism exists, but absolutism and precise formulas supersede it in all cases.

This leads to the last point. "All things are relative" is an absolute statement, but how can this philosophy have an absolute premise? If I say that all people breathe oxygen, there is no exception; this statement is absolute. If I write that all raindrops contain H_2O, this is also an undeniable absolute. If I assert that all people are over six feet tall, however, that premise is false because it is a misrepresentation of people. To claim that *all* things are relative is a contradiction in itself and dismantles the whole ideology of relativism, making it invalid.

Absolute Morals

The logic is the same concerning morals, which are also absolute, regardless of the culture or framework in which one lives. Cultures have divergent value systems, but some values are better than others. For example, many human rights issues, such as freedom of religion without fear of government reprisal, are applicable to all cultures. Some values are neutral, making them neither superior nor inferior to each other. For instance, some cultures eat raw fish, while others prefer to cook their fish. Although in the United States we are frequently warned about the dangers of eating undercooked meat, we don't consider eating raw fish to be immoral. Architecture, sports, and leisure activities are a few areas where value systems are neutral. But moral absolutes include honesty, not stealing, fidelity within a marriage, not coveting others' possessions, and honoring your father and mother. Other absolutes include the unalienable, God-given laws of nature and the social compact upon which our tremendous nation was founded.

Hollywood provides many examples of replacing absolute, God-given morals with relative, man-made substitutes. People can choose to use illicit drugs, heavily consume alcoholic beverages, engage in promiscuous acts (both heterosexual and homosexual) with multiple partners, smoke two packs of cigarettes a day, divorce and remarry for frivolous reasons, get an abortion, engage in criminal activity, and eat a junk food diet, among other behaviors. Consequences come with participating in behaviors that result from violating moral absolutes. People die of drug overdoses, others steal to get their fix, work productivity decreases, and on-the-job accidents increase. Some are arrested for driving under the influence or charged with vehicular homicide after killing someone while operating a vehicle in an intoxicated state. Families are divided, children are raised in broken homes, and STDs are contracted in increasing numbers. Gangs and a life of crime entice children. Emotional distress and physical ailments occur, cancer and other diseases become more common, and the ramifications go on.

Only a fool would argue that divorce, illness, emotional distress, crime, and other troubles occur even when one abides by an absolute moral code. This sentiment is true. Accidents and problems still occur, but instances of such misfortune grow exponentially when people engage in dangerous, immoral activity. Luke 17:1 says, "Then He said to the disciples, 'It is impossible that no offenses should come, but woe to him through whom they do come!'"

Dangers of Relativism

Relativism is dangerous because it breaches a person's mental and moral strength until, as Plato writes, "he is driven into believing that nothing is honourable any more than dishonourable, or just and good any more than the reverse."[36] Samuel Adams powerfully authored, "He who is void of virtuous Attachments in private Life, is, or very soon will be void of all Regard for his Country. There is seldom an Instance of a Man guilty of betraying his Country, who had not before lost the Feeling of moral Obligations in his private Connections."[37]

Neither life nor people are perfect; despite elitists' futile efforts to create a utopian world through legislation, man will never be able to do so. But this does not mean that we should encourage and give equal status to all behavior based on the philosophy of relativism that promotes irresponsibility and rebellion. More importantly, government should not legislate deviant behavior under the pretext of equal rights and nondiscrimination policies.

Besides, relativism is really absolutism because all its practitioners are being rebellious. Tattooing, sexual immorality, multiple piercings, huffing (intentional inhalation of chemical vapors to get high), tongue splitting, embedding, branding, and other behaviors may have different art, styles, and methods, but they all have the same purpose—to disfigure, destroy, and dishonor the human body. Paul reprimands believers in 1 Corinthians 6:19–20: "Or do you not know that your body is the temple of the Holy Spirit who is in you, whom you have from God, and you are not your own? For you were bought at a price; therefore glorify God in your body."

The selection of different modes of self-mutilation does not make the behavior relative; the absolute is that people are damaging and destroying their bodies, minds, hearts, and souls. The other absolute is that they are trying to fill a spiritual void by engaging in such behaviors and defiling God's temple in the process.

SELF

The third component of the liberal, relativistic socialists' trinity is self. These people do not believe in the existence of a transcendent God. They deny the existence of a sovereign, omnipotent, omniscient, omnipresent God, so something else must replace that vacuum in their lives. When one denies God, He is not simply removed from the mind, soul, heart, and spirit; once God is expunged, someone or something else takes His place. In past cultures and once-powerful empires, people worshipped a number of gods or idols in place of the real God. Statists reject God, but they have not replaced Him with Baal, Asherah, or another idol. Instead, they have replaced Him with self.

Man as God

Yes, man is the center of his own universe. He controls it. He can solve its problems, mysteries, and perplexities; and he can master it through the application of science and math. It is he who possesses the ability, power, and knowledge to do all things, including "solving problems." These two words are in quotes because many "problems" are either manufactured to advance his agenda or beyond his capabilities to solve. His "solutions" often worsen the so-called problem or create an unpredictable complication where one did not previously exist.

Examples of poor attempts to solve problems include the following:

- New mercury lightbulbs supposedly benefit the environment, but the process of discarding them is extremely harmful to users and the environment.[38] (It's interesting that in twelve years I have changed only 15 of the 119 lightbulbs in the two places where I have lived.)
- A gas additive (MTBE), which allegedly emits a cleaner byproduct, pollutes water to such an extent that boiling it does not remove the contaminant.[39]
- Electric cars reportedly produce less pollution, but the battery production for the engines and the contamination caused by battery disposal create more environmental detriments than benefits.[40]

- Windmills kill millions of bats annually.[41]
- Denmark's feeble attempt to increase the use of wind power as an energy source has led to several retributions: Denmark uses 50 percent more coal-generated power to cover supply gaps during times of low wind, thus increasing its overall carbon emissions by 36 percent. It has incurred the highest electricity costs in all Europe, and it has lost 2.2 jobs for every "green" one created.[42]

Other problems, both real and imagined, reportedly being resolved by socialist-leaning liberals include man-made global warming, insensitivity, intolerance, bullying in schools, illness, aging, poverty, and so forth.

The Ruling Class Rises

According to liberals' beliefs, man is his own god. For this reason they can make up the rules as they go along and change them whenever doing so is convenient for them; hence we find the connection to relativism as discussed above. But even though all people in this scenario create their own relative values and morals upon which to live, they require others to monitor them and provide guidance. This thinking leads to the need for an aristocracy, or small ruling class, to lord over the masses despite the rulers' incompetence in knowing what is best for their subordinates.

Actually, the ruling class is not really concerned about what is best for its subjects; rather, it is selfishly interested in what benefits itself. But this notion contradicts the precept that all people are the center of their universe, does it not? Since when do obvious contradictions impair the socialist-leaning liberals' agenda? Moreover, all liberal philosophies share the same fault, a weak and unstable foundation. In every society a class of people believes it has reached its existential pinnacle or realized self-actualization;

this small group erroneously supposes it has earned the right to govern others. This belief is not about government of, by, and for the people; no, it is about acquiring power and dominance over the populace.

Let's summarize the main points of this discussion. First, God is excised out of society or a people. Second, when this occurs, He is replaced with another god—man himself in this case. Third, despite the socialists' mantra that capitalism and democracy breed class conflict, societies have always had classes of people. For the socialist, this reality translates into two classes—the ruling class (aristocracy) and the governed (or controlled subordinates). The two classes are far from equal not only in quality of life but also according to the perception of the ruling class; here, the rulers prosper while the masses suffer through the rulers' pathetic, alleged attempts to create utopia.

Several examples illustrate this point well. Social Security is a savings plan into which the general population is required to pay, though Congress is exempt from contributing to such a poor investment. Now that government-controlled health care has been forced upon citizens, the members of government will not be affected by its restrictive parameters because they maintain unfettered access to high-quality services. While politicians reject a voucher system that would allow parents to enroll their children in schools of their choice, wealthy congressmen send their students to elite, expensive private schools. Though elected officials discourage the consumption of fossil fuels by the populace, socialist-leaning liberals consume it in their private jets, large SUVs, multiple mansions, and pool houses (some of which are larger than the homes of many; no names will be mentioned here). Although they utter compassionate rhetoric about their constituents and the poor, their actions betray their intentions and shatter their credibility.

The point is that elitists in positions of authority truly believe they are messiahs or gods as they worship their egos and accomplishments. This is not to imply that every elected official or authority figure subscribes to such beliefs, but many do. When you hear officials discuss the importance, benefits, and requirement of big government (including schools); the need to help people understand what is best for them; the necessity to restrict freedom due to contrived crises; and the detriments of family, faith, patriotism, and America's founding principles, you know you are listening to socialist, aristocratic liberals. In their rhetoric they talk about "saving" and preserving America, but in reality their intentions contravene such sentiments. Their actions betray their real intent, which is to transform the magnificent United States of America into a socialist country that tramples on our freedoms while advancing a powerful government that wields its strength against a dependent, powerless citizenry.

SUMMARY OF THE STATE RELIGION

The trinity of the statist comprises the environment, relativism, and self. All these are ingredients in the education system's program of indoctrination. The environment replaces the Holy Spirit, relativism substitutes for the Son, and self stands in place of the Father. In turn, the statist incessantly attacks the Trinity in addition to faith, family, and patriotism so people will transfer their trust from these foundational cornerstones of America to an authoritarian, socialist, tyrannical government, which plays god, becomes parent, and expects reverence to it alone.

The faith of socialist-leaning liberals in the environment, relativism, and man has evolved into a religion. Their religion comprehensively permeates our culture, emanating from music, television programs, the news, and our education system. When people talk about separation of church and state, remember that the Founding Fathers forwarded no such concept. Faith is always present; therefore, religion is present as well. The question becomes this: What is the predominant faith and religion of our culture? Our nation was founded on Christianity, though it allows others to practice the faith of their choice. As Christianity is gradually removed from society, another religion must take its place. The above presentation illustrates that when people reject God, they must replace the true God with another god. Today's substitute is man himself.

CHRISTIANITY IN U.S. EDUCATION

One cannot establish a solid argument for separation of church and state. Christianity has largely been removed from the public school and higher education systems, although many schools were founded as Christian institutions with Bible study integrated in instruction, which is symmetrical with the beliefs our Founding Fathers expressed. Consider the following:

- Harvard (1636), Yale (1701), and Dartmouth (1769) were founded as Congregational colleges.
- William and Mary (1693) and Columbia (1754, originally named King's College) were founded as Anglican colleges.
- Princeton (1746, originally called the College of New Jersey) was founded as a Presbyterian college.
- Brown (1764, originally called Rhode Island College) was formed as a Baptist college.
- Rutgers (1766, originally named Queen's College) was opened as a Dutch Reformed college.
- Penn (1751, originally named The Academy) was founded as a nonsectarian college.[43]

Harvard's "Rules and Precepts" stated that students' main life goal was "to know God and Jesus Christ which is eternal life (John 17:3) and therefore lay Christ…as the only foundation of all sound knowledge and learning."[44] The goals and purposes of other colleges listed above intimate the same desire to propagate the Christian faith, learn the precepts of Christianity, know Jesus Christ, and lead a godly life.[45] Public school education also once emphasized Christianity. *The New England Primer*, for example, used Bible lessons to teach the ABCs and included other biblical truths and information, making it the second best-selling book in the colonies after the Bible.[46] Noah Webster, considered the "Father of American Education," stated that Christianity should be "one of the first things in which all children, under a free government ought to be instructed....The Christian religion must be the basis of any government intended to secure the rights and privileges of a free people."[47]

THE EDUCATION PHILOSOPHY CHANGES

The belief system of the founders and citizens of early America contradicts that of the modern education system, which under the architecture of John Dewey seeks to minimize, if not eliminate, God from its confines. According to Dewey, "There is no God, and there is no soul."[48] Benjamin Bloom, the creator of Bloom's Taxonomy, which explains the cognitive (mental), affective (emotional), and psychomotor (manual or physical) domains of learning, believed that the pinnacle of intellect was reached when one perceived no difference between right and wrong. Christian beliefs and morals have been supplanted by environmentalism, relativism, and glorification of self. This is the religion of the public education system.

Encouraged by the federal and state governments, the local public school entity promotes the "faith" as discussed above. In doing so, it teaches only the parts of issues it needs its clientele to know to advance its religion. This technique is called indoctrination. If you enter a school and examine its resources, you will discover all things liberal, including biased textbooks and curriculum; periodicals, such as *Time* and *Newsweek*; websites and news programs, such as CNN and MSNBC; newspapers, such as the *New York Times* and *Washington Post*; supplemental resources, such as the previously discussed *Forest Voice*; and standardized test questions that promote the liberal agenda. Furthermore, the teachings of relativism encompass a number of liberal causes, including multiculturalism, diversity, same-sex marriage, homosexuality, and sex education in general (often as early as kindergarten).

Keep in mind that no concept such as "separation of church and state" exists. Christianity has been excluded and replaced with the liberal, socialist religion of the environment, relativism, and self.

AN EDUCATIONAL MODEL TO COPY?

The "Released Time Education" model in South Carolina would be good to emulate in returning to our foundational ideals. This program allows public school students to leave school early once a week to participate in a Bible study class at a local church. The program is legal for the following reasons: parents give permission for their children to participate, the public school endorses the program, church volunteers transport and teach the students at no cost to the school, and private donations cover the cost (so no taxpayer dollars are expended). In at least one school district, volunteers also agree to tutor students one hour per day, and they also assist with school projects and programs.[49] Therefore, in a manner reminiscent of colonial times, students receive instruction in Christian precepts while still attending the public school. Also, a positive partnership has been forged between the school, church, and local community. One volunteer, Ella Mae Colbert, said it best: "I've noticed that young people are troubled, and they don't really know why. And whoever gets to them first, that's what they take to."[50]

Based on the attack against our Christian faith and the desire of statists to create an air of dependence on government, it is doubtful that such a concept will be imitated on a large scale, even though education leaders typically love to borrow ideas.

TEACHERS

Let me talk briefly about teachers, who play a critical role in shaping students. Most have a genuine passion to help students learn, grow, and improve; they are dedicated professionals with good intentions who want the best for pupils. As professionals, they do what they are asked to do by following policies, protocol, and the law. Many continue in their chosen careers to raise their families or to avoid starting over in a new career.

A certain number of educators recognize that this nonsense has impregnated schools, but they do their jobs as they were trained. Many reject the current philosophy that dominates the system and embrace a contrary perspective on how it should be operated. They too are frustrated with the expansive bureaucracy, the irresponsibility of students and parents, and the epidemic of poor behavior and effort; they bear the burden for these as well as a multitude of maladies and ill-founded expectations; they criticize the day care role they have been forced to assume and would willingly and gladly return to a challenging atmosphere that genuinely educates students in a strict, disciplined environment; they long to teach both sides of issues, develop students' analytical skills, and truly educate pupils. But they are a decreasing minority.

Teachers can't do anything to combat the system. They are required to teach the written and tested curriculum and to follow school policies and procedures that foster dependence on the school. Even if they do recognize the weakening of our education system, they often do not perceive the new faith, the attack on family, the destruction of patriotism, and the resulting long-term effects of those realities. Some lack the intellectual capability to comprehend the intricacies of issues; others are proponents of the ideology through choice or the indoctrination they received in the public school system and institutes of higher learning. Those who buy into the philosophy and strive to fulfill it are often administrators and key decision makers who determine policy.

Teachers have a big impact on students and communities. My favorite teachers and strongest colleagues maintained high expectations, stressed student responsibility, and meted out consequences for noncompliance with rules. It is vital to shift the system back to its intention—teaching children how to learn, think rationally, develop problem-solving skills, and shape an informed electorate that can discern between competing ideologies and opinions, right and wrong, truth and deceit.

Despite their frustration, it is curious that teachers vote in large numbers for liberal, socialist politicians who favor this state of education and promote the policies that continue to hamstring the system. Educators need to overlook monetary concerns and choose candidates who will negotiate the system away from its current philosophical course. If that were to occur, a large force of competent professionals are qualified and willing to execute a plan to reinstitute a rigorous education program.

PARENTAL PHILOSOPHY SHIFT

Why the moral shift in the general population away from worshipping a transcendent God, who rewards or punishes people based on their behavior, to a faith in self? Part of the responsibility for this problem lies with parents, especially those who grew up prior to the 1960s rebellion but who raised their children in the 1970s and 1980s. A multitude of these parents bought into the notion that their children needed to attend college to train for a professional career. Raising children to go to college and attain a higher level of education is noble; the problem occurred when parents deemphasized faith in their homes and simultaneously allowed their children to be instilled with a relativistic, humanistic value system in schools. The focus shifted from acquiring a job or working in a trade one enjoyed for the glorification of God and the raising of one's family to placing high value on achievement—grade point averages, SAT scores, athletic accomplishments, and professional (white-collar) employment.

Today this value shift has expanded to include membership in clubs or community organizations, leadership positions held in those activities, community service and volunteering, acceptance into academic honor societies, gaining employment while in high school, and receiving awards and recognition in any of these activities.

The focus is on achievement and résumé building. Many students compile a laundry list of high school activities in which they minimally engage to impress employers and college admissions officials, but they are void of experience, skills, deep knowledge of these activities, or dedication to any of them. Therefore, the participation and accomplishments of many students can be taken at face value because pupils engaged in too many extracurricular activities to attain mastery of any of them. Remember the old adage "jack-of-all-trades, master of none." Yet parents, students, employers, and colleges are proud of the "accomplishments" of these students.

Improvement, achievement, and accomplishment, all stressing self, helped instill this worship of self into the spirit of our nation. Of course, accomplishment is not bad, and neither is self-improvement. But taken out of context and separated from a desire to glorify God, self becomes a god; and self can neither satisfy itself through its achievements and acquisition of power nor really help anyone apart from the divine author.

WHAT HAPPENED TO DIVERSITY?

Diversity is a concept that destroys, disunites, damages, and discourages. Put simply, diversity is natural and good, and we should encourage it but not emphasize it. Mainly, diverse people who have common values create order and success; diversity in the realm of divergent values, however, leads to confusion and failure. Notice that *div*, the prefix of *diversity*, is the same prefix for *divergent* and *division*. If we focus on diversity, it causes division. We can see this truth in sports teams and any organization successful through teamwork.

A school functions through diverse people who possess varied interests and specialties, whether math, English, social studies, science, or foreign languages. Educators work hard toward the common goal of developing students by following shared principles of hard work, determination, sacrifice, and high expectations. A football team is composed of diverse people with diverse skills who play a variety of positions—lineman, quarterback, receiver, linebacker, and kicker—striving toward the common goal of winning a championship by abiding by a set of shared values. A family is often composed of diverse people with various personalities, and the family's shared values make it a strong unit. A nation populated by diverse people from a plethora of countries, backgrounds, cultures, and languages built the strongest nation in the history of the world due to a grasp of the shared principles of hard work, morality, sacrifice, rugged individualism, and a desire to enjoy and protect God-given freedoms. Those who possess the same goals and principles to achieving them experience accomplishments, while those who engage in dissension endure struggle and hardships.

However, diversity of thought must exist. When schools provide only the liberal viewpoint, students are indoctrinated. When issues are discussed, both sides of the issue must be presented. When this occurs, students are then provided with the necessary information to formulate an intelligent, logical opinion. Why does this sound unreasonable? Why is the conservative viewpoint smothered? Why is conservatism rarely, if ever, heard? Why has our Christian history and heritage been purged from our institutions of learning? The answer is simple. If both sides of an issue are equally represented, the relativist liberal loses; the majority will agree with the conservative point of view. Therefore, schools controlled by socialist-leaning liberals must eliminate opposing viewpoints and facts to force their agenda on the electorate—again, indoctrination hard at work.

To entrench environmentalism, relativism, self, and socialism in the American psyche, they must exclude Christianity, family, faith, and our founding principles. So the next time you hear some liberal cry "censorship" when some immoral, deviant material is removed from a school, remember what you have read here.

CHARACTER EDUCATION

To add insult to injury, schools across the fruited plain have adopted "character education" programs to instruct students on a variety of positive traits, such as integrity, forgiveness, and tolerance. Each month a new characteristic is highlighted as the word of the month. Bulletin boards, lesson plans, and announcements are dedicated to defining the trait and explaining its value to the student body. Again, this initiative, though altruistic in nature, is a poor substitute for the absolute morals Christianity imparted in public schools for many decades. After liberals booted Christianity from public schools, they had to replace it with something when they observed student behavior and effort steadily decline, including lower standardized test scores, increased dropout rate, more instances of teen pregnancy, proliferation of drug use, multiplication of discipline referrals, and higher absenteeism. These are perfect problems for the liberal, who can propose extending the school day and school year as well as institute various programs of indoctrination, such as character education to "help" children.

The Separation of Church and State Fantasy

Therefore, the concept of separation of church and state in schools is a fantasy. Socialist-leaning liberals have launched a successful campaign to smear Christianity and expunge it from our schools as well as society as a whole. In its place they have implanted the faith I have illustrated. Although the public school system has been dubbed a secular institution, it anoints our children with this religion. As a result, our children are being indoctrinated in the statists' faith, a violation of the First Amendment, which states that Congress shall make no law respecting an establishment of religion. Technically, Congress did not make a law establishing religion in this institution; however, schools offering prayer were not doing so at the insistence of Congress either.

Through an over-reaching Supreme Court, Christianity has been removed from our schools and many parts of our society; therefore, by default that same Supreme Court and the federal government are responsible for allowing a pseudoreligion to be substituted in its place. Since the judicial branch advocated this fundamental change in our culture, it is responsible for that which fills the void. The judiciary has also become a tool of statists, who abuse it to force American citizens to abide by their agenda when it is rejected outright at the ballot box. Christianity has been purged from our schools, while the religion of environmentalism, relativism, and self has been infused in its place.

CHAPTER 5

SPAWNING SOCIALISM: FROM STRENGTH TO WEAKNESS

HOW DOES THE statist's religion promote socialism? As previously described, when faith is eradicated from an institution, something else must take its place. When the traditional family is eroded, another entity must fill the void. These two institutions, religious faith and stable families, cannot be removed from society as a benign tumor is extracted from someone's body. On the contrary, they are comparable to vital organs in the body that need to be replaced with other organs when they are removed. In this case, they have been replaced by a man-made, imitation organ that is far inferior in operational capability. This counterfeit, corrupt, ineffective mechanism is government. As government usurps power from people, the latter become dependent on the former.

CENTERS OF THE COMMUNITY

Essentially, all policies, initiatives, and regulations in the public school system are intended to increase dependence on the local government, in this case the school at the expense of parental authority and influence. I previously discussed attendance policy, dress code enforcement, character education, and other examples of schools assuming influence in people's lives, as described in chapter 3. The struggles schools experience in these areas are the direct consequence of the dissolution of the family and the attack on faith. The more power the school accumulates, the more services it provides, and the more dependent students, parents, and communities become. The school system assumes responsibility for students and parents, parents cede their authority to the local socialist government, the government usurps further responsibility, parents sacrifice more authority, and the cycle continues. Elitist educational and national leaders want this cycle to happen. It allows the school to become the center of the community and invites dependence on all forms of government to grow.

Educational leadership programs actively promote the center-of-the-community concept. Once established, dependence on the school cannot be restricted to or corralled within the local government, as stated above. As this dependence becomes infused in the mindset of the populace, citizens expect the state and federal governments to provide similar services. This thinking leads to reliance on government and ingrains socialism in our nation, where people lack the tendency to help themselves. Each school system ("little brother") becomes its own little communist country, through which the federal government ("big brother") and influential pro-socialist members of society control the development of its subjects.

The following examples of public schools assuming increased responsibility support these accusations. A multitude of education leaders have stated that the most important thing in a child's life is the school. They have uttered this message in seminars, college classes, and even meetings in local school systems. I always believed families held this honor, but the socialist does not think the same way. Here is how the socialist operates:

- In the area of discipline, school personnel are responsible for initiating behavioral plans and scheduling appeal hearings when students are suspended.
- The school must make multiple contacts concerning attendance and grades.
- The school is required to motivate students to attend school, perform well, graduate, and meet minimum federal and state requirements.
- The school must encourage students to work hard and employ interventions to combat at-risk behavior.
- The school must provide instruction regarding diet, personal hygiene, organizational skills, sex education, and other issues.
- The school must develop a myriad of crisis plans in the event that a disaster impacts it or the community.
- The school must offer counseling at the elementary level to encourage students to be polite, helpful, generous, honest, and so on.
- The school must assume the central role of fundraising and charitable work in the community.
- The school must provide breakfast because of difficult economic times.
- The school must provide transportation home at the conclusion of after-school activities.
- The school must offer after-school tutoring, supervision, and a snack to students in its care because parents are not yet home from work.
- The school must babysit students during the summer.

To ensure that pass rates and graduation rates meet minimum requirements, student behavior is acceptable, pupils are properly supervised, and children are adequately nourished, the school must take on these extra responsibilities. As a result, the school naturally becomes more intrusive in peoples' lives, and state and federal legislation push schools in that direction.

As previously stated, some school actions are reasonable and expected, such as offering after-school tutoring. But at what point does the school cross the line, become too intrusive, and substitute for the parent and family? When parental authority is usurped, parents and students are indoctrinated into relinquishing their personal responsibilities to the local government; they become conditioned to rely on the school system to complete certain functions for them or repeatedly remind them to do so. Dependence on the "little communist country" increases and becomes the norm. When did schools become the center of communities with new buildings that look more like palaces than schools? At one time the school's function was limited, but now it dominates. The important centers in a community are usually the most luxurious, an attribute once relegated to churches.

This process explains how citizens naturally and gradually increase their reliance on the school or local government. To review, each generation of school customers expects more, and each generation of leaders expects and yearns to offer more. Dependence on the local government increases over time, and socialism results because this reliance on local government is transferred to the state and federal levels. The resulting consequence is a squeeze from both sides—leaders in government and education on one side, parents and students on the other—that produces a socialist society.

Leaders at state and federal levels continue to enact legislation to promote bigger government. The government itself cannot replace families throughout the country, at least not initially. The only way to achieve this end is to divide and conquer, and the way to do so is through local school districts, in which the large majority of our children enroll due to mandatory attendance laws. After a few decades of indoctrination and continuous bombardment against the family, faith, and patriotism, the federal government could feasibly assume control over the indoctrinated population, though the "small communist countries" will continue to play a role in the statists' schemes.

Values have been changed, morals redefined, attitudes transformed, history revised, patriotism obliterated, Christianity eradicated, and families destabilized to such an extent that politicians flaunting socialist ideals can be elected into office. A large opposition to this trend toward socialism is present in America, but it is up against a formidable opponent. This opponent has been brainwashed not only to accept government care but to believe it deserves and has a right to such care. This opponent is allied with the relativist elitist, who is also powerful and controls the public and higher education systems, media, and popular culture.

This is a sad hypothesis, is it not? Liberals encourage irresponsible behavior and reliance on government in order to control the people; they ingrain a childlike mentality that encourages citizens to depend on a perpetual parental figure; they indoctrinate people into believing they are incapable of helping themselves or are victims of some imagined social injustice. Their objective is to perpetuate a welfare state, in which the socialist government cares for its populace from cradle to grave. In this state a small, powerful, pseudointellectual ruling class experiences conspicuous prosperity at the expense of a large, miserable, poor lower class. Does this description sound familiar? It should. This was the condition among many monarchies and feudal systems that existed for centuries before the founding of the free, God-fearing, independent United States of America. It is also the condition in every former and current communist or socialist nation—the Soviet Union, East Germany, Cuba, Venezuela, North Korea, and Vietnam.

WEAKNESS PROMOTED

Another major impact of this expansion of government power, which forces socialism on American citizens and creates an atmosphere of dependence on it, is weakness that affects the mind, body, and spirit. As the populace succumbs to weakness, it relies on the government to solve its problems or alleviate the pain caused by natural disasters, health issues, STDs, the inability to attain home ownership, unemployment, and more. The government sometimes promotes such reliance. When national disaster declarations began with the Eisenhower presidency, Mr. Eisenhower issued 107 proclamations in eight years (13.4 per year).[1] In comparison, President Clinton declared 381 (47.6 per year) in his eight years in office, and President George W. Bush issued 458 (57.2 per year) during his two terms as president.[2]

When events do not go their way, people whine and complain that life is too hard, complicated, or inconvenient. They struggle with maintaining a house, staying in good health, repaying debts, rebuilding after a tragedy, and fulfilling the demands of a job. Taking a pill is easier than exercising or eating a well-balanced diet. It is more convenient to stay in an air-conditioned home and fuss about allergies than to engage in physical activity outdoors. Demanding other people's money and government services is easier than families, neighborhoods, churches, or community organizations helping themselves and each other. It is simpler to collect unemployment and stand in traffic, holding a sign that invites others to give you food or money, than to get a job. Some businesses even post help-wanted signs on their windows in view of such bystanders. After all, one may "not like" that type of work. Ingesting medicine for herpes is easier than abstaining from sexual promiscuity. Accepting free needles to inject oneself with illicit drugs is more convenient than resisting deviance. It is simpler to murder an unborn child than to abstain from sex or raise an unplanned baby. Getting a divorce is easier than working through marriage difficulties.

It never used to be this way in America. People once accepted their circumstances and worked through them, adversely viewing state welfare. People once accepted that they would face hardships, knowing that they could rise above them through hard work. People came to America to experience the American Dream, leaving whatever they had behind or coming with meager possessions to take a risk in the land of opportunity. People demonstrated physical, intellectual, emotional, and spiritual tenacity.

In a relativistic society that insults inhibition and celebrates licentiousness, it is no surprise that we experience the problems encompassed by this list and a multitude of others not written here. When these problems occur, it is easier to criticize God for allowing them to happen (even when one expends zero effort to worship God) than to seek and obey God with all one's heart, soul, mind, and strength. It is easier to reject His sovereignty and question His lack of intervention than to practice restraint, wisdom, self-denial, and responsibility. Plato wrote, "Instead of throwing the blame of his misfortune on himself, he accused chance and the gods, and everything rather than himself."[3] Revelation 16:9 says, "They blasphemed the name of God…and…did not repent and give Him glory." Of course, no one is perfect. Problems will come, and individuals will make mistakes. But unfortunate occurrences increase exponentially when God is denied, ignored, and forsaken.

Physical, emotional, mental, and spiritual strength—these important characteristics encourage success, joy, peace of mind, prosperity, and probably a number of other benefits of life.

Physical Weakness

People seem to be more ill than ever before and require more attention for real or imagined sickness. Doctor's visits are more prevalent. Sick days from work or school are taken in higher numbers. Allergies were practically unknown when I was growing up in the '70s and '80s. Medication has become a trillion-dollar industry as many ingest a wide variety of pills for a myriad of illnesses and other problems. More people, especially children, choose to stay indoors instead of going outside to play because it is too hot, cold, windy, or humid. Or else they stay indoors because the heat index, wind chill, UV index, pollen count, or air quality is not ideal. These excuses are not necessarily their own. Various media professionals often provide them to prevent illness, sunburn, or even discomfort. In many cases news outlets have convinced people that staying indoors is safer than going outside and sweating or sneezing, being too hot or cold, damaging the skin, becoming infected with Lyme disease or West Nile virus, or inviting some other problem.

Laziness has risen to new heights. Many, especially children, spend an increasing amount of time surfing the Internet, playing video games, or watching television. Sadly, television commercials must encourage youth to go outside and play for sixty minutes a day. When I was a child, we were outside for hours at a time regardless of weather conditions, temperature, sickness, amount of sunlight, or what have you. Moreover, we did not apply sunblock; take along tissues, Band-Aids, or antibacterial cream; or put on helmets, knee pads, or elbow pads. We did not worry about taking snacks along so we would not get tired or lose energy. We did not tote water bottles to maintain proper hydration levels or practice any other nonsense society instructs parents to do with their offspring today. And we, in addition to previous generations, survived and were better off than the "protected" youth of today. With society constantly scaring people on a variety of issues and promoting inactivity, we wonder why ailments such as obesity, injury, and diabetes are on the rise. Plato addressed such inclinations in *The Republic*:

They are always doctoring and increasing and complicating their disorders, and always fancying that they will be cured by any nostrum [questionable remedy] which anybody advises them to try....They deem him their worst enemy who tells them the truth, which is simply that, unless they give up eating and drinking... and idling, neither drug nor cauter[ization] nor spell nor amulet [charm worn against evil] nor any other remedy will avail.[4]

Plato also wrote that men "require the help of medicine...just because"[5] and that "man is always fancying that he is being made ill, and...in constant anxiety about the state of his body."[6] Our obsession with health definitely parallels the mindset of ancient Greece.

Let us briefly examine the pharmaceutical industry. In 2008 the profits of the top twelve pharmaceutical companies alone were $51,938,200, which was an increase of $11,841,700 from the previous year.[7] The pharmaceutical industry has been one of the most profitable ones since 1995, ranking first from 1995 to 2002 and being among the top three from 2003 to 2006. The exception is 2005, when it ranked fifth.[8] Overall, the top ten pharmaceutical companies earn more profits than the rest of the Fortune 500 combined.[9]

I do not have a problem with drug manufacturers making profits; on the contrary, I support the free market economy and the principle of supply and demand. My intent is to illustrate society's increased use and dependence on medication. Whether pharmaceutical companies encourage such consumption is immaterial. In the end people control their choices. Data indicates that more people are deciding to ingest medication to feel happy, energized, stable, pain free, and so on.

Air-conditioning may be one technology that provides more detriments than benefits, and none pertain to the environment. People wake up in their air-conditioned homes, get in their air-conditioned cars, and go to air-conditioned workplaces, shopping malls, restaurants, or movie theaters. They return to their air-conditioned homes in their air-conditioned cars and sleep in their air-conditioned houses. Then we wonder why people have allergies and find the heat intolerable. In regions that experience cold winters, people complain about cabin fever during the winter months. Then when the temperature hits seventy degrees in the springtime, they enclose themselves in their air-conditioned homes. This is weakness. People who lived many decades with simple fans for cooling suddenly cannot tolerate the heat once they begin dwelling in an air-conditioned environment.

One cannot live in a purified environment. Attempts to do so preclude the body from building defenses against allergens, bacteria, viruses, even the sun due to lack of exposure to them. Children contract more illness than adults because their bodies have not yet had the opportunity to strengthen their immune systems. As people age, they are typically healthier after developing tolerance to strains of sickness to which they have been exposed. Attempts to remove all contaminants through sanitizers, air purifiers, sunblock, and other means prevent the body from becoming strong due to the "purified" environment in which it exists, causing it to become ill once exposed to certain inputs.

I hypothesize that excessive application of sunscreen can harm the skin and lead to higher incidents of skin cancer. If someone prohibits his skin from being exposed to the sun and one day acquires sunburn due to a lack of protection, I believe the skin has impaired defenses against that rogue moment of exposure, possibly increasing a person's probability of developing skin cancer. This does not insinuate that one should never use sunblock; instead, I point out that exposing skin to the sun's rays is probably important because it allows the skin to build a defense against the sun's potentially harmful side effects.

The ramifications of physical weakness include increased health costs, overreaction to minor health issues, increased labor costs due to missed work, fear of going outside and being active, a higher propensity of injury due to inactivity, and laziness. These problems translate into an erosion of strength. Many people can barely walk more than a short distance, let alone engage in strenuous physical activity. Young athletes often become overheated when playing a sport because they are accustomed to sitting in air-conditioning all day. Because of this reality, coaches often cancel practice when the temperature reaches a certain level. In the past kids were outside much of the time, so they became accustomed to the heat and were able to be active in it, even when not drinking liquids. When people become inactive, injury and other health problems more readily occur because the body loses strength, flexibility, muscle mass, and endurance.

When injuries cause an employee to miss work, productivity drops or the business incurs extra costs to hire a substitute or to pay others to work overtime. Today, many use minor ailments as excuses to miss work, even when they can satisfy the job demands. The more benefits people receive, the more inclined they become to take advantage of them for spurious reasons. When my dad began working in a factory in 1965, he received zero sick days during his first ten years on the job. Yes, you read that accurately—zero sick days for an entire decade. Today's workers are not only granted multiple vacation and sick days but also encouraged to miss work for the slightest symptoms of illness. Of course, weakness breeds weakness, and society slowly declines into a worse condition.

EMOTIONAL WEAKNESS

Based on my observations as both a supervisor and employee, the emotional state of Americans is not much better than their physical condition. People's feelings are hurt more often and more easily. They lack self-discipline and are unable to resist self-gratifying thoughts. They do something because they feel like doing it, not because it is the right or best thing to do. Kids dislike their parents for frivolous reasons. Many are unable to manage their problems without first referring to self-help resources, daytime talk shows, or government services. This leads to a host of consequences, including therapy; disability diagnoses, such as ADHD; and a bevy of other "disorders," such as obsessive-compulsive, oppositional defiant, and bipolar disorders; as well as excuses and justifications for their inability to be strong.

This problem then leads to an abundance of further implications resulting from emotional weakness, including the following:

- A confused populace that seeks an ailment or diagnosis to excuse its behavior or weakness
- A mentality in which people want to one-up each other concerning the severity of their sickness or the state of their desperation
- A lack of personal responsibility to manage the consequences of behavior and thus a tendency to blame others
- An expectation that the government should compensate people monetarily or via services
- Lawsuits when people feel they have been manipulated or treated unjustly by an "evil" corporation though their own incompetence often caused the problem
- Statements such as, "I don't feel like . . ."
- Marriage ending in divorce because of the words "I love you, but I'm not *in love* with you"
- Children who become insubordinate to their parents
- Parents who are unable to raise their kids because they do not want to upset them, hurt their feelings, or lose their friendship

- Many become incompetent and unreliable because they acquiesce to their emotions and become ineffective parents, friends, neighbors, spouses, and employees. Weakness breeds weakness, and culture steadily slides into a deeper state of it.

Much of the blame for this mentality rests with the media and the education system. The media relentlessly broadcast emotional weakness by focusing on feelings (not to mention stories that highlight the exception). The education system has also increased its focus on affective, or emotional, learning. As long as students feel good about themselves, everything runs well. If students do not feel like doing their work, they are excused. If someone feels like following a rule, fine. If not, we must express sensitivity toward his decision. During discussions, students are asked how they feel about a topic instead of what they know or think about a topic. When I was a social studies teacher trainee, my classmates and I were instructed to inject emotion into debates because tension stirs up people and inspires discussion. It did not matter whether their arguments were rational, informed, or intelligent; rather, what mattered was that students were confident in expressing their feelings. It was unimportant that opinions were irrelevant or historically inaccurate as long as students had the opportunity to share how they felt. How often are questions phrased as "How do you feel about something?" instead of "What do you think about something?" It is much easier to feel than to think.

Intellectual Weakness

This emphasis on feelings evolves into intellectual weakness as people lose the ability to think and reason for themselves. Much of this phenomenon may be the result of increased television viewing, which requires no individual effort. Watching television doesn't require reading, listening, thinking, or responding; one just sits on the couch and watches people do things and tell them stuff. It is important to point out that hearing is not equal to listening; the latter requires effort on the part of the message's receiver. The mind eventually becomes weak and dependent on this type of input and stimulation, losing its ability to think and reason. An unused muscle atrophies. The same is true for a mind that is not properly exercised. As with a muscle, we can rehabilitate the mind to function properly, but the battle is a tough one; and the battle for the mind may be more arduous than one for a muscle.

Once people succumb to a state of "mind atrophy," they will believe anything they see on television, hear on the radio, and read in a magazine, e-mail forward, blog, or newspaper article. Just as dependence on local government leads to reliance on the federal government, once people develop this state of mind, they essentially lose the ability to think intelligently.

Therefore, liberals can create an uninformed and gullible populace that believes foolish doctrines, such as the notion that man is causing climate change or that all weather phenomena—from cold to hot, rain to snow, drought to flooding, tornadoes to hurricanes—are the results of man-made global warming. People will believe the lies that pro-life individuals are terrorists and that terrorists are misunderstood youth. They may also fall prey to thinking that redistribution of wealth via punitive income taxes on achievers will create prosperity or that the United States is an evil, imperialistic nation (even though it has singlehandedly spread freedom throughout the world more than all other nations combined).

Any truth is accepted as false, and any falsehood is considered to be truthful. The Bible teaches in 2 Timothy 4:3–4, "For the time will come when they will not endure sound doctrine, but according to their own desires, because they have itching ears, they will heap up for themselves teachers; and they will turn their ears away from the truth, and be turned aside to fables." Furthermore, Isaiah 5:20 says, "Woe to those who call evil good, and good evil; who put darkness for light, and light for darkness; who put bitter for sweet, and sweet for bitter!"

Those who oppose or criticize the maladjusted mainstream value system are labeled as nazis, fascists, neoconservatives, racists, homophobes, and a bevy of other disparaging adjectives. Of course, because nobody wants to be so adversely labeled, he capitulates when bombarded by such monikers, especially if he is mentally weak.

Education

In education, with the exception of a few courses geared toward the brightest college-bound students, expectations are low, performance is poor, behavior is unacceptable, and the curriculum expounds the socialist, relativistic, secular value system. Education leaders can talk about pass rates on end-of-year exams all they want, but the curriculum is dumbed down and easier than it used to be. It is not only easier; it is revisionist history, environmentalism, multiculturalism, sex education that excludes or discourages abstinence in many cases, evolution without creation, "values clarification," and socialism. The volume of taught material has been dramatically reduced, some content has been completely omitted, and the required work is often simple at best.

Instruction is based on "differentiated learning," through which different methods of instruction are employed to prevent boredom and address all learning styles. The activities associated with this methodology are often unchallenging, but they make students feel good. They can help students learn, but the strategy focuses more on fun and entertainment than on intellectual development. It seems as if this method of teaching needs to be incorporated to compensate for the low value of education many students possess.

Charts, graphs, games, group work, and the like are emphasized, guiding pupils through learning instead of putting on them the onus of studying and learning. Though these types of activities have a place in the classroom, they should not be primary teaching tools. They are simply too easy and do not challenge students to work hard or grow intellectually.

Furthermore, homework has been minimized, if not eliminated altogether. As a result, students complete all or most work in class, negatively impacting efficiency and requiring the volume of material to be reduced due to time constraints. Partly because of this phenomenon, many are proposing the aforementioned extension of the school day, school year, or both. However, an efficient system would not require such a measure to be enacted. Moreover, missed work can be made up any time without penalty, reducing responsibility on the part of students, increasing lethargy, and lowering expectations.

The brightest students gladly cruise through the coursework and earn straight As, while their parents are ecstatic with their performance. When these students are genuinely challenged, which is atypical, their grades may drop. But through encouragement and motivation they become excited about the subject and enthusiastic about learning, rising to the challenge to perform at a high level. As a matter of fact, this is true of all students. Although the majority of high school students may not have the ability or desire to succeed in a college-level class, they still rise to the level of expectations their teachers demand. With encouragement, motivation, some fun mixed in, and a positive relationship with their teachers, students achieve at a higher level when teachers expect them to. I know—I have done it. And I have been successful with all types of students, regardless of race, gender, income, background, ability, or goals.

Who is to say that many more students do not have the will or skills to perform well in a college-level class? If expectations were increased across the board, beginning at the elementary school level, who can say how many more children would be ready for more challenging coursework by the time they reached high school?

Gearing instruction toward the middle or lower ability level brings down the whole classroom, school, and society. Instead of lessening the workload so students can feel good and asserting that our students are experiencing success, it would be more beneficial to genuinely increase the standards in education and raise everyone to a higher intellectual echelon. This plan is superior to uttering empty rhetoric and catch phrases about having high expectations and realizing achievement. Such phrases include "All kids can learn," "It's about what is best for kids," "Think outside the box," and "Child-centered education." If someone really needs to proclaim that all kids can learn, we have a problem. Even paramecia (slipper-shaped protozoa that move by cilia) can learn; therefore, it is common sense, I think, that all children can learn. Some may not believe in the potential of all students, but that does not mean it should be a slogan for the education system.

"Thinking outside the box" is far from original or creative. Educators use this cliché as if they coined it. Have they forgotten that the Founding Fathers formulated the greatest government on earth, that innovative thinkers (some of whom spurned the public school system) developed many inventions we take for granted, or that many businesses grew out of new, original ideas? I would say probably so since they have been indoctrinated by revisionist history. The American way is to think outside the box within certain boundaries to improve society.

For liberals, relativism removes boundaries that allow them to institute inappropriate ideas and engage in a Pandora's jar of behaviors, as previously discussed. It may also be a good idea to return to the box when it comes to education; maybe then the system could be put back on track so real teaching, learning, and achievement could be experienced. But that will not happen because tradition and our founding principles are enemies of the socialist-leaning liberal.

A program of teacher training that indoctrinates future teachers in the realms of relativism, socialism, and revisionism also corrupts the system. Eventually teachers who did not face indoctrination retire and are replaced by those who did; eventually the school system employs teachers who received liberal indoctrination beginning in kindergarten and continuing through their college years. It is this group that has been fully equipped by at least seventeen years of the statists' indoctrination program, which propagates the elitists' agenda in the classroom, thus perpetrating socialism on a country through the mandatory public school system.

Then the ruling class easily prescribes change because education providers have been effectively brainwashed through a liberal teacher training or school-administration curriculum. They, in turn, instill secularists' values into students, who then are also efficiently indoctrinated. Parents who have graduated from the public school system within the last twenty years and work in any sector in the nation have been trained that the state should care for their children because that belief coincides with their experiences.

Diversity

Diversity is another platform by which liberals have weakened our intellectual ability. We all know people are different—and that is a good thing. We all know that different abilities, interests, and experiences make an institution work. As a matter of fact, diversity is a natural occurrence we should recognize, not emphasize. For example, a sports team cannot function without diversity due to the different types of athletes required to fill various positions. A school cannot teach all subjects without diversity. A family has naturally diverse parents and children. What makes all these entities successful is similarity.

The National Football League has thirty-two professional teams, but only one wins the Super Bowl at the end of the season. Although various factors such as injuries can impact a team's ability to win a championship, the key to victory is similarity. Similarity involves sharing common values, including a hard work ethic, sacrifice, dedication to excellence, discipline, teamwork, and integrity, to name a few. If all team members do not exhibit these traits, the team fails. It is not diversity that preludes success; it is adherence to the same value system to achieve a defined goal. All teams have diversity, but not all teams succeed.

When we focus on America, we see that diversity was natural because people immigrated here from all over the world and continue to do so. For decades we recognized our diversity but did not emphasize it. Immigrants migrated here to experience American freedom, contribute to American exceptionalism, and become Americans. America became strong due to its traditions of rugged individualism, hard work, and freedom; and immigrants adopted these values, adding to our strength.

Today, many emphasize diversity more than being American; they magnify differences—race, gender, social class, and age—over similarities. Emphasizing differences causes division and counters the prevailing unity that made America unbeatable. Division weakens a nation. Remember the old adage "to divide and conquer" and the wisdom that "a house divided against itself cannot stand." The latter is rightly attributed to Abraham Lincoln, but he borrowed this statement from Jesus (how many students learn this fact in their revisionist history classes?). Jesus said in Matthew 12:25, "Every kingdom divided against itself is brought to desolation, and every city or house divided against itself will not stand." If our nation becomes divided, then liberty, the three cornerstones I described, and government by the people will fall to the religion of the state, socialism, and tyranny.

In the previous chapter I mentioned the importance of teaching diverse opinions on various topics; however, taken to the extreme, diverse ideas can be dangerous. Have you ever participated in a brainstorming session with a group of people in an organization? In theory, ideas of all types are respectfully heard as equal. The rationale is not to criticize others' suggestions so feelings are not hurt and dialogue can be kept open. In practice, to make presenters "feel good," participants listen only halfheartedly to absurd ideas before quickly casting them aside, so this is a game of smoke and mirrors. Unfortunately, leaders considering various policies for our nation have corrupted this process, leading to the acceptance of ideas that were once considered "crazy" or unimaginable.

Consider the following absurd notions:

- Development has been curtailed to preserve the habitat of the sloth beetle.
- Providing needles to drug users reduces crime and incidents of HIV or TB.
- Sex education must begin in kindergarten.
- Teens require gender clarification training in schools and through television programming.
- Cow-produced methane causes global warming.
- Increasing taxes leads to job creation.
- Killing unborn babies reduces the carbon footprint of the earth's inhabitants.
- The U.S. Constitution is confusing and outdated and has no binding power.

Schools need a diverse faculty and staff to teach all subjects and fulfill various school responsibilities. But if all teachers do not possess the same work ethic, dedication to student success, high expectations, and ability to motivate, schools will struggle and possibly fail. All it takes is 10 percent of a faculty—only ten teachers out of a faculty of one hundred—to deviate from the core values for a school or school system to fail. If ten teachers refuse to enforce the student code of conduct, their students will push other teachers to do the same. Rotten apples will spoil the bunch, so to speak. As time goes by, more teachers concede the fight, and disciplinary problems increase. Those who stay strong continue to do well, but the school as a whole loses because negative forces eventually outweigh positive ones. Even though negative forces can be a minority, their influence is powerful and damaging.

If enough employees refuse to follow procedures, it is easy to see why any system in any profession can struggle. It takes only a teaspoon of dirt to contaminate a five-gallon bucket of water. Relativism causes this dilemma as those who have been conditioned by its ideals decide to abide only by the rules they "feel" are appropriate.

Factor into the equation those who formulate or influence school policy, including school board office personnel, school board members, board of supervisors, state and federal officials, teachers' unions, and other interests, and it is easy to comprehend why schools are mediocre. Each of these groups has values—some similar, some different—that affect how schools should be run. Government officials, though the least qualified, have the largest input.

Only one leader or group of leaders can proclaim that students should not get zeros for failing to complete work (which does occur) or should not be held accountable for refusing to participate in gym class, and the system is hamstrung. An edict stating that we need to make adjustments to grading based on race, gender, income, and disability compromises the system. Of course, the special interest group references some type of research to support its assertion that a policy will benefit students; actually, such initiatives usually further weaken students and work toward the expansion of the socialist government upon which these students will depend.

Furthermore, one can uncover "research" that supports any claim despite its level of frivolity. Research is more often a pursuit to find evidence that supports an assertion than a hypothesis proven or disproven through accepted research methods.

It takes a strong mind to overcome this indoctrination, especially when the media and popular culture bolster it. Fewer Americans are able to endure the attack with each passing generation. Even if teachers fulfill their job responsibilities, the legislation, regulations, and education philosophy generated by the socialist mindset are often the cause of a weakened education system that impairs the intellectual capacity of our citizens.

The consequences of our intellectual demise include a population that is easily misled—and intentionally so—about innumerable issues. As a result, incompetent or disingenuous politicians elected to office drive the nation further to the left and down the road to socialism. Also, people will believe whatever supports their lifestyle. It does not matter if something is right or wrong, good or bad, weak or strong; as long as individuals reap some benefit, a poor policy is all good. What is beneficial for the country is sacrificed for individual self-interests. This, of course, takes us further down the path of weakness and self-destruction since this intellectual rupture affects the physical and emotional realms as well.

As I wrote above, doing what is easy is more convenient than doing what is right. In other words, it is easier to "feel" than to think. The fewer analytical skills people develop, the more easily they are influenced to make poor choices. The more easily they are controlled, the more readily they are to subscribe to socialist ideas and policies that make them depend on big government. Sadly, a large percentage of the population cannot think logically. The sadder part is that much of the nonsense being spewed in our society, such as the many topics listed above, is considered rational thinking. The saddest part is that once intellectual thinking has been redefined, it may not be possible to reverse its course.

Weakness breeds weakness, and our nation gradually declines into a deeper condition.

Moral Weakness

Moral strength is the final thread damaged by the liberal, relativistic, socialist agenda. Honesty and integrity are endangered when people accept that it is okay to say anything to avoid consequences or to get their way. One can change his mind at any time. Although the picture is not presented in this fashion, people can rationalize that they did not lie last week because they have a different feeling this week. Leaders carefully choose their words so when they fail to abide by their election campaign promises, for example, they cannot be accused of lying. In reality, they intentionally and unethically mince words to hide their true objectives.

The media habitually misrepresent, misreport, confuse, and lie to the public. If the media and liberals were honest about any issue, they would not be able to enact their desired policies or win election into office. Also, the popular culture has redefined morals and glorified instant gratification. As a result, character is weakened, ethics are in a state of confusion, the three cornerstones are eroded, and the concept of having a guilty conscience is lost.

Popular Culture

Compare the programs on television today to those twenty-five, thirty, or forty years ago. When I was a youth, I watched *Leave It to Beaver*, *Happy Days*, *What's Happening!!*, *Good Times*, *Laverne & Shirley*, *Hee Haw*, *The Lawrence Welk Show*, *The Cosby Show*, *Family Ties*, and *Sanford and Son*, among others. Compare the themes of these programs with those of *Two and a Half Men*, *Cougar Town*, *Friends*, *Desperate Housewives*, *Beverly Hills 90210*, and a host of others. Then consider reality shows *Temptation Island* and *The Bachelor* or talk shows such as *Maury* (sometimes known as *The*

Maury Povich Show) and *The Jerry Springer Show.* And we wonder why our teenagers and adults exhibit questionable behavior.

Compare the fathers in these modern programs with those from the past. Today we see a bunch of incompetent buffoons; past shows portrayed men who were strong, upright, and capable of being reliable family leaders. Sadly, adult actors portray these immature, unrestrained, immoral, prepubescent-minded characters; these performers act like perpetually immature adolescents who refuse to grow up. Paul said in 1 Corinthians 13:11, "When I was a child, I spoke as a child, I understood as a child, I thought as a child; but when I became a man, I put away childish things." Celebrities need to heed this counsel.

Those born after the mid to late '80s think that what they view on television has always been the norm; on the contrary, licentious sex, lust, adultery, homosexuality, drug use, and other forms of deviance were rarely if ever broadcast on commercial television. Watching these programs is unnecessary because their advertisements alone are crude enough to dissuade me from tuning them in.

Movies shown in theaters are not much better. They are brimming with portrayals of various kinds of deviance, alleged oppression caused by overbearing parents, disparagement of Christianity, and condemnation of patriotism. Contrast these movies with those from three or more decades ago, in which behavior was normal, parents were espoused, women were respected, our Christian faith was reverently expressed, and love of country was portrayed. Moreover, the men were masculine, strong (showing physical, emotional, intellectual, and spiritual strength), faithful, respectful, and resilient. They are unlike the soft, crying, emotional sissies depicted today.

As with television, this type of entertainment has caused incidents of questionable conduct, along with the negative consequences that accompany them, to reach epidemic proportions.

Overall, the movie industry has played a crucial role in the erosion of our morals, families, faith, and patriotism.

The music industry has devolved into a state of moral turpitude as well. Again, compare the songs and artists of several decades ago to those of today. When I was growing up, music was mostly innocent, clean, and fun. Today, one cannot escape crude lyrics, sexual overtones, messages about drug and alcohol consumption, and disrespect for women. The highly visual music videos shown on MTV, BET, VH-1, and CMT only magnify this problem. Listen to the music played over the public address system at your child's high school before and during events or at school dances. Parents don't complain because their children listen to the same garbage at home. Adults who have become desensitized ignore content once considered inappropriate. Students cannot comprehend that their music is debased because they have been consistently exposed to its corrupt lyrics.

Finally, innumerable pornographic websites feed the sexual appetite. This topic could fill another book, so I am not going to write extensively on it. In the end a large segment of contemporary pop culture can be proud of the fact that it shows no shame and considers nothing sacred except its own despicable behaviors, beliefs, attitudes, and productions. No, my friends, contemporary pop culture does not exemplify American values; instead it tramples on our traditional morals and replaces them with a vulgar, perverse, debased substitute.

A recent television commercial for Sirius XM Radio illustrates this point. In its advertisement, Sirius XM states that Elvis Presley, Michael Jordan, Richard Pryor, and Howard Stern changed music, sports, comedy, and radio, respectively. The problem with these personalities is that all but one, Michael Jordan, negatively impacted our culture by leading it down the path of vulgarity and licentiousness. Only Michael Jordan is an appropriate role model who has provided a positive influence on people of all ages, especially youngsters.

In our society we tend to glorify those who have promoted the erosion of our founding principles. We uplift models of impropriety above those of uprightness. We lionize personalities who personify wickedness over those who exalt goodness. We idolize rebels instead of those who epitomize strong moral character. The prophet Isaiah cautioned, "Let grace be shown to the wicked, yet he will not learn righteousness; in the land of uprightness he will deal unjustly, and will not behold the majesty of the Lord" (Isa. 26:10).

The implication of this moral decline is the acceptance of deviant behavior and the ridicule of conduct once considered normal. For example, those who abstain from sex are ridiculed and portrayed as prudes. As a result of the repercussions of promiscuity, assemblies in schools warn against the risks of premarital sex without "protection" and promote abstinence only occasionally. Unfortunately, students see such presentations once a year at the most, but they witness undesirable behavior every day of their lives.

GOVERNMENT INTERVENTION

As I noted, the government has assumed an active role in caring for people by providing advice on health, diet, exercise, and so on. As permissiveness escalates, restrictions slowly increase. As mentioned, relativism permits others to dress however they want, so the school must lay down the law on what is acceptable.

A better example is the nationalized health care legislation President Barack Obama signed into law. The government will likely determine who receives care based on age, severity of affliction, and the lifestyle in which one engages. Maybe someone does not deserve treatment for AIDS if he engages in promiscuity by sleeping with multiple partners or taking illicit drugs. Today, liberal relativists encourage you to experiment with your body and reject the values of your parents and grandparents; tomorrow, socialists will deny you health care because they are unable to pay for it. Similar decisions can be extended to those who smoke, drink, vacation at beaches, consume too much fast food, do not exercise, or purchase too much soda on their grocery store discount card.

What I am about to say may sound outlandish but is not beyond the realm of possibility. General Electric aired a television commercial in which it touted its electronic medical records technology. This innovative technology stores medical histories in a single, secure place with the purpose of aiding collaboration between doctors. In the ad a patient speaks to his doctor, who asks a question about the patient's medical history. The scene cuts to an auditorium filled with physicians. Five stand to describe a portion of the patient's medical history, including past advisement to quit smoking. Like the previously described Audi commercial, this one was more creepy than encouraging. Will federal health care legislation decline treatment for a patient who ignores his doctor's suggestion? What if a doctor noted a patient's confession to eating too much red meat? What if a patient refuses to take prescribed medication because he doesn't like swallowing pills?

Thanks to relativism, what was once right is now wrong and vice versa. Who decides what is right, wrong, excessive, or not enough? Values are skewed. Smoking has been demonized, but marijuana use is glorified. Over one thousand marijuana dispensaries have opened in Los Angeles since California legalized medical marijuana in 2005, so the city council is trying to pass an ordinance to dramatically reduce their number.[10] This example, though apparently confined to Los Angeles, epitomizes the ramifications of bowing to relativism and altering our nation's value system. One may smoke marijuana, but he cannot get a suntan because it may lead to skin cancer. For now the marijuana smoker receives compassion, while the sunbather is excoriated for not caring for his body and burdening the health care system. Thanks to relativism, the rules are always at risk of being changed, and we do not know how often change will occur. It all depends on the needs or values of the relativists in charge at the time.

Do you think this claim is beyond reason? Look at how close the country came to having government-run health care forced on it in 1993. Then compare that to what happened in 2010. The push in 1993 died (no pun intended) relatively quickly. Unlike the 1993 effort under President Clinton, all five congressional committees that have health care jurisdiction passed a version of reform in 2009,[11] and the disastrous latter effort was debated for months in 2009–2010. Liberals and proponents who expected a rampant passage and signing of a health care law were shocked by the amount of dissatisfaction, "tea parties," debate, and delay it aroused.

H.R. 3200 and Education

Ponder a provision in the new health care bill (H.R. 3200, "Patient Protection and Affordable Care Act") that will create a federal workforce whose job is to visit homes and gauge whether parents are properly raising their children. The legislation will provide resources to families to help the government be certain that children are eating a proper diet, learning according to their age level, and experiencing overall appropriate development.

Under "Title IX: Miscellaneous Provisions" in Section 1904, Subpart 3, Section 440, we find, "Home Visitation Programs for Families with Young Children and Families Expecting Children." Section 440a states that the provision's propose is

> to improve the well-being, health, and development of children by…providing voluntary home visitation for families with young children and families expecting children. [12]

It continues under Section 440a, 3, A, C, and D.

> The State shall identify and prioritize serving communities that are in high need of such services, especially communities with a high proportion of low-income families or a high incidence of child maltreatment....The State will promote...collaboration with other home visitation programs...and...provide referrals to other programs serving children and families.[13]

It is common knowledge that low-income people vote for Democrats, so here is another entitlement that guarantees their vote for socialist-leaning liberals. Section 440f, 1, A explains the use of expenditures for "voluntary home visitation for as many families with young children (under the age of school entry) and families expecting children as practicable."[14]

The best part comes from Section 440f, 1, A, v, I–VII, which states that parents will be provided with

> knowledge of age-appropriate child development in cognitive, language, social, emotional, and motor domains...[and] realistic expectations of age-appropriate child behaviors; knowledge of health and wellness issues for children and parents; modeling, consulting, and coaching on parenting practices; skills to interact with their child to enhance age-appropriate development; skills to recognize and seek help for issues related to health, developmental delays, and social, emotional, and behavioral skills; and activities designed to help parents become full partners in the education of their children.[15]

States must file annual reports with the federal secretary, describing the services offered, the attributes of the program, its providers and recipients, the cost and outcomes of the program, and "other information deemed necessary" by the federal government. The secretary can also provide independent evaluations of state programs and must provide regular reports to Congress. Of course, the omniscient federal secretary will provide training, technical assistance, and best practices to the states.[16] How much would such a program cost? Keep in mind that this is just one small section of the massive health care bill. The amount of money reserved for this initiative alone (Section 440m, 1–5) rises from $50 million in 2010 to $250 million in 2014.[17] That is a fivefold increase over a five-year period.

The most ludicrous portion of H.R. 3200 is the part of the title that calls it "affordable." If this program alone will cost $250 million by the year 2014, how much will the remainder cost? More importantly, why does the state think it knows best how to raise and train children in all facets of development? It doesn't. In fact, it wants children to be raised the way it deems, not according to parental preference and certainly not according to the Bible.

I can only imagine the "modeling" and "coaching" the state would provide, especially in areas of health and wellness. Will state officials demonstrate how to properly inject meth in addition to the current practice of distributing needles? Will they provide sexual demonstrations or simply tell children to do what feels right and provide contraceptives? Will their consultation include direction on fulfilling any type of relativistic moral behavior one feels like doing? Will they further promote dependence on the government and encourage subjects to report on neighbors, friends, relatives, and even parents if they dissent?

Hitler said that those who control textbooks control the country. What happens if that control expands to include parenting and teaching? Then the state shapes its subjects in the fashion it deems best, which allows for easier control. One of the above provisions says that the "state will identify and prioritize." Again, the federal aristocracy interferes in the personal lives of its citizens and in the process tramples on the precept of government by the people.

The bill begins by focusing on poor families or mistreated children but also mentions identifying as many families as is feasible for this project. As with other federal programs, it does not take long for them to metastasize into gargantuan proportions. Moreover, the federal government always sells programs in a gentle, friendly light, but often the intention is for later expansion to shackle as many citizens as possible. Annual reports typically allow for the identification of "best practices" that can later be mandated for all to implement.

What is the definition of low income? During the election of 2008, if the rich were considered to make two hundred fifty thousand dollars, where does that place the middle and lower classes? The 2009 SCHIP (State Children's Health Insurance Program) legislation (H.R. 2) provides health coverage to families making up to three times the federal poverty level.[18] The average family size based on the 2000 census was 3.14,[19] or 3 if rounded down. According to the U.S. Department of Health and Human Services, the 2009 poverty level in the contiguous United States and the District of Columbia for a family of 3 was $18,310.[20] Triple that number, and you get $54,930. This figure may provide a sense of what those who authored H.R. 3200 consider low income to be.

The term *voluntary* is also compelling because it would eventually evolve into *mandatory*. For example, increasing the legal drinking age to twenty-one was "voluntary" until states were threatened with losing federal funding if they did not make the change. The same occurred with raising the speed limit on interstates to a minimum of sixty-five miles per hour.

The previously cited provision for "collaboration with other home visitation programs" so they can "provide referrals to other programs" is a way to ensnare victims. As programs work together, they provide multiple services to families and trap them in an inescapable state of dependency. Finally, the annual reports to and by the secretary would allow the federal government to legislate best practices; set timetables stipulating when families and children should attain certain levels of development; adjust delivery to guarantee successful indoctrination and dependence; and monitor programs so the government can provide interventions for those programs, providers, and recipients not meeting improvement or achievement goals, possibly due to resistance and insubordination.

At Opencongress.org, you can read H.R. 3200 and vote in opposition to or in favor of it. As of August 4, 2010, a whopping 78 percent of the 10,284 votes cast were in opposition to the bill.[21] Does the federal government really need to "help parents become full partners in the education of their children"? Is this for real? Is the central government living in the "valley of exceptions" when it devises such schemes? In what other venues do these elitist aristocrats yearn to help their subjects become "full partners"? Such involvement is expected in North Korea but not in the United States of America. This is just one example, my friends; just one example. Who knows how many other areas of our lives the government is planning for us?

Based on the direction in which our tremendous nation is headed, while more and more people become amenable to government control, it won't be long before a small, socialist group of statists will make these decisions for us. How will these decisions be made? They may ask these questions: What is the fiscal situation at the time of the decision? What is the country's population? What is the global temperature? What is the yield of the grain crop? How much do Americans consume compared to the world population? Who is related to whom in the federal government? Who donated a generous sum of money to a politician's campaign? Who donated money to a liberal or conservative organization? What coach gave someone's daughter playing time when she was not very good at her sport? Who is the principal at someone's son's private school?

This is just a short set of questions a small cabal may ask when deciding what is and isn't right for its subjects. If you think the last few questions are an exaggeration, think again. People expect high school principals to make exceptions for reasons such as those. Leaders regularly base decisions on those types of factors. I have probably been a beneficiary because of someone I knew. This is normal human thinking, so such tendencies are not unlikely when a group of socialist leaders make decisions for their subordinates.

CONSEQUENCES OF WEAKNESS

What you end up with is a small group of powerful individuals making decisions for the large, incapable, weak social class. Spiritual infirmity that forsakes our Christian faith creates a moral vacuum that allows the government to insert itself into God's rightful place. We see no clear direction because there are no absolutes; everything is relative. Therefore, precepts, values, morals, and desires can instantly change on a whim.

This is where spiritual, mental, emotional, and physical weakness lead; these four areas are interconnected, weaken congruently, and decline in one component causes decline in the rest of the body. To be honest, if a nation possesses spiritual tenacity, the remaining three characteristics will be strong. Otherwise, all four areas will languish. Our spiritual strength in the United States of America comes from our Christian faith, and our greatness proceeds from our Christian foundation. Our weakness is the product of our abandoning faith in Christ, and our demise is the result of our decision to forsake our God.

Recall the discussion about faith and religion always being present. If one type of faith is eliminated, another must take its place. As liberals eradicate Christianity from society, they replace it with environmentalism, relativism, and self. The same pattern is true of power. A finite amount of power exists in our country. At the birth of our nation, this power was divided between the state and federal governments (federalism), between the three branches of government (separation of powers), and between state and local governments. The people hold the power of government, as Abraham Lincoln said at Gettysburg in 1863: "government of the people, by the people, for the people." The preamble to our Constitution begins, "We the people."

In modern times people are in peril of losing their power through usurpation by a group of liberal, relativistic statists who have an insatiable appetite. The more citizens weaken, the more power they lose to this small group of socialists. Sometimes power is freely given away due to laziness, stupidity, or ignorance. But more often weakness in the four areas described above allow the federal government to assume more power at the expense of Americans they are supposed to serve.

The time is not only right but also critical for people to reassume their personal responsibilities and stop making excuses for their circumstances, mistakes, and decisions. With relativism, problems are never anyone's fault. Instead, he points the finger at others. Returning to our Christian roots for guidance instead of turning to a fallible government is vital. Right now is the critical time for families to reestablish their stability and role of raising productive, moral, civilly responsible citizens rather than looking to an inept government. Right now it is imperative that we return to our founding principles of a limited government based on liberty and the unalienable rights provided by our Creator. We should take this step instead of allowing socialism's principles of restricting freedom, discouraging hope, and perpetrating tyranny to hijack our unique government. The relativistic, weak mentality that nurtures the growth of a strong central government took strong hold of our spirit with the 1960s hippie rebellion.

Revisiting the Rebellious '60s

We often fondly remember the 1960s as a period of personal growth, drug experimentation, free love, rock and roll music, removal of the shackles of restraint, and uninhibited self-expression that came and eventually went. Of course, the decade itself passed on, but many of the behaviors, attitudes, and values from that unfortunate time have lingered, expanded, and infected our culture to epidemic proportions. Unfortunately, many who flaunted those behaviors and adhere to them today hold positions of power in government, corporations, education, media outlets, law firms, hospitals, and other areas of influence.

My interpretation of the 1960s is simple: it was the rebellion of a bunch of spoiled-rotten white kids against authority, including parents, teachers, pastors, police, and other authority figures. During the civil rights movement, while blacks fought a righteous cause against discrimination, Jim Crow laws, and vicious acts of violence, whites whined about their parents and other authority figures. Evidence of this conflict is bountiful in movies and television shows, in which characters are always blaming their parents for their problems. Two words summarize this tendency: grow up.

Black Americans were often victims of lynchings, beatings, inferior schools, loss of jobs, firebombs, and other injustices that made them second-class citizens in the land of the free. I believe white kids subconsciously did not appreciate the attention blacks were getting, although most agreed that the civil rights cause was just. Many whites wanted to see equality for blacks come to fruition, but, doggone it, they were going to benefit from something as well; therefore, they needed to fight their own battle. Thus was born the rebellion against authority, social norms, morals, and tradition. While blacks organized for justice against oppression, whites assembled for the freedom to get high, have sex with multiple partners, be lazy, and rebel against their parents.

I should say at this juncture that I do not hold a grudge against people for making errors in judgment, admitting their transgressions, and adjusting their behavior accordingly. My displeasure is with those who continuously engage in purposeful behavior that is unethical, illegal, and immoral. They not only defend and justify their mistakes but also condone and promulgate such behavior or worse. Romans 1:29–32 warns against those who are

> filled with all unrighteousness, sexual immorality, wickedness, covetousness, maliciousness; full of envy, murder, strife, deceit, evil-mindedness; they are whisperers, backbiters, haters of God, violent, proud, boasters, inventors of evil things, disobedient to parents, undiscerning, untrustworthy, unloving, unforgiving, unmerciful; *who, knowing the righteous judgment of God, that those who practice such things are deserving of death, not only do the same but also approve of those who practice them.* (emphasis added)

Today, though the status of blacks has much improved, we continue to fight both battles, one good (civil rights) and one bad (hippie revolution). As society takes on skirmishes to guarantee civil rights to blacks, it also fights the nonstop encroachment of the 1960s relativistic hippie uprising. The civil rights battle brought positive advancements, but the hippie revolution brought negative consequences and complications.

What a dismal, perverse legacy the spoiled white generation of the 1960s and its descendants have left for America compared to the sacrifice, unselfishness, perseverance, faith, and hard-fought victories the same decade's black generation and their predecessors have bequeathed.

Unfortunately, relativism, elitism, and socialism have infected several of the self-proclaimed contemporary civil rights leaders, and this ideology has victimized the movement itself. For more information about this occurrence, I highly recommend the book *Enough* by Juan Williams.

CHAPTER 6

SPAWNING SOCIALISM: COMMANDEERING THE EDUCATION SYSTEM

THE SINGLE, UNDERLYING lesson of history is that nothing occurs without a prompt, that things happen for a reason, that for every action there is a reaction, or, most commonly, that every effect has a cause. What impetus drives the agenda of elitist, socialist-leaning liberals? We can easily ascertain that their goal is the accumulation of power. Everyone knows that power corrupts and that many who possess it want to acquire more of it. But why power? What induces a group of people to want to control the masses? Is this thinking an offshoot of evolutionary theory that states only the strong survive?

In this case the strong amass power to control—I mean help—the weak. What if you intentionally guided a populace toward a weaker state of mind, body, and spirit, enveloping their intellectual, emotional, physical, and moral well-being (as described in chapter 5)? Is it not true that weaker people require a greater level of paternalism and care? Societal evidence points to that reality since more attention is necessary for babies and young children, the learning disabled, those undergoing physical therapy for an injury, senior citizens residing in nursing homes and other facilities, and patients needing surgical procedures.

Let's look at the example of babies and young children. Is it not true that newborns require more care than infants, who require more care than toddlers, who require more care than teenagers, who require more care than adults? What if the education system were organized to perpetuate a childlike mindset in students so they demanded constant parental attention? What if this system commenced in kindergarten and continued through the college years, meaning that a dependent mentality was instilled from ages five to at least twenty-one? What if the federal government assumed the role of the parent?

If citizens of a nation cannot think for themselves except in the ways in which they are indoctrinated, are they not easily controlled and influenced? Since this plan would be premeditated and carefully calculated, the concept of natural selection would be uprooted and discarded; and we know statists believe in evolution. Furthermore, since liberals believe they are gods, they can arrogantly intervene in the evolutionary process as the arbiters of mankind's welfare. (I must add that I believe in the biblical creation and am using evolution only to illustrate the relativists' philosophy.)

So then power and control are key motivators for relativistic liberals. I should probably cease from calling them "secular" since they worship the environment and themselves. They are using this religion to supplant Christianity and any faith that worships a transcendent God. One may argue the role of evil intentions and the Devil's influence here, but I will not delve into that arena. However, an evil presence is definitely associated with the insatiable desire to control people.

I must note that reasonable control is good. Such control is the purpose of laws that protect people and their property, responsible parents who nurture productive and moral citizens, and religion and faith in the training up of children and adults in the way they should live. Police, teachers, pastors, and other authority figures provide invaluable roles in an orderly society. Without authority, chaos reigns (as we see with relativism).

Oppressive control is a different concept. An authoritarian who raises and disciplines his child is one thing. Controlling parents who abuse or neglect their child is an entirely different realm. A representative government that institutes reasonable controls is a far cry from a repressive regime that oppresses its people, sometimes forcefully. As I already discussed, the hippie revolution was an act of rebellion against authority, morals, tradition, and order. How ironic is it that the same liberals who rebelled against reasonable authority in the 1960s are today advocating an authoritarian, controlling government?

My hypothesis is that something from the past has become ingrained in the aristocrat's brain, and he has been working to construct its blueprint in society for some time now. That stimulus from the past is *The Republic*, the book Plato wrote in 360 BC. In his tome Plato advances an interesting interpretation of the state. In my opinion, liberal socialists have adopted his outline for society and have been striving tirelessly for at least fifty years to implement it in America. They have conquered the media, education, the entertainment industry, even the Supreme Court to do so. They have also attacked Christianity, faith, family, and the United States to achieve this end. They have intentionally lied, misreported, revised, and indoctrinated the citizens of America to institute this plan. So then, let us examine *The Republic*.

THREE SOCIAL CLASSES

Plato observes that society comprises three social classes: the working, busy-bee class (trader); the military class (auxiliary); and the ruling class (guardians, counselors, saviors, or philosopher kings).

I begin with the latter, the ruling class, which is the smallest of the three and represents the wisdom of the state. The members of this class receive the most extensive education. After attending regular school until age twenty, students who possess a philosophical nature and ability are chosen for further education that will prepare them for the role of philosopher king.[1] At this point, they study dialectic, or the art of reasoning, for ten years. At age thirty, the most proficient students from this group are chosen to pursue an education that will allow them to attain "absolute being."[2] In essence, these students study philosophy until the age of thirty-five. Between the ages of thirty-five and fifty, pupils hold military or political office to acquire life experiences and determine whether they will stand firm in their training as philosophers. Those who have proven themselves after this point spend the rest of their lives pursuing philosophy, beholding absolute good, and occasionally holding public office for the good of the public. These philosopher kings also train their successors, equipping them to maintain the proper governance of the state.[3]

In short, Plato's rulers must strongly demonstrate the abilities of reason, restraint, and wisdom in the pursuit of absolute good (or truth), and they have to prove that they will not be corrupted by the world, which is one of the purposes of the fifteen-year apprenticeship as an officeholder. That time is "an opportunity of trying whether, when they are drawn all manner of ways by temptation, they will stand firm or flinch."[4] Assuming that students do not begin school until the age of five, they spend forty-five years preparing for this vocation.

These kings, considered infallible, would never disagree with each other due to the inculcation of a universal instruction, possession of a clear vision of truth and good in all things, and conviction that they would not be swayed by temptation to pursue evil or falsehood. Since they are wise and infallible, they plan society for everyone else. This includes barring unnecessary activities they believe waste human resources while encouraging beneficial traits; the latter are developed to perfection, thus creating the ideal society.

The second social class is the auxiliary class. These individuals also attend school through the age of twenty, but afterward they enter into a military career. Since the members of this class possess a natural trait of combativeness, their role is to perform the military functions of the state, including fighting enemies of the state, maintaining balance in society, enforcing temperance (moderation) in the populace, and supporting the rulers.[5]

The third social class, labeled the trader class, comprises the bulk of society. These busy bees engage in production, business, and trade. The traders can also attend school through the age of twenty and pursue a career in the commercial sector. Although they begin school in childhood, attendance is not compulsory.[6] Education for all three classes includes a moral component that promotes temperance, obedience to authority, and control over sensual desires.[7]

Once the education system determines someone's place in his respective class, mobility between classes does not exist. Once people are in their proper place, movement allegedly does not need to occur because they are content. According to Plato, justice results from each person doing his one work.[8] The three classes are not allowed to intermix; however, children within a class ascend or descend to a different class based on their natures and abilities.[9] Moreover, the ruling class controls the members of the latter two classes; the philosopher kings believe they are doing so as a service to others and the state.

According to Plato, the auxiliary and trader classes are subordinate to the ruling class because only the aristocratic philosopher kings possess a firm grasp of truth and thus the ability to create and maintain a just society. Again, justice is fulfilled when everyone is in his proper place. All members of society can attend school until the age of twenty. The education system's mission involves building moral character and promoting temperance in citizens. Today, "proper" moral disposition is created through character education programs and the indoctrination that occurs in the education system.

Plato's Social Classes in the U.S.

Let's compare and contrast Plato's social classes with our modern society. Who belongs to which social class in our world? That is fairly easy to ascertain. The philosopher kings are the politicians, primarily those at the federal and state levels but especially at the federal level. It is they who dictate policies for states and local governments to follow. They include unelected officials, such as members of the president's cabinet and federal justices. Federal officials are the elite, wise rulers who have the knowledge and ability to tell others how to live. Aides, state and local officials, lobbyists, and others are members of the trader class who perform busy work as the kings dictate.

The middle group, or auxiliary class, includes military and law enforcement agencies, such as the FBI, ATF, CIA, state police, and local police force. Again, they are charged with protecting society, maintaining balance, and enforcing temperance.

The third social class, the trader class, comprises everyone else—educators, doctors, lawyers, businessmen, mechanics, coal miners, cooks, nurses, bankers, custodians, artists, farmers, actors, athletes, and so on. All professions are included as part of the trader class. These workers labor at various jobs, professions, and tasks, allowing society to function smoothly and properly.

Separation of social classes occurs within our system to a degree. Students possess diverse academic abilities and ambitions. Strong students attend more prestigious universities than weak ones do, and the large majority of both groups choose careers within the commercial sector. Regardless of whether students go to college, they more than likely enter the trader class. The only exception is those students who enlist in the military or enter the law enforcement profession, thus comprising the auxiliary class.

An important distinction between real life and Plato's scenario is that people in our nation can experience class mobility; they do not necessarily remain in the social class they originally choose. For example, it is not unusual for soldiers to leave the military and find employment in the private sector, for private sector workers to join the military, and for some citizens to perform in both roles, as members of the National Guard and as employees in the private sector. Members of the ruling class are primarily trained in the most prestigious universities, such as Ivy League schools, Stanford, Duke, MIT, and Georgetown, though not all students who graduate from these institutions enter the ruling class. Although our process deviates from that of Plato in some ways, it is in these prestigious universities, mostly but not exclusively, where the philosopher kings are trained.

Therefore, from where or—should I ask—from whom do the philosopher kings come? For many decades national leaders were born, raised, and developed anywhere in America. Today, however, the elitists come from the elitist class, which breeds and trains its own in "knowledge," "wisdom," "truth," and "reason." Is it not interesting that liberals defend the mediocre public school system while sending their children to elite private schools? They are labeled "elite" schools because the "elite" are intended to attend there. Socialists vociferously oppose the school voucher system, which would allow average citizens to choose the best schools for their children, so they can guard the means by which their offspring receive a high quality education at expensive private schools.

The process works like this: The descendants of socialist-leaning liberals attend schools where the curriculum is rigorous, expectations are high, and achievement is realized through hard work. Through the process the next generation of kings receives the "wisdom" to allegedly rule efficiently. This is the training ground. The number of years is less than Plato's requirement, but it is the same process. On the other hand, the majority is attacked on two fronts: first, the public school system indoctrinates it in the statists' value system; second, liberals excoriate the cornerstones of family, faith, and patriotism.

Their stance on this issue has nothing do with expense. A voucher system would allow common students to receive a quality education at less-expensive alternatives and remove them from the umbrella of public school indoctrination. Moreover, the common folk cannot be permitted to contaminate the philosopher kings' training ground with inferior blood. Statists have the gall to talk about caring for the poor and ending class division, yet they promote class conflict by barring others from sharing in their opportunities. Although the ruling class asserts that no privileges exist for any class, it clearly has the privileges of lording over the masses, controlling society, and enjoying luxuries others are not allowed to possess. The notion of a classless society or one in which no class has privileges over others is a myth.

Many celebrities consider themselves part of the ruling class (they do carry much influence within it), but they are mistaken. Instead, they are upper-tier members of the trader class, who are merely pawns statists maneuver to advance their agenda. Many retro-hippie celebrities praise tyranny (as evident in their commendations of Fidel Castro and Hugo Chavez) and the progression toward socialism as they sit in places of honor, showered by the adulation of the masses. They enjoy a life of luxury while condemning the design that permits their indulgent lifestyle; at the same time, they discourage others from aspiring to that life because they consider themselves superior to the masses, from whom they receive worship, believing they deserve special privileges.

Due to their elevated position in society, they claim the qualifications to pontificate on all issues, but many dwell in a fantasy their whole lives. They play pretend roles that cause them to think they are experts in those particular realms, yet they wander far from reality. Since the multitude has sacrificed reason for sensual values transmitted from the pop culture, it allows celebrities to rise to this level of honor. But again, celebrities are elitists but not rulers. Plato wrote, "They are glad to be honoured by lesser and meaner people,—but honour of some kind they must have."[10] He was not referring to celebrities in this passage, but his words certainly apply to them.

Within today's trader class, one can find a number of subclasses based on income level. Athletes, businesspeople, celebrities, educators, and service workers make different amounts of money and therefore experience divergent standards of living based mostly on material possessions. Income is not the basis of membership in the trader class, however; it is instead the role one plays in society. All these individuals provide a service to society in some way, shape, or form. Athletes and celebrities entertain their audience, businesspeople offer goods and services to their customers, teachers indoctrinate students according to the precepts of liberalism and socialism, and service workers provide an important function in society by cooking meals, collecting garbage, assembling products, and more. A multitude of careers in addition to these also fit within the trader class. Just because life is more complex in the twenty-first century does not preclude the statists' ambition to formulate a society based on Plato's *Republic*.

The three-tiered republic duplicates itself in the trader class. Celebrities claim the top rung of the hierarchy, though they do not rule from its elevations. In a sense they are leaders who possess much influence over the culture as they provide negative examples by living immoral lives, but they are neither kings nor rulers. A large majority of celebrities have bought into the 1960s hippie revolution counterculture; have abandoned traditional religion; have supported attacks against faith, family, and patriotism; and have both condoned and promoted a barrage of popular, deviant behaviors. Many in Hollywood and the pop culture publicize any concept that runs counter to traditional values and morals once considered normal. They worship the environment, relativism, and self to fill the void left by their rejection of God, especially the Christian God.

Similar to Plato is the fact that students are not bound by their parents' social class; rather, they can become members of a different social class based on their ability or goals. But, as previously mentioned, the large majority of students who do not enter the military become members of the trader class regardless of whether they attend college or the level of prestige of the university in which they enroll. They may earn different salaries and belong to different subclasses, but all are part of the commercial class.

Exceptions do occur. Some bright students who possess gifts compatible with leadership and politics may find themselves within the ruler class, but such is a rare occurrence. When I ponder the top students in my high school class, I note that all are part of the trader class. Compared to their parents, many have climbed the social ladder, which is part of the American Dream and a good thing. But they remain connected to the large trader class.

In review, subclasses exist in the trader class from lower to upper and to those in between. Therefore, improving one's position in life is still possible, making the American Dream alive and well. A divergent view of this dream is that the ruling class controls these citizens' lives and that these individuals have been brainwashed into wanting the ruling class to manage their lives.

Remember, the philosopher kings allegedly achieve an indivisible wisdom; therefore, they formulate the plan for society to run smoothly and perfectly. Also remember that socialist-leaning liberals have adopted a prescription for life that is neither the philosophy upon which America was founded nor based on the framework the founders laid out for America—a truly enlightened, wise, Providence-inspired construct that became the greatest country in the history of the world.

LIBERAL PLAYBOOK: *THE REPUBLIC*

One can discern that the state described in *The Republic* and the United States of America do not match each other perfectly. The American government and way of life impair full implementation of Plato's caste system. America greatly contrasts with Plato's state, and it would have been impossible for him to prophesy about the changes in culture over the millennia; nevertheless, the attitude of statists has not changed. I hypothesize that the direction in which statists have guided society over at least the last fifty years (and possibly longer) has been based on Plato's writings. *The Republic* is an important playbook liberals have employed to fulfill their conceived world order, a socialist government in which the masses depend on a small, aristocratic ruling class. How good it is for elitists when such a government is not forced on the people, when they choose it for themselves after careful guidance (or indoctrination) from those in charge, the philosopher kings.

This ideal explains the need for statists to remove faith (Christianity in America) from society and replace it with an alternative (environmentalism, relativism, self). It also explains their need to control all their subjects' activities to attain the perfect society; all have heard the government mantra about caring for citizens "from the cradle to the grave." Those in government do not offer this control as benevolence but to permit the establishment of a small aristocracy that oppressively controls its subjects.

Unfortunately, Plato's vision and that of liberal statists diverge from each other; in fact, they are at opposite poles. Plato's goal was to create a just society based on absolute good and truth, and his state had a place for God. As a Greek he referred to the gods, but he also recognized the Creator, Providence, and divine order.

Though some of his ideas definitely exuded socialism and control, his intentions were to avoid evil and tyranny. On the other hand, the socialist's objective is not to search for truth, justice, reason, or goodness; it is to control others through the acquisition of power and to promote the tyranny Plato loathed as the worst form of government.

The Republic and the U.S.

I will analyze and apply Plato's *Republic* to our nation today. Many facets of the *Republic* apply to our current state of affairs. Some of Plato's observations appear to be coincidental to our culture, while liberals, I think, intentionally apply others to it. My purpose in reading Plato's *Republic* was to examine his views on education, which I was introduced to while studying for my teaching license. After writing the rough draft of this book, I delved into his tome and was surprised by his description of government and society in the fourth century BC. I was most fascinated by how closely it parallels our nation; some of the things I had written were present in Plato's culture over two thousand years ago. I knew I had to include those relevant equivalents in my book. I believe you will be equally captivated by these comparisons, by their danger to society, and by their threat to permanently alter our fantastic, glorious, Christian-based democratic experiment.

Plato's Ideal Government

Plato considered aristocracy (government by a privileged class) as the ideal and most just form of rule. He ranked timocracy (an intermediate government between aristocracy and oligarchy), oligarchy (government by a small faction of persons or families), democracy (government by the people, majority rule), and tyranny (absolute power held by a single ruler) behind aristocracy from most to least appealing and from just to evil. In Plato's mind, democracy was the second most evil form of government, and tyranny was inevitable.

In his aristocratic regime Plato identifies various traits of socialism, including the following:

- Discouraging innovation because it creates complexity
- Maintaining a simplistic lifestyle in the realms of music, poetry, sports, and education
- Censoring poets, writers, and musicians
- Purging luxury from the state
- Limiting laborers to one vocation
- Emphasizing the state over the individual
- Promoting wealth redistribution
- Restricting health care
- Approving abortion
- Engaging in selective breeding
- Requiring government consent of marriages
- Unifying subjects through persuasion
- Granting rulers (and rulers only) the right to lie to benefit the state

Training Citizens in Schools

Plato believed education was the primary instrument in forming his state. The purpose of education in his ideal republic, he believed, was to create a temperate citizenry by nurturing it in the ways of the state. The state accomplished this objective by directing the school system and "properly" educating students, beginning at a young age, via a method more beneficial to the state than to the individual. "The beginning is the most important part of any work, especially in the case of a young and tender thing; for that is the time at which the character is being formed and the *desired impression* is more readily taken"[11] (emphasis added). Recall the examination in chapter 5 of the federal government's "Home Visitation Programs for Families with Young Children and Families Expecting Children" that is included in H.R. 3200, also known as "Obamacare."

The purpose of this simple, basic education was to build character and identify students for their appropriate careers and social class based on their natures, strengths, and preferences. This philosophy has progressed in our nation to the point that education leaders call for third graders to take career surveys and sixth graders (yes, eleven-year-olds) to begin developing career plans so they can be placed in an education track that provides preparation for a particular career. An eleven-year-old? Are they serious? Does that not sound like communist China or the former Soviet Union?

Plus, a goal is to have the state's "desired impression" permeate the child's character, beginning at age five. The modern American education system is being used in this fashion; it has been constructed to indoctrinate students in the ways of the state, which I have described in this book. Recall Ms. Colbert's quote in chapter 4 regarding students taking to whoever gets to them first. This intentional plan is based on Plato's provisions for an ideal, utopian state. Some argue that socialism is the best type of government and that its failure is the result of improper implementation. Such advocates have not conceded this view and are trying to implement their ideology through the education system.

Plato wrote about the importance of indoctrinating students through the education system: "The authority which we exercise over children, and the refusal to let them be free until we have established in them a principle analogous to the constitution of a state, and by cultivation of this higher element have set up in their hearts a guardian and ruler like our own, and when this is done they may go their ways."[12] He also wrote, "For good nurture and education implant good constitutions, and these good constitutions taking root in a good education improve more and more, and this improvement affects the breed in man as in other animals."[13]

Educating and nurturing children are good priorities, but today's goals extend beyond improving children to indoctrinating them according to the socialist belief system. Moreover, parents should be teaching morals and values at home, while the school supports that instruction. That is how education used to be done. Today, Christian teachings have been expelled from schools and replaced with those of the socialist-leaning liberals' religion. Parents have passively submitted to this theocratic instruction and thus allow the public schools to care for their children.

In early America education goals included the creation of an informed, literate, Christian electorate; such an electorate is the best way to allow people to govern themselves and maintain a democracy. Remember, Plato's preeminent government was an aristocratic one and that today's socialist-leaning liberal is an aristocrat. The goal of today's education system is to nurture students who willingly desire and accept a strong government upon which they can depend, thus sacrificing their freedoms. Now citizens are being guided to follow a certain ideology (liberalism) instead of "a principle analogous to the constitution of a state," which is our Christian faith and the U.S. Constitution. The goal is to implant the socialists' mindset into a populace so it becomes the natural way of thinking and takes deeper root in each successive generation.

In this scenario state interests supersede those of the individual. "And therefore we must consider whether…we look to their greatest happiness individually, or whether this principle of happiness does not rather reside in the State as a whole. But if the latter be the truth, then…*all* must be *compelled* or *induced* to do their own work in the best way. And thus the whole State will grow up in a noble order"[14] (emphasis added).

Not only is the state's happiness valued more than that of the individual; the latter must be "compelled or induced" to work toward the former's health and contentment. Moreover, citizens must be gradually convinced of this fact. "In the present generation...; there is no way of accomplishing this; but their sons may be made to believe in the tale, and their son's sons, and posterity after them."[15] Therefore, liberals concede time in their effort to realize this objective, and the move toward socialism has been gradual and steady. Furthermore, is not Plato's use of the word *tale* intriguing?

The good news is that realizing their objective may take longer than they planned. Recall the statists' reactions to the patriotic outpourings and religious zeal that followed 9/11 despite forty years of efforts to diminish them in our nation. The bad news is that the shift is still taking place. Moreover, liberals have recently adopted the practice of expeditiously passing federal legislation in response to the latest "crisis," encouraging socialism to become ensconced in society more rapidly than ever. Examples of this strategy include the Troubled Asset Relief Program (TARP, 2008, $66 to $356 billion), American Recovery and Reinvestment Act (2009, $787 billion), and Education Jobs and Medicaid Assistance Act (2010, $26 billion), among others. This sentiment runs counter to the foundational precepts of the United States and against the principles of liberty upon which the government serves the people instead of the opposite. When free people exercise freedom within the restraints of religious morality and faith in God, this action leads to a society in which people and government contentedly coexist in a mutually beneficial relationship.

Health Care and Medicine

Since government interference in health care is at the forefront of our minds, what does Plato say about the medical field? He says much. I quote several of his thoughts here. First, "excessive care of the body...is most inimical [adverse] to the practice of virtue."[16] Furthermore, Plato honored Asclepius, the god of medicine, because "bodies which disease had penetrated through and through he would not have attempted to cure....He did not want to lengthen out good-for-nothing lives, or to have weak fathers begetting weaker sons;—if a man was not able to live in the ordinary way...a cure would have been of no use either to himself, *or to the State*"[17] (emphasis added). Finally: "Those who are diseased in their bodies they [physicians] will leave to die."[18]

If this does not resonate with socialized medicine and the nationalized health care bill, nothing does. Though society sometimes takes extreme care and has developed a hypochondriac, overcautious mentality, we should not deny care to those who provide no benefit to the state, whatever that means. In any case such ideals are often hidden in the words of those who promote government-controlled health care.

Redistribution of Wealth

On the topic of the redistribution of wealth, Plato believed the rich and poor were at war with each other. He wrote that if we "give the wealth or power of persons of the one to the others, [we] will have a great many friends and not many enemies."[19] This statement should remind us of the "benevolent" New Deal and much liberal policy since that decade. How does a politician or political party gain favor? By giving people what they do not possess, by buying votes through promises and entitlements, by taking wealth from those who have worked hard to achieve success and giving it to those who, often by choice, are less fortunate.

Socialists would have our country run this way despite the fact that "poor" Americans are wealthier than most of the world's population; despite the fact that many are in challenging situations due to poor decision making; despite the fact that one can move from poverty to prosperity through hard work, thrift, perseverance, and sacrifice; despite the fact that millions have improved their standard of living and achieved the American Dream; and despite the fact that hundreds of thousands annually immigrate to America out of oppression to access our dream.

The 2008 presidential election campaign was rife with promises and entitlements—from homes to health care, to happiness, to racial harmony, to well-educated citizens, to a temperate climate. And this was all for free—that is, if you neglect to calculate the amount of taxpayers' wealth that would be confiscated and redistributed to the so-called have-nots. Liberals recruit "friends" in exchange for promises, many of which go unfulfilled. Then when the promises fail to materialize, statists blame the "rich," manufacture class and racial conflict, make further ill-conceived promises to the beleaguered "poor," and author more legislation that shackles the population. Then the cycle repeats itself.

Frankly, many Democrats of the sixties assented to civil rights because they saw the proverbial writing on the wall; they recognized that civil rights for blacks were inevitable, so they voted for the legislation in exchange for the privilege of bribing blacks for their votes, just as they were doing with their other constituents. As a result, dependency grew, self-sufficiency eroded, and the nation advanced further toward a socialist government.

Marriage and Child Bearing

In his discussion of state-approved marriage and controlled procreation, Plato writes about undesirable unions. He says there will be "strict orders to prevent any embryo which may come into being from seeing the light; and if any force a way to the birth, the parents must understand that the offspring of such a union cannot be maintained, and arrange accordingly."[20] These words are reminiscent of both standard and partial-birth abortion.

Ancient Greece and America

I could write many pages comparing Plato's ideal republic to the challenge currently facing our society. It makes me wonder what Greek life was like in 360 BC compared to American society in AD 2011. Did Plato study the progression of Greece from a timocracy to a tyranny? When he wrote *The Republic*, was Greece somewhere between the poles in that spectrum? Was Plato frustrated with his country's political landscape? Did he witness decadence, laziness, unethical behavior, and an obsession with pleasure? Were he and his fellow Hellenes cynical about the state and direction of their country?

I sense these ideas in his writings; furthermore, I believe contemporary America is in a position similar to Greece during Plato's time. Greece was heading in the direction of a fallen empire, the end of which occurred about three hundred years later. I believe Plato was trying to prescribe the cure for his nation's ills. To repeat, I think the United States is in a similar, precarious position. However, we do not need to search for a new government. On the contrary, we need to return to the foundational precepts of liberty granted by a generous, merciful, benevolent God.

Returning to Our Christian Roots

Exaggerated environmental concerns are not going to destroy our planet; rather, the moral upheaval glorified in our culture is consuming our society and will destroy it from within. The Romans, Greeks, and ancient Israelites did not perceive their destruction while it happened. I fear we are in the same precarious position in the United States today; we are too ignorant, secular, and self-absorbed to realize our brilliant nation is being decimated before our eyes due to moral decadence, rejection of God, and the refutation of our Christian foundation.

Contrary to the warnings of environmentalists, what will remain amid the rubble of a nation that was once powerful, wise, virtuous, and reverent toward Providence are the land, water, plants, wildlife, and air. Voting for conservative candidates to attain tax cuts and preserve our highly advanced health care system is not enough; we must return to our Christian foundation and adjust our declining and reprehensible behavior.

We need a revival that will redirect us toward our Christian roots, traditions, and heritage (unlike ancient Greek polytheism), a faith that allowed us to be shaped into the greatest nation in the history of nations. Otherwise, we will follow in the footsteps of empires that preceded us—broken, troubled, hard-pressed, defeated, forsaken by our God.

PLATO'S RESERVATIONS

The point should be clear that a multitude of Plato's aristocratic, socialist ideas are being imitated in our nation today. Consider the following: state control and power over many facets of our lives, state interests prized over those of the individual, a state-directed education system, a small group of philosopher kings ("rare plants," according to Plato) who preside over their subjects, possess the wisdom and propensity to guide and nurture their inferior subordinates, and set the course of our entire lives. I believe liberal, socialist-leaning statists have melded themselves to these principles and through their application are trying to forge Plato's ideal, utopian society.

But even Plato admitted that instituting his perfect state was a fallacy: "Then you must not insist on my proving that the actual State will in every respect coincide with the ideal."[21] He asks, "And is our theory a worse theory because we are unable to prove the possibility of a city being ordered in the manner described?"[22] In the search for a perfect state, the discussion was "not with any view of showing that they [the ideals] could exist in fact."[23] The socialist statists are not dissuaded. In their pride, arrogance, and self-worship, they believe they can create this utopia. They believe they are not only greater than the gods; they believe they *are* the gods. They want the perfect state, they dream of the perfect state, and they will trample on others' freedom to conceive the perfect state.

PLATO AND GOD

Unlike today's messiahs and elitists, Plato's goal was to create a nation based on justice, absolute good, reason, and divinely inspired wisdom. He magnified the Creator of the heavens; God, the maker of all things; God as perfect, good, unchanging, and incapable of lying. Plato envisioned justice as the heavenly way, heaven as the reward for just behavior, and hell as the punishment for evil actions. Moreover, he recognized that the just man was blessed and the unjust man was cursed, that injustice was the offspring of evil, and that the soul was divine and immortal. These beliefs are harmonious with Christianity, are they not?

In our age "leaders" who wish to establish their aristocratic utopia have the delusion that they are superior to God and can fulfill His role. They reject heaven, hell, and evil in the process. Plato warned, "And you know that a man who is deranged and not right in his mind, will fancy that he is able to rule, not only over men, but also over the gods."[24] Statists need to delegitimize God so they can take His place; they need to purge God from society so people will turn to them instead of to Providence for guidance. Plato noted, "Every one had better be ruled by divine wisdom dwelling within him; or…by an external authority, that we may be all…under the same government, friends and equals."[25]

The choice is ours. Will we allow God, our Creator and Savior, to rule? Or will we relinquish His sovereignty to an external authority, a socialist, paternal government that perceives itself as god?

AMERICA'S PHILOSOPHER KINGS

Not all federal politicians are proponents of the statists' desire to control the populace through such a republic. We can easily discern those who are supporters of this philosophy from those who are not. Adherents of the socialist ideology are those politicians who advocate reductions of liberty, drown hope by hyping various problems or crises (both real and imagined), strive to expand federal government power to the detriment of the people (in contravention of the Constitution), and convince citizens of their inability to control their personal lives in combination with the federal government's capability to do so. These statists, relativists, and socialist-leaning liberals are committed to the scheme that a small group of philosopher kings (though they may not render that term) need to show people the way, the truth, and the life.

Such reasoning is beyond the grasp of many individuals, who exhaustively labor in their professions, not realizing they are the tools of socialists. People are consumed with working, running errands, raising their family, and transporting their children to manifold activities. They often have neither the time nor energy to become fully knowledgeable about this threat or to defend themselves against the attack.

Educators are preoccupied with fulfilling federal and state mandates; teaching classes; sponsoring extracurricular activities; completing mountains of paperwork; analyzing an abundance of data; and tracking student progress, behavior, attendance, or attitude changes. They have been saddled with a burdensome workload that allows them only to complete the mind-boggling volume of tasks commanded by the statists who control the system.

In their effort to form a republic where a small cabal asserts power over the masses, socialist-leaning liberals have attacked freedom, family, and faith; indoctrinated the population; and strived to expunge hope from America. As hope diminishes, emptiness and despair multiply—one of the statists' goals. Why would someone want to perpetrate a sense of hopelessness on the citizenry? Is this logical? Most would say no, but since when are power-hungry relativists rational? Their objective is to satisfy their appetites so they can control others while shattering the dreams of those they wish to subjugate.

The reason is simple, as we see in the movie, *The NeverEnding Story*. In the film an entity wants to strengthen what is called "the Nothing" while people's hopes and dreams correspondingly diminish. A wolf, who serves the entity behind "the Nothing" and works to achieve its objective, states the reason for pulverizing peoples' hopes: "People who have no hopes are easy to control, and whoever has the control has the power."[26]

The members of this ruling class actually believe they are superior to their subjects in knowledge and wisdom; actually they believe that without their existence, society would self-destruct. They believe they are a privileged class that needs to save people from themselves. If you listen to what they say in their media sound bites, they quickly reveal their intentions. Given that they have embraced this mentality, it is easy to understand why these arrogant people view themselves as gods. As I previously detailed, they worship themselves and their achievements, rejecting God. Therefore, something—or someone—else must replace God, and they see themselves as the answer, the messiahs of the world.

They acknowledge faith only because the foolish masses believe in such mythology; giving false recognition to their outdated religious conceptions is better than fighting a conspicuous battle against them. They primarily fight surreptitiously, using the pop culture to ridicule citizens' faith and the education system to delegitimize it, thus gradually purging it from the culture. Consider the increased emphasis on Santa Claus and the Easter Bunny over Christ's birth, death, and resurrection in today's society compared to several decades ago. In their alleged service to others, the statists restrict and indoctrinate others in the "proper" lifestyle to create the perfect, balanced society, as written in Plato's description of the philosopher-king class.

This explains why religion must be attacked, destroyed, and replaced with character education programs and other forms of values clarification instruction. The way to achieve this aspiration is to indoctrinate students through the education system. The products of the education system become adults (some of whom become educators) and parents; they are accessories in the indoctrination of their offspring, who become voters and by choice elect these narcissistic socialists into office.

Only a fool would believe that man can create the perfect society; only a fool would be oblivious to the truth that God's foolishness is wiser than man's wisdom. First Corinthians 1:20, 25 says, "Has not God made foolish the wisdom of this world?...Because the foolishness of God is wiser than men." Plato recognized that the perfect state could not exist. In exploring the ideal standards of a state, he was doing so "not with any view of showing that they could exist in fact"[27] and requested that no one "insist on my proving that the actual State will in every respect coincide with the ideal."[28]

I previously detailed that the rulers will promote beneficial activities, while deterring those they consider detrimental to society. To accomplish this objective, other influences must be eradicated, denounced, and declared illegitimate, including family, faith in God, and patriotism. Remember, at America's birth, Christianity was taught in schools but has since been subordinated to secular values in our contemporary schools. Constituents cannot declare loyalty to matters that run counter to the statists' aristocratic, socialist view of society. Citizens cannot depend on their parents, God, or the precepts on which our nation was founded because the values of that powerful triumvirate contradict those of the rulers. Those influences must be destroyed for the aristocratic state to become established.

Philosopher Kings and Education

What is one place where this objective can be achieved because all students are required to be there? The mandatory public education system. According to Plato, the way to found the ideal state is to "take possession of their children, who will be *unaffected by the habits of their parents*; these they [kings] will train in their own habits and laws,…and in this way the State… will soonest and most easily attain happiness"[29] (emphasis added). According to Plato, one intent of the education system is to build moral character in its students. This goal may sound altruistic on the surface, but it becomes twisted and evil when the ruling class uses the system to indoctrinate its citizens in the values it wants to promote while ridiculing and breaking down values it opposes because they inhibit the development of the three-tiered republic. Actually, socialist-leaning liberals could care less if it were a three- or ten-tiered republic, just so long as they were controlling it.

Of course, some educate their children at home or in private schools. Such competition stirs up revulsion in socialists because they have no control in such places. One must also keep in mind that many private schools are also liberal, adopt the same secular curricula and textbooks as the public schools, and follow state guidelines for the education of children. Therefore, the statist viewpoint is alive and well in numerous private school settings. Nevertheless, the socialist, who must have total control, abhors any autonomous system that competes with his own.

The Mighty Strong Beast

In his book Plato describes a "mighty strong beast." This term refers to those who use fallacious reasoning in their arguments and whose wisdom is the reiteration of the opinion of their followers. In my opinion this "beast" is a fair portrayal of our current education system.

The tempers and desires of a mighty strong beast who is fed by him—he would learn how to approach and handle him, also at what times and from what causes he is dangerous or the reverse, and what is the meaning of his several cries, and…when… he is soothed or infuriated; and…that when, by continually attending upon him, he has become perfect in all this, he calls his knowledge wisdom, and makes of it a system or art, which he proceeds to teach, although he has no real notion of what he means by the principles or passions of which he is speaking, but calls this honourable and that dishonourable, or good or evil, or just or unjust, all in accordance with the tastes and tempers of the great brute. Good he pronounces to be that in which the beast delights and evil to be that which he dislikes; and he can give no other account of them except that the just and noble are the necessary, having never himself seen, and having no power of explaining to others the nature of either, or the difference between them, which is immense.[30]

Let's break down this quote. First, the "mighty beast" is the education system. The so-called experts have learned how to "approach and handle" it by thoroughly studying it, learning its tendencies, and discovering its aspects and nature. As a matter of fact, they have acquired advanced degrees in their pursuit of mastering the beast, and they surmise that they have grasped its "times," "causes," "cries," and "tastes." In "attending upon him," they have experimented, conducted mountains of research (killing numerous trees in the process), and analyzed reams of data (more dead trees), believing they have perfected the beast to the point of calling it an "art." They "proceed to teach" the art in teacher education programs, conferences, professional periodicals, faculty meetings, and staff development sessions. However, they do not have a strong grasp of the "principles or passions" of which they philosophize. They are passionate about children and shaping the future, but nothing in what they say is concrete; their slogans are empty and vague.

Fickle is what is "honourable and dishonourable," "good or evil," "just or unjust"; what is "honourable" today is "dishonourable" tomorrow. This year's good is next year's evil. What is just for this generation is unjust for the subsequent one, and this sense of justice reverses again in later years. Their principles are constantly changing based on opinion, new research, further data analysis, and public sentiment.

The "good he pronounces" usually involves the allocation of federal, state, and local money; grant money; and resources, in which "the beast delights." It also involves the maintenance of power and control over the system via a monopoly, while the reverse is the "evil…he dislikes." Education leaders are unable to "give account" of the "just and noble" due to their hollow catchphrases, such as "We do what's best for children," "All children can learn," "Child-centered approach," "Think outside the box," and "Understand diversity in a changing world." High expectations are recognized but rarely produced; they are often dismissed in favor of feelings, emotions, and self-esteem.

Public education funding deserves a brief discussion. Since we are in a challenging economy, many advocate a significant reduction in funds allocated to public schools. Although I believe a majority of localities, excluding the district where I worked for twelve years, have overfunded education, considerable cuts to school coffers are inappropriate at this time. Those who have spent excessively, including most districts, can tolerate a decrease in spending, but enacting sharp, punitive reductions is unwise. Removing school finances is not the solution to improving a mediocre system. Instead, a philosophical transformation is necessary to reestablish a rigorous, effective education system. To benefit students, parents, teachers, communities, and our nation, we must turn away from the socialist-leaning liberal ideology that grips the system.

I may be wrong about this "mighty strong beast." Maybe the beast is liberalism as described in this book; maybe the beast is relativism with its acceptance of all notions that violate norms, morals, and traditions. Maybe the beast is the master of Pandora's jar, who has persuaded men to unlock its cover and unleash its evil on our culture. Perhaps the beast is the Devil, who has convinced society that neither he nor God is real and that man is truly god. The serpent told Eve in the garden of Eden, "Your eyes will be opened, and you will be like God" (Gen. 3:5).

Higher Education

Once students enter college, statists have free reign to indoctrinate youth. Parents not only are absent from campuses of higher learning but also give more freedom to their children to allow them to grow, mature, and become independent. At the same time, students are strongly encouraged to experiment and break free from the restraints of their parents' "oppressive" value system. This freedom often leads to the uncontrolled and irresponsible behaviors common on college campuses. Refer back to the legacy of the 1960s. Blacks broke the shackles of slavery and discrimination, while whites shed the chains of their parents' discipline and that of other authority figures. The values of the rebellious '60s have infected righteous causes and all society, leading us to self-destruction.

The visible promotion of college enrollment includes the opportunity to pursue a certain profession, develop high skills, earn a higher paycheck, and access an improved standard of living. In 2005 a high school graduate, a college graduate with a bachelor's degree, and a college graduate with a master's degree earned $583, $937, and $1,129 per week, respectively.[31] Therefore, a graduate with a bachelor's degree made 37.8 percent more than a high school graduate did, while a graduate with a master's degree earned 48 percent more. Unemployment in 2005 was more than double among high school graduates (4.7 percent) compared to students who possessed a master's degree (2.1 percent).[32]

The hidden reason to encourage all students to attend college, once a mantra of former President Bill Clinton, is that it provides an unrestrained opportunity to indoctrinate young, impressionable students. Do you consider it a coincidence that twenty-one-year-olds vote liberal in large numbers? At one time the norm was that students attended a university for four years. Today's students are encouraged to stay for five or six years; some majors are designed to piggyback a master's degree onto a bachelor's degree, which requires students to stay enrolled for six years. As majors become more complex and in higher demand, students remain enrolled for over six years as they pursue law, medical training, education, and other degrees.

How many careers should not require a college education? I can name one for sure: communications. Instead of spending sixty thousand dollars at a university, most communications majors could learn the skills of their trade through apprenticeships with a company within their profession; apprentices could even pay a fee to the company for such an opportunity. Within two years, students would be trained in the skills of their profession.

In the past most students finished college with a bachelor's degree. Today, most in their mid to late twenties have earned their master's degrees, and many have earned a PhD. The sad part is that many of these academically proficient learners develop a sense of intellectual superiority over those who do not attain such levels of achievement, causing them to see themselves as philosopher kings in their respective realm of authority or profession. They believe their acquisition of higher levels of education provides a rite of passage into the realm of the elite, making them wiser than their subordinates and those who do not attain such status. Often these people are far from intellectual, wise, or rational. The sadder part is that I know those with high school diplomas who possess more common sense and wisdom than a dozen PhDs put together. The saddest part is that many with PhDs are running and ruining our superb nation.

Graduates who complete the requirements for a PhD (most of whom remain in the trader class) enroll in college-level classes for a minimum of eight years. Tack onto that the number of years spent in the public school system, and they were enrolled in the liberal, relativistic, socialist-leaning education system for twenty-one years. This time spent in education reflects another difference between Plato's *Republic* and modern society. In *The Republic* only the philosopher kings spent a large number of years acquiring education. In our world everyone is encouraged to improve himself by obtaining education beyond high school. The reason, of course, is the further indoctrination of students in the value system of the ruling class, which is easily accomplished in the far left-leaning higher education system.

Liberal universities indoctrinate naïve students in socialistic ideals so they will adopt contemporary liberalism. This ideology imparts class envy, antireligious sentiments, antimilitary and unpatriotic beliefs, and relativism, which is composed of values clarification instruction on a wide array of moral and behavioral issues. As I previously stated, graduates ingrained with the socialist philosophy become promoters of the agenda because universities are breeding grounds of liberal thought that usually generate a liberal product, strengthening the voice of socialist, relativistic ideals. The longer one is in the system, the more predisposed he becomes to embracing its convictions due to a continuous, unrelenting, flagrant assault on the mind.

I have seen conservative-leaning colleagues change into statist-agenda proponents while spending years in post-secondary education pursuing their PhDs. The more who are indoctrinated through the education system, the easier it is to pass such instruction on to future generations. This pattern is in accordance with

Plato's *Republic*. Recall that part of his education system's mission is to instill moral character and a value system that benefits the state over the individual; furthermore, he dictated that fulfillment would occur only after such dogma was implanted in successive generations.

Considering the host of recent crises identified and reforms enacted, it is intriguing that no one has called out inflated tuition charged by colleges and universities. This is especially surprising since socialists, who are supposedly anticapitalist and continually attack prosperity and business profits, run these institutions. Then again, the socialist media, politicians, and interest groups protect their left-leaning brethren. Also, liberals' stance against capitalism and the free market is not an aversion to money but a testament to their desire to accumulate and control it.

Today's kings believe they serve others by controlling them and that their subjects want to be controlled by them. They institute a "moral" program that advances their agenda so they can control their subordinates by their subordinates' choices. Through this program they annihilate families, faith, and patriotism. Through their values clarification ideals, they glorify the environment, relativism, and man above God, Christian precepts, and our founding principles. Faith in God and family inspires many to be strong, to develop character, to maintain discipline, to overcome adversity, to avoid bad influences, to raise strong families, and to build a stable society. But liberals replace this faith with trust in government.

BIG GOVERNMENT GROWS

Achievement for the majority occurs but on a much lower level than that of the elitists. In the process the education system rears loyal followers of the kings. Many endorse the liberal agenda as they follow in the footsteps of hippies by demanding entitlements and naively falling for the belief that they need the government to care for them. The number of those who acquiesce to the socialist ideology increases in size with each passing generation.

Many wonder how an inexperienced candidate such as Mr. Barack Obama could have been elected president based on his campaign platform, but the process is simple. With each passing year, greater numbers of Americans accept the brainwashing they receive. Almost every segment of society has accepted the premise that it needs or deserves a government handout—from the poor to the middle class, to the elderly, to minorities, to teenagers, to business owners, to homeowners, and so on. Most, if not all, citizens belong to more than one of these groups.

When the government offers a bailout, almost all accept it, even if they believe in small government. How many people are enrolled in the national do-not-call list operated by the federal government? How many then turn and argue for a smaller government? How many car dealerships participated in the cash-for-clunkers program the federal government instituted? How many then voted conservative to receive lower business taxes? A better question is, how many actually received their reimbursements from the government for the clunkers program? How many insurance companies supported President Obama's health care reform, withdrawing consent only after discovering that the bill's penalty for not having health care was too low?

How many people make their decisions based on what benefits them most at the time instead of exhibiting a solid value system? Such practices are antithetical to acting according to one's values and what is best for society, highlighting the damage relativism and selfishness inflict on a culture, as I discussed earlier in this book. How common is this behavior?

I am not surmising that the federal government should never provide programs or that no one should benefit from them when it does. The point is, how many unnecessary federal initiatives exist that should be either beyond government purveyance or instituted by private organizations? The three listed above represent only a few grains of sand in an expansive desert.

First, the entitlement mindset needs to change. Second, citizens must reject government interference, even if they benefit from it. Integrity means doing right when no one is looking and others are compromising. If you reject socialism and instead believe in small government, individual responsibility, our founding principles, democracy, the free market, our Christian foundation, or some combination of those, then you must refuse to participate in federal government programs and initiatives.

The Ruling Class Promotes Conflict

Conflict is an instrumental weapon statists employ to advance their agenda. Everyone has heard of the divide-and-conquer strategy. When the trader class is divided, the relativist comes to the rescue to solve its conflict. For example, now that relativism has dictated that homosexuality is normal behavior and equal to heterosexuality, many are fighting for gay marriage as a right, and the federal judiciary is legislating this right. Since many still reject this deviant lifestyle, only legislation can force its acceptance in society. In addition, indoctrination in the education system through mandated curricula as well as brainwashing through the media and entertainment industries garners further acceptance of homosexuality, making it a technical knockout for the statist. A deviant behavior is normalized, a traditional value is rejected, a new norm is created, and people are forced to accept it. Family is damaged, faith is uprooted, and the state redefines morality.

Once a behavior, such as sexual promiscuity, is accepted, the culture is irreversibly contaminated. The only way to proceed is to go further in that particular direction. For instance, once a steak is cooked, it cannot be uncooked; the choice is between maintaining its current condition or cooking it further. Rotting fruit presents a better illustration. Once the rotting process begins, it cannot revert itself; the rotting continues until the fruit is completely decomposed. Likewise, an eroding culture continues to decline into a further state of destruction.

Another example of government intrusion is in the realm of racial tension. When a judge declared O. J. Simpson not guilty of murder, the media reported that the nation was divided down the middle according to color. They alleged that blacks supported the decision while whites opposed it. To support their premise of a divided nation, they played video clips of blacks celebrating in the streets and whites hanging their heads in disappointment. Their reporting could not have been further from the truth. Many people of both colors agreed or disagreed with the verdict. I would say that the large majority of Americans, regardless of race, color, gender, or religion, believed O. J. Simpson was guilty.

The media successfully creates a pretend conflict, allowing the government or its media cronies to arrive on the scene to alleviate the problem, counsel others, and point them in the right direction; as a result, people become accustomed to the government solving their problems through its interference, whether active or passive. Due to racial tension provoked by intentionally exaggerated and misleading media reporting, the government is needed to restore order and to encourage or initiate some type of sensitivity training for citizens. The same script plays out whenever conflict springs up between other groups: rich versus poor, children versus parents, immigrants versus citizens, old versus young, man versus woman, or weak versus strong. Moreover, the media creates conflict when it otherwise does not exist to cause further division and create a circumstance in which the government must come to the rescue. This practice is similar to a fireman committing arson so he can be a hero by extinguishing the flames.

As you can see, a complex interplay occurs between and within groups. In the end the relativists aspire to achieve their ideal state in which a small, wise ruling class manages the rest of society. These rulers use the military for self-protection and to enforce the republic's norms for behavior as they foolishly try to craft utopia on earth.

If you have observed how countries like China (think Tiananmen Square in 1989) and Iran (recall the 2009 peaceful presidential election protests) use their military to suppress their citizens, you have witnessed how kings would have used the military in a republic such as Plato's. Remember, part of the military's role, according to Plato, is to maintain balance and temperance. In the statists' utopian and egotistical fantasy, no war or conflict will exist between nations since all kings will be in concordance concerning their ruling philosophy. Then they will unite under a one-world regime to create the perfect world. But conflict will occur because "only the dead have seen the end of war."[33] In the elitists' deluded mind, they think they can achieve a one-world government. Only one enemy would be left if that society were realized, the oppressed people. Therefore, the military would be necessary to keep the people in line.

The problem with this whole plan is that America has gotten in the way—that pesky America with her freedom, Christian faith, hard work ethic, independence, rugged individualism, unalienable rights, and government of, by, and for the people. If not for our radical nation, *The Republic* would have come to fruition years ago. This explains why mostly aristocratic leaders and their subjects who are accustomed to being controlled by their government despise America. Therefore, a war against democracy and freedom has raged in the United States since nearly its inception.

CHAPTER 7

THE 235 YEARS' WAR: THE CAMPAIGN AGAINST DEMOCRACY, FREEDOM, AND CHRISTIANITY

W HEN WE LOOK at the monarchies of Europe, we see that essentially two types of kingships existed—constitutional and absolute. Absolute monarchs had total authority and complete rule over their country, though they learned that it was a good practice to consider the opinions of the military, the church, and the wealthy. Often these kings believed God had chosen them to rule (known as "divine right"), thus they ruled with solitary authority over their people. Constitutional monarchies, often referred to as "limited monarchies," were constrained by a constitution and a legislature, such as the English Parliament. In either case monarchs ruled. A privileged, aristocratic class of people, such as royal officials, judges, the military, businessmen, and church officials, also existed. This small class experienced more privileges than other inhabitants of the nation, although the bourgeoisie, or middle class, and a large lower class were also present.

FEUDALISM

What was the social order before the rise of the monarchs? During the Middle Ages, also known as "medieval times," feudalism was the social order from about AD 700 to 1100. In this arrangement, a monarch gave land to men (lords or vassals) in exchange for loyalty and military support. This land included an estate (fief) with its peasants (serfs). The fief was considered a lord's private property, which his sons inherited. The beneficiaries of this inheritance became knights, who provided military service to the royal army.

Nobles were of various ranks. A lesser noble could serve a brother of higher rank, making the former a vassal; hence, a noble could become a vassal to a noble greater than he and a lord to a noble lesser than he, thus fulfilling both roles—lord and vassal.

Lords assumed and executed the large majority of powers government typically held but remained loyal to the king. In small villages, called manors, serfs were bound to the land and provided labor for their vassal in exchange for food, shelter, and protection. The serfs worked for vassals (or lords), and vassals worked for the king. In this hierarchy kings ruled at the top (smallest class), lords (known as nobles) of various ranks occupied the middle (middle class), and serfs dwelled at the bottom (largest class). In essence the nobles in power controlled the general population, which found itself at the mercy of the whims of these authoritarians; therefore, the majority sacrificed their freedom and power to paternalistic lords.

MONARCHY

In the 1100s, feudalism lost dominance, and monarchs reestablished their role as the primary form of government in Europe. Strong nobles seized control of the throne and strengthened their power. They did so by defeating other lords in battle, increasing the size of their armies, and raising taxes to support what became permanent armies. As these monarchs gained power and solidified their claims to the throne, other feudal lords submitted to their authority. At the same time, monarchs established the tradition of the eldest son inheriting the throne, appointed to royal office townspeople and clergy who showed loyalty to the king, granted self-government to towns to discourage allegiance to their feudal lord, and acquired territory and power through marriage.

The monarchical system survived for approximately seven hundred years, but a few events, which seemed innocuous at the time, eventually transformed this style of government. Columbus discovered the New World in 1492; the Spanish established the first permanent European settlement in America at St. Augustine, Florida, in 1565; the English settled Jamestown, Virginia, in 1607; and the Pilgrims founded Plymouth, Massachusetts, in 1620. Aristocrats, monarchs, bourgeois, or any class at the time had no inkling that these events, combined with the Enlightenment in Europe during the late 1600s and early 1700s, would transform the shape of human government.

BRITAIN'S AMERICAN COLONIES

As American colonies grew after the establishment of the first permanent English settlement at Jamestown in 1607, the British king still controlled them and his subjects. Dual obstacles, however, impaired King George III's ability to rule over American colonists. First, the distance between the two land masses—the British Isles and North America—made monitoring the Americans a challenge. Second, the American spirit of independence, fostered because of that distance, changed the relationship between ruler and subordinate.

Locke, Blackstone, Hobbes, and others enlightened the world regarding government by writing about social compacts and a government's responsibility to rule justly. The Americans developed a growing spirit of independence and self-reliance; after all, neither the monarch nor parliament could take the credit for colonial survival and expansion. Though Britain planted royal officials in

America to maintain and enforce royal legislation, containing the new American psyche was a battle inevitably to be lost. Twenty-first-century sports spectators often hear references to athletes whom opponents "can't stop but can only hope to contain." In the case of American colonists, the British crown could neither stop nor corral their independent spirit, self-reliance, or the government the American character would eventually devise.

The American Spirit

During the 169 years from 1607 until the issuance of the Declaration of Independence in 1776, "Americanism" matured. The colonists established freedom of religion, private industry and the free market, land ownership, and representative legislative assemblies (Virginia's House of Burgesses, 1619; New England Confederation, 1643; Virginia Assembly, 1765) in their experimental government. Though imperfect, the Founding Fathers authored an original form of government that became deeply rooted in American life, a government based on the traits of self-reliance and hard work. It was a government established on the principles of Christianity, God-granted natural rights, and liberty. This was a government devised for "we the people." The Founding Fathers did not think outside the box; they ingeniously developed a new box that metamorphosed the world.

Tension with the King

After the 1763 French and Indian War, in which the British and American colonists successfully defended American territory against the French and their Indian allies, King George III found himself in a financial quandary due to war costs. Britain had incurred a debt of 140 million pounds and wanted the colonies to assume one-third of this expense through taxes and enforcement of the Navigation Laws.[1] Legislation enacted by King George to increase taxes or reduce profits for his subjects across the Atlantic included the Sugar Act (1764), Stamp Tax (1765), Townshend Duties (1767), and the tea monopoly granted to the British East India Company (1773). The main colonist complaint against these taxes on paper, glass, paint, lead, tea, sugar, playing cards, and other items was the lack of representation for them in the English Parliament, so they denounced them as "taxation without representation."

Furthermore, King George restricted Americans through edicts, including the Proclamation of 1763, Quartering Act (1765), Intolerable Acts (1774), and Quebec Act (1774). This legislation restricted settlement, forced colonists to provide room and board to British soldiers, impacted business and commerce, and affected various rights, such as assembly, trials, and religion. The colonists responded to these acts through the Boston Massacre (1770), the Boston Tea Party (1773), the scuffles at Lexington and Concord (1775), and the Battle of Bunker Hill (1775), which led to the Declaration of Independence on July 4, 1776.

Declaration of Independence

In the Declaration, the founders presented several precepts the British Crown had violated, including taxation without representation, natural rights, and the social compact existing between the king and those he governed. Natural rights included the God-given unalienable rights to life, liberty, and the pursuit of happiness. Since Providence naturally granted these rights to man, a government could neither award nor restrict them. If a ruler was unjust toward those he governed and if differences were irreconcilable, the governed, as a last resort, could break the social compact and formulate a new government, which the Founding Fathers did by issuing the Declaration of Independence. The founders initially desired reconciliation with their king, but such a possibility was lost after the skirmishes at Lexington, Concord, and Bunker Hill.

For 169 years Americans had been developing in their spirit this notion of independence and self-government. Because the settlers lived so far away from their king and country, survival was up to them. They had to grow food, hunt, fight disease, build residences, and provide self-defense; they had no time to seek government approval or assistance. These were literally do-or-die living conditions. Over time the unique American traits of rugged individualism, self-discipline, and hard work became ingrained in the colonists' psyche, thus forming the American spirit. Being oppressed by an authoritarian, immoral, unjust monarch was no longer tolerable. As we know, the Revolutionary War led to the independence of the colonies and the founding of the United States of America.

235 Years' War

What most scholars, historians, politicians, intellectuals, and others neglect to recognize is that the outcome of the American Revolution ignited the war between aristocracy and democracy, between big government and small government, between liberty and tyranny, between a small ruling class and government by the people, between an old world order and a new world order. Ever since that moment in time, those who errantly wished then and desire now to reinstitute aristocracy and authoritarianism into its perceived proper place of superiority have instigated a war against freedom and democracy. The focus of their war has been on the one nation that precludes their ascension to godlike status—the United States of America.

When the United States was founded, its government was regarded as the great experiment in democracy. Also, many world leaders firmly believed that the experiment would quickly fail, that the coalition of colonies forming the United States would collapse, and that European monarchs would reestablish their preeminence in the New World. It is not uncommon for nations to adopt multiple governments; for example, since 1776 France has had fifteen governments, and Brazil and Poland have had seven since 1822 and 1921, respectively. Afghanistan has had five since 1923, and Russia has had four since 1918.[2]

Whiskey Rebellion

Two early incidents in America tested her foundation and strength. The first was the 1794 Whiskey Rebellion in southwestern Pennsylvania; this was a protest against an alcohol tax because it was a levy on an economic necessity. This challenge tested the stability of the newly formed government and the fortitude of its first leader, President George Washington. If the rebellion was not suppressed, it could spread like wildfire throughout the states. The nascent government could topple before it ascended very high off the ground. But President Washington handled the blowup with the support of militias from several states, proving to the world that the newly formed government was stable and respected by its citizens.

Election of 1800

The second incident occurred after President Washington set the noble precedent of not running for a third term in office, starting the self-imposed tradition of a two-term presidency. One must be suspicious of those who talk about flouting this tradition. Plato wrote, "The State in which the rulers are most reluctant to govern is always the best and most quietly governed, and the State in which they are the most eager, the worst."[3] Nevertheless, Mr. Washington presided over the nation from 1789–1797 and declined a third term to prevent the development of a monarchical, authoritarian mentality in the young country. True to the principles upon which the nation was established, this would be a government that represented the people. President Washington also added "so help me God" to the conclusion of the presidential oath of office, a tradition most presidents have since followed.[4]

Mr. Washington's act of selflessness led to the election of John Adams in 1796 as the second U.S. president. However, Mr. Adams' bid for reelection in 1800 led to a contested presidential race between Aaron Burr and Thomas Jefferson; Burr was actually Mr. Jefferson's vice presidential candidate. Both men had seventy-three electoral votes, meaning that the House of Representatives needed to break the tie. After thirty-six ballots, Thomas Jefferson was finally elected as the third president of the United States.

Because the two key contenders, Mr. Adams and Mr. Jefferson, advanced competing ideologies concerning the role of the central government, some believed the contest would cause a rift in the young nation so severe that it would not be able to withstand the fallout from the losing side. Some thought the losing party would not accept defeat, thus leading to an internal conflict that would doom the nation to dissolution. Some were apprehensive about the change in power from the Federalist Party of Mr. Adams to the Democratic-Republican Party of Mr. Jefferson. Again, the "experts" were wrong; the nation accepted the election results and moved forward in unity.

War of 1812

Therefore, United States citizens and the government proved they could survive adversity, accept compromise, and settle differences of opinion. But what would happen if the blossoming country were forced into war? This opportunity arose in 1812 when the United States went to war against Britain a second time. This time the contention was over British impressment of American sailors (capturing and forcing them into the British navy), the plunder of American shipping, the arming of the Indians, and border disputes.

Britain was disappointed with America for giving trade preference to France and purchasing Louisiana from her. After the Revolutionary War, the U.S. western border extended to the Mississippi River. The 1803 Louisiana Purchase extended this border, more than doubling the acreage of the United States. As a result of its enlarged territory, the United States struggled to manage the vast expanse and secure its borders, which the British exploited at will. Therefore, the War of 1812 commenced.

Many favored the powerful British to win this war, though the underdog had crushed them in the Revolutionary War. Many anxiously anticipated a British victory so the states could again be divided among the European powers. For the third time since the Revolutionary War, the authoritarians were disappointed. Though this war ended in a draw instead of an outright victory for the United States, it was not a loss either. The underdog again proved it was a formidable opponent by holding its own, winning key battles against the superior British fleet, and crushing Britain's military in the January 1815 Battle of New Orleans. This final victory occurred after peace had been negotiated but before it was communicated in the states. America's prowess and the world's respect for this young, gritty nation were steadily growing.

The monarchs were probably more than a little disillusioned by these unfolding events. After all, thirty-eight years had passed since the daring experiment had begun, and no one had expected it to last this long. During those years, U.S. territory had expanded, while that of France, Spain, England, Sweden, and the Netherlands had shrunk. Though the United States had held off the strongest military in the world on two occasions, the aristocrats bided their time and patiently waited for the young democracy to implode.

Mexican War

The next opportunity came in 1846. Americans entered into war with Mexico over the Texas territory and assaults Mexican raiders had conducted against Americans in that land. The Mexican army was considered better skilled, better trained, and better armed than its American counterpart. Again European powers expected a rapid defeat of the poorly trained, inexperienced American army.[5]

Forgive me if I sound monotonous, but the United States again dashed the dreams of European authoritarians for the fourth time (Whiskey Rebellion, 1794; election of 1800; War of 1812; and the Mexican War, 1846–1848). The reputation of and respect for the United States were steadily growing when this implausible democratic experiment turned seventy-two years old at the conclusion of the Mexican War.

Slavery

European hope for America's collapse did not completely dissipate in 1848. Another opportunity to topple this gritty nation and bury democracy in favor of aristocracy arose with the Civil War in 1861, if not sooner in 1860 when the South expressed its dissatisfaction with the election of Abraham Lincoln as president. The South's discontent with the North's increasing sentiment to end or restrict slavery was both audible and becoming more frequent throughout the first half of the nineteenth century. The 1850s had been no exception.

The abolition of slavery had been a point of contention in the states, beginning with the drafting of the Declaration of Independence. Upon hearing a provision in the Declaration to end slavery, South Carolina protested by leading an exodus of southern colonies from the convention. Only when Thomas Jefferson's antislavery provision was expunged from the document were the southern, slave-owning colonies of South Carolina, North Carolina, and Georgia willing to ratify it. Unfortunately, the thirteen colonies agreed, at the suggestion of John Adams, that only a unanimous vote would allow them to present the Declaration to King George III.

After that initial discordance, the North and South combated each other over the slave issue on a number of occasions, including the Three-Fifths Compromise (1787); Northwest Ordinance (1787); Missouri Compromise (1820); Gag Resolution in Congress (1836); Compromise of 1850, which contained a more stringent Fugitive Slave Law; Kansas-Nebraska Act (1854); Dred Scot Decision (1857); LeCompton Constitution in Kansas (1857); and the concept of popular sovereignty, which allowed citizens of a territory, upon admission into the Union, to determine by popular vote its status as a free or slave state.

Private initiatives dedicated to the abolition of that "peculiar institution" of slavery included William Lloyd Garrison's antislavery newspaper, *The Liberator* (introduced in 1831); *Uncle Tom's Cabin* (1852) by Harriet Beecher Stowe, which sold one million copies worldwide; speeches by Frederick Douglass, a former slave who had escaped his bondage; and the Underground Railroad, through which thousands of blacks escaped to freedom.

Maybe the depth of this conflict would be the impetus to cause permanent division of the Union, both ideologically and politically. If a fracture occurred, dividing the United States, would it be reparable? The internal strife within the country that had been building for over a half century could certainly have divided it between North and South. The resulting weakness caused by the fissure could have permitted European powers to reenter the United States and divide its territory among themselves, could it not? When Abraham Lincoln was elected in 1860, the world soon learned the answer to that question.

Civil War

On December 20, 1860, secession began with South Carolina and ended with Tennessee on June 8, 1861. Eleven out of thirty states left the Union, and four states—Missouri, Maryland, Delaware, and Kentucky—chose neutrality. If the South had won the war, the United States would have lost approximately half of its land. European monarchs and aristocrats probably watered at the mouth when they considered the possibility of such a scenario coming to fruition. Once the land was divided, European powers could have easily reaffirmed their influence in America and at last put an end to this ludicrous governmental experiment. President Lincoln wisely warned that a house divided against itself could not stand (Matt. 12:25); however, the Founding Fathers warned against this disunity as well, especially in "Federalist Paper No. 5" by John Jay. It clearly illustrates the vitality of a strong, single Union compared to the distresses experienced by a divided nation due to the breakdown of that Union.

Mr. Jay's benefits of union included the ability to secure liberty, the elimination of animosity between independent republics, the promotion of trade between regions, and the effective defense against enemies.[6] If the Union were partitioned between North and South, slave and free, European powers would have expeditiously made treaties with individual states or separate regions of America. Mr. Jay based this proposition on the history of conflict between European nations. The states or regions would naturally develop rivalries over land, resources, interests, power, and influence. According to John Jay, the close proximity of separate republics to one another would more likely invite conflict between them as opposed to conflict from afar, leading to alliances with European nations for protection from each other rather than unifying together against Europe.[7]

Therefore, various states or sectors within America would engage in conflict against each other as was common in Europe, causing alliances to regularly form and change. Overall, a divided nation would lead to quarrels, wars, distrust, envy, fear, inequality, tension, jealousy, and discord.[8] Democracy and liberty in America would have been in peril due to dissension and division from within. This would have motivated monarchical regimes to intervene and become established, with freedom possibly succumbing to tyranny.

The Confederacy's army was stronger and more experienced than that of their northern brothers, so many expected it to expeditiously win the war that would cause this fatal division of America. The commoner in Europe rooted for the North and its ideals of freedom, while the aristocracy favored its like-minded Southerners.[9] Some argue that such polarized sentiments in Europe were exaggerated due to the varied interests within the proletariat and government.[10] However, it is clear that the overriding factor discouraging foreign diplomatic recognition of the Confederacy as a nation that would spawn direct intervention on its behalf was not slavery; instead, the South's inability to convincingly win enough battles to prove it could win the war kept foreign assistance at bay. If the North won the war, no European nation wanted to face its diplomatic, military, or economic wrath for allying with its adversary.

The nations of Europe partial to the Confederacy, especially England, closely observed the progression of the war from a distance. To commit on the side of the Confederacy would mean retribution if the North won and the Union remained intact. England had to be certain the South would be victorious before it could join the fracas, demonstrating the respect the United States had earned on the world stage. France took a similar stance before entering the Revolutionary War as an ally of the Americans. It did so only after the patriots proved they could defeat the British, which they did with victories in Trenton, New Jersey, in 1776; and in Saratoga, New York, in 1777.

The Nation Preserved

Of course, the North was victorious, slavery was abolished, and the Union was saved. Gone once and for all were Europe's chances of dividing America, handicapping democracy and freedom, preserving aristocracy, and expanding a powerful central authority. Lyrics from "The Battle Hymn of the Republic" sum up the northern victory.

> In the beauty of the lilies Christ was born across the sea,
> With a glory in His bosom that transfigures you and me;
> As He died to make men holy, let us die to make men free,
> While God is marching on.

Thanks to divine favor, the North won the war, slavery was abolished, the Union was preserved, and concerns about European interference dissipated. The preservation of the United States also meant the perseverance of liberty, exceptionalism, rugged individualism, the American Spirit, and the unalienable rights to life, liberty, and the pursuit of happiness as granted by God. In addition, God left intact His chosen nation so it could fulfill its purpose of proclaiming the gospel to the world; Jesus stipulated in Matthew 24:14, "And this gospel of the kingdom will be preached in all the world as a witness to all the nations."

Europe again witnessed this democratic experiment's determination and will to survive as well as its strength, spirit, perseverance, and sacrifice. The divergent views of the slave and free states were insufficient to create an irreparable division in the United States. Similar to the opposing philosophies behind the election of 1800, only on a much grander scale, the magnificent nation proved to the world that it would survive internal conflict and dissension; in this case it took a war, but the nation survived and began the process of healing its wounds. Of course, fallout from the abolition of slavery that led to continued discrimination, abuse, and oppression of blacks caused internal strife in our nation that culminated with civil rights gains in the 1960s and continual struggles for equality up to today.

The nation survived, and freedom and opportunity spread to other groups in society. Though it was a sad, unfortunate struggle, only in America could those once denied freedom climb the ladder of opportunity to achieve the American Dream and more. One could presume that Europe would want to emulate such success, but one would be wrong.

It is important to recall that the common man in Europe rooted for the North and the principles of freedom the United States espoused, while the aristocrats pulled for the South and its principles of bondage, control of others, and rule by a minority group of aristocratic leaders. Why was this the case? The South was aristocratic in nature and replicated the governmental institution of Europe; a small group of powerful landowners kept a large proportion of their population in an oppressed, dependent state. The European aristocracy instituted a similar practice in Europe, though it did not implement slavery as the southern colonies had. Instead, it firmly restricted all citizens, who experienced a lower standard of living, fewer freedoms, and less opportunity than did the ruling class.

A defeat of the North and dissolution of the Union would have translated into the destruction of freedom and democracy. The division of the states would have permitted the continued expansion of Europe's authoritarian system of government, as Europe would have reestablished its influence in the United States. Even European leaders' subjects recognized the value of American government and were encouraged by it. This realization led to mass emigration from those nations so many could gain access to the American Dream, a variety of freedoms, and unlimited opportunity in the land flowing with milk and honey where the streets were "paved with gold."

As we have seen, America and its new government survived a number of challenges to their existence. The common man was elated, but the ruling classes were dumbfounded. By the conclusion of the Civil War in 1865, the American experiment had lasted eighty-nine years. Who would have thought?

The century would end with no other threats to American sovereignty. The 1898 Spanish-American War was a minor incident in the annals of history, but it did not threaten the American way. In fact, soon the world began to rely on America for both protection against tyranny and the spreading of democracy, as seen in the instrumental role played by the United States in the two world wars.

The United States was powerful, influential, and charitable. The Cold War brought fierce competition between communism and democracy for world influence and power, and nations influenced by democracy realized much greater prosperity than those molded by communism. The United States and the Soviet Union provoked one another on various occasions from 1945 to 1991 in a number of arenas, but as a whole democracy was accepted. The American experiment was an irrefutable success and an integral part of culture. The battle between aristocracy and democracy was over.

235 Years' War Changes Venue

Or was it? The war has simply changed venues. It moved from battlefields into classrooms, from war rooms to the media and entertainment industry, from the war culture to the pop culture. Especially since the hippie revolution of the 1960s, the fight has morphed from a physical altercation to an intellectual scrum. As I have written, statists have attacked the family, Christian faith, and patriotism to advance their goals and destroy America. Once they have neutralized those three enemies of aristocracy, they will use the government to fill the resulting voids. The socialist government then becomes the parent, the entity, the idol to be loyal to.

Patriotism means being dedicated to our nation's precepts, ideals, and spirit. Statists want us to reject those values and instead declare loyalty to socialism. Though they talk kindly of America, they want to redefine it. Liberals believe only they possess the wisdom and knowledge to instruct us on how to live in order to create their utopian society. Relativists suppose they are blessed with these innate traits we do not have and cannot understand. In addition, socialist-leaning liberals worship the environment, relativism, and mankind. This is their trinity.

Since aristocrats believe only they have the ability to rule others, they must accumulate the power to do so. A finite amount of power in the world is divided among its peoples. Statists want to gather this power to the detriment of the righteous concept of government by the people. In this scenario, freedom is consumed by tyranny, and citizens suffer for the benefit of the statists.

You no longer need to ask yourself, "Why does a politician advance a foolish policy?" or "Why does a political party want to enact ludicrous-sounding legislation?" or "Why does an international body, such as the United Nations, take an illogical stance on an issue?" Now you know the answer. This war has been waged since 1776 and has been fought continually for 235 years. It is a war of tyranny versus liberty, aristocracy versus democracy, statists versus the people.

Socialists will not rest until they have won the war. Liberals talk about wars against "crises," such as health care, global warming, the swine flu, deforestation, and more. But, as Plato warned, the tyrant "is always stirring up some war or other, that the people may require a leader."[11] These diversions distract many from the real war (as described here) and provide statists with opportunities to expand their power as they engage in their conquest against America's ideals, to the detriment of the free American people.

Democracy as a Weapon of Statists

Do you not think this increase in power is feasible in the land of the free and the home of the brave? If not, think again. Plato wrote that "tyranny naturally arises out of democracy, and the most aggravated form of tyranny and slavery out of the most extreme form of liberty."[12] He further stated, "Because of the liberty which reigns there…[,] he who has a mind to establish a State…must go to a democracy."[13] Therefore, when the voting record, sound bites, actions, and proposals of liberals confound people; when statists' policies, procedures, and regulations that harm America baffle citizens, the answer to their perplexity is this: socialist-leaning liberals use our freedom to destroy what they hate and what inhibits their rise to power—freedom and the awesome nation that promotes it. They use what America offers to hijack the nation, destroy it, and establish tyranny. In other words, relativists use the United States because they can; the nation's liberties permit such an attack, so citizens must be cognizant of Plato's observations and practice discernment at all times.

The populace cannot develop a lackadaisical, apathetic mentality as it lives its comfortable and prosperous lifestyle. This indifference permitted socialists to begin the takeover of our fabulous nation, and at least fifty years later, America is at the brink of transformation. The following news headlines from one day, May 28, 2009, should startle us: "Texas Woman Told to Remove 'Offensive' United States Flag from Office," "Gay Male Voted Prom Queen at Los Angeles High School," and "Couple Ordered to Stop Holding Bible Study at Home Without Permit." These represent attacks on patriotism, family, Christianity, and absolute morals—all in a single day, all in the United States of America.

Extreme Sense of Liberty

Why does this happen? Because "liberty, getting out of all order and reason, passes into the harshest and bitterest form of slavery."[14] This occurs because the democratic man "is drawn into a perfectly lawless life, which…is termed perfect liberty."[15] "Democracy…has evil cupbearers presiding over the feast, and has drunk too deeply of the strong wine of freedom."[16]

The correlation between Plato's writings and the presence in today's society of licentiousness, relativism, lack of self-control, and pursuit of every pleasure is obvious. Of course, lawlessness and disorder eventually lead to control and domination; the absence of self-control leads to government regulation. An inability to self-discipline leads to a state program of coercion and indoctrination. "The insatiable desire of this [freedom] and the neglect of other things introduces the change in democracy, which occasions a demand for tyranny."[17] This is why the founders wisely recognized the importance of Christianity and morality to the survival of the democratic nation they were forming; they knew the latter would not survive without the former.

Plato vividly describes the condition of the United States over two thousand years before its existence. He was not a prophet but an observant philosopher. Plato recognized that the health of a nation changes according to the spiritual strength of its people and thus their desire to acquire wisdom, truth, and absolute good by pursuing the likeness of God. Otherwise, they crave foolishness, deceit, and evil, which are attained by feeding the insatiable, sensual desires of the flesh. I quote *The Republic* at length because of Plato's accurate description of modern-day America.

Parent-Child Relationships

"The father grows accustomed to descend to the level of his sons and to fear them, and the son is on a level with his father, he having no respect...for either of his parents; and this is his freedom.... The master fears and flatters his scholars, and the scholars despise their masters...[;] young and old are all alike;...and old men...are lo[a]th to be thought morose and authoritative, and therefore they adopt the manners of the young."[18]

Children seemingly fail to honor their parents more so today than at any other time in our history. Children expect money, food, clothing, and shelter, but they neither appreciate nor respect their parents other than as a resource. In addition, how many adults adopt the behavior of their offspring instead of the brood following the ways of their parents? We see this trend in the tattoo craze that has gripped our nation over the last decade or so.

Parents are supposed to teach and shape their children. This statement is in strong contrast to the recently accepted notion that the younger generation is commissioned to enlighten adults and find its own way while formulating its own differentiated value system. Proverbs 22:6 says, "Train up a child in the way he should go, and when he is old he will not depart from it." When they age, adults who have trained themselves based on moral relativism do not depart from their individualized value system. More importantly, their offspring digress into a further state of revulsion as a result of poor modeling, parents' inability to establish a higher standard (out of guilt or a feeling of hypocrisy), parental incompetence, and the continued indoctrination inculcated through the socialist-leaning education system and relativistic pop culture.

Pets

Consider what Plato says about animals and pets: "How much greater is the liberty which the animals who are under the dominion of man have in a democracy than in any other State."[19] The "rights" provided to animals in our culture can exude only from a democratic society that has perverted liberty. American pets receive better health care than multitudes of people in the world; they have health care plans, day care services, medications, and holiday costumes. Come on, America! This is ludicrous and shameful, and it reveals how deeply the environmentalists' religion has become rooted in our culture.

Oversensitivity

Plato writes about oversensitive demeanors, sensitivity training, changes in terminology to avoid offending others, and other exaggerated reactions. He also mentions disregard for laws, policies, and procedures if they are not convenient to one's needs or desires. He writes, "See how sensitive the citizens become; they chafe…at the least touch of authority…[and] cease to care even for the laws, written or unwritten."[20] Do these words not resonate with the 1960s rebellion and relativism? Furthermore, once dependence becomes expected and accepted, the people seek out someone who will provide greater protection, advice, or service. "The people always have some champion whom they set over them and nurse into greatness."[21]

Fickleness

The following quotes from *The Republic* summarize the general mindset Americans are embracing in greater numbers:

> Those then who know not wisdom and virtue, and are always busy with gluttony and sensuality, go down and up again as… they move at random throughout life, but they never pass into the upper world;…neither are they truly filled with true being, nor do they taste of pure and abiding pleasure. Like cattle,…they fatten and feed and breed, and, in their excessive love of these delights, they kick and butt at one another…and kill one another by reason of their insatiable lust. For they fill themselves with that which is not substantial.[22]

He lives from day to day indulging the appetite of the hour; and sometimes he is lapped in drink…[,] then he becomes a water-drinker, and tries to get thin; then he takes a turn at gymnastics; sometimes idling and neglecting everything…[;] often he is busy with politics, and starts to his feet and says and does whatever comes into his head; and, if he is emulous of anyone who is a warrior, off he is in that direction, or of men of business; once more in that. His life has neither law nor order; and this distracted existence he terms joy and bliss and freedom; and so he goes on.[23]

How many obsessions do Americans have? Eating, drinking, sex, happiness, a variety of entertainment venues, exercise, shopping, self-esteem, health, comfort, the environment, security, attire, a myriad of addictions, and any number of material collections. We move mindlessly from one fad to the next without care about possible consequences of the new or remembrance of joys or blessings of the old. We endeavor to occupy our existence with meaningless pleasures in the attempt to fill the spiritual void left because of the exclusion of God from our lives.

Have you ever watched those who are not proficient runners participate in a marathon? Thousands torture themselves because running is the latest fad or so they can say they participated in the event. Runners struggle, limp, gasp, and wheeze to fulfill this compulsion; they carry water bottles around their waists like a bullet belt, listen to music to distract themselves, and monitor their heart rates to ensure they are reaching their maximum level of fitness.

This is ridiculous. It is one thing to exercise but quite another to engage in self-torture because it is the latest craze. The apostle Paul exhorted against such behavior in 1 Timothy 4:7–8: "Exercise yourself toward godliness. For bodily exercise profits a little, but godliness is profitable for all things, having promise of the life that now is and of that which is to come."

Many who do things in excess focus on satisfying fleshly desires while neglecting the logical and spiritual needs of the body and soul. Passion and desire drown out reason and absolute good from their lives; therefore, they do not experience what Plato called the "upper world" or "pure and abiding pleasure." This happens when one removes God from his life; such excess is an attempt to fill the void that remains. This is the heritage of a religion in which one worships the environment, relativism, and self; however, such religion is futile compared to the Creator, Counselor, Rock, Mighty God, Prince of Peace, Redeemer, and Everlasting Father.

Accepting Shameful Behavior

The following explains our descent into depravity:

There are jests which you would be ashamed to make yourself, and yet on the comic stage, or indeed in private, when you hear them, you are greatly amused by them, and are not at all disgusted at their unseemliness;…there is a principle in human nature which is disposed to raise a laugh, and this which you once restrained by reason, because you were afraid of being thought a buffoon, is now let out…; and having stimulated the risible faculty [tendency to laugh] at the theatre, you are betrayed unconsciously to yourself into playing the comic poet at home….And the same may be said of lust and anger and all the other affections.[24]

In this way unacceptable ideas, behaviors, and attitudes gain acceptance; they gradually become entrenched in a culture over time. Think about the slow and steady decline of television content over the last few decades; programming that was once shocking to one generation is now normal to the next one. People have become desensitized to what they once found objectionable—for example, promiscuity, drug use, profane language, and other offensive behavior.

Recall the metaphor about cooked meat and rotting fruit in the previous chapter. This problem is not confined to the above-quoted "comic stage" but extends into our homes via various entertainment outlets. Ideas once deemed shameful have become notions of aspiration. Although the circus has diminished in recent years, the freak show lives on, and its portal is the popular culture (recall the discussion in chapter 5).

THE REPUBLIC IS MODERN AMERICA

How could Plato have been so wise? From where did he attain his wisdom? How is it that the descriptions throughout his book fit the American landscape so snugly? My hypothesis is this: Plato wrote his book in 360 BC, which was near the end of the Greek empire's strength. I sense cynicism in his tome about the state of Hellenic culture, a similar cynical attitude many others and I share about contemporary American culture. I believe his book is based on his knowledge of the history of Greece, the realities of his age, the direction in which his culture was headed, and his supposition as to how to cure its ills or formulate a new, stable state. As I often say to friends and colleagues, "You must know where you were to understand where you are to determine where you are going." Plato had a firm grasp of this truth.

I believe the condition of Greece during Plato's time runs parallel to America's current state and possibly that of the world. Greece's prowess declined shortly after Plato's writings, if the erosion had not already begun. In 2011, I believe the United States is in the same precarious situation Greece faced during the fourth century BC. I believe the United States is teetering toward self-destruction unless it returns to its moral Christian heritage; I also believe it is in desperate need of a spiritual Great Awakening like those of the 1740s and early 1800s if it is to avert this implosion. (By the way, in most cases the Great Awakening has been purged from our textbooks.) I believe our decline will occur more swiftly than Greece's due to our technological, faster-paced culture. Without spiritual revival, I believe the United States will incur God's wrath for forsaking His Word and rejecting His route to salvation through His Son, Jesus Christ.

Plato's Folly

It is important to note here that my view of the ideal government diverges from Plato's. He believed that aristocracy provided the best government, whereas I pledge loyalty to our representative, democratic government based on God-given freedoms. The weakness in Plato's argument is his focus on man's ability to seek and follow reason, rationality, and truth. Though he mentions God, divinity, and Providence, he emphasizes man's ability, or lack thereof, over God's supremacy. He also adheres to the Greeks' polytheistic beliefs by referencing the gods numerous times.

Plato was not far off the mark in his search for absolute truth and good; although he touched on divine inspiration, his wisdom omitted the one true God due to his lack of exposure to Him. It is captivating to discover that Plato's writings mirror those of Solomon, who authored Ecclesiastes circa 931 BC. They both discuss life, government, justice, wickedness, corruption, goodness, wisdom, folly, and eternity. Solomon also mentions the tendency of life to repeat itself and that nothing new is under the sun, which may be our situation today—the United States repeating the pattern of ancient Greece.

The difference is that Solomon finds justice and grace in God, the Father, as opposed to man or the many gods of Greece. Though Plato recognizes the Creator, he does not discuss Him. Solomon, known as the wisest king to ever rule, glorified God as the source of wisdom, righteousness, and knowledge instead of exalting man to that stature. Ecclesiastes 7:23 summarizes Solomon's conclusion after examining life and searching for wisdom: "I said, 'I will be wise'; but it was far from me." Ecclesiastes 12:13 adds, "Fear God and keep His commandments, for this is man's all." The first verse alludes to our inability to discover wisdom on our own, while the second verse admonishes us to fulfill our duty of obeying God's decrees.

Plato's folly, which man considers wisdom, is intimated in two more verses from Solomon. Ecclesiastes 7:29 says, "Truly, this only I have found: that God made man upright, but they have sought out many schemes." Ecclesiastes 8:17 says, "Then I saw all the work of God....For though a man labors to discover it, yet he will not find it; moreover, though a wise man attempts to know it, he will not be able to find it." People can try to find wisdom, but, as with Plato, if they seek it apart from God, they will fail; instead of finding wisdom, they will impart foolish schemes. Although Plato exuded wisdom in his writings, his solution was errant and fallible. Paul wrote in 1 Corinthians 1:25, "The foolishness of God is wiser than men." Our government was developed with the goodness of God's Word as its foundation, making it the greatest nation in the history of the world. But it is also the most despised nation to evil men who desire to control and handicap their fellow man.

America's Vital Christian Faith

Our democracy was founded on Christian principles and the recognition that the nation would flounder if it abandoned those moral precepts. Daniel Webster proclaimed, "If we abide by the principles taught in the Bible, our country will go on prospering and to prosper; but if we and our posterity neglect its instructions and authority, no man can tell how sudden a catastrophe may overwhelm us and bury all our glory in profound obscurity."[25] Foreign visitors recognized our Christian faith and heritage. The Frenchman Alexis de Tocqueville wrote in 1830, "The religious aspect of the country was the first thing that struck my attention....

Not until I went to the churches of America and heard her pulpits aflame with righteousness did I understand the secret of her genius and power."[26] Do you think our youth ever read or hear these or similar quotes in the relativistic education system?

Returning to Strength and Morality

According to the traditions of our nation, it is up to the people to fight indoctrination promoted through the education system, the media, pop culture, and the judicial branch. Resist weakness and train yourself and your children to be strong emotionally, physically, intellectually, and spiritually (or morally). If you choose to be weak, that is because the nonsense relativists have been injecting into minds for at least fifty years has conditioned you to be so. Protect your mind. Shield your mind. Screen your mind. An "open mind," unprotected by the filter of discernment, provides a chasm through which a litany of debris, garbage, and contaminants may enter. This pollution impairs one's capacity to discard poor influences in favor of beneficial ones, eventually leading to tolerance of the former to the detriment of the latter.

Remember that this is intellectual warfare. Liberals have been indoctrinating you and your offspring through the education system, media, and pop culture for half a century. You are a product of whatever you allow to enter your mind. Reject secularism and relativism. Reject sexual promiscuity and divorce, which break down the family. Reject criticism and ostracism of America's foundational principles. Reject indoctrination from both the public and higher education systems. Reject the lust, immaturity, and crudeness promoted by the entertainment industry.

THE WAR CAN BE WON

With a tough mind, a strong will, enduring Christian faith, and a desire to save our nation and way of life, we will win this war. It will require resolve and sacrifice similar to those of the greatest American generation that fought and won World War II, but the battle may be harder to win thanks to the weakness the statists have perpetrated on our citizens. If you support socialism, promote secularism, and worship the environment and man, then my plea does not apply to you. But if you think you are exempt from the oppression wielded by those whom you support, you have another thing coming. You are in fact a pawn whom statist puppeteers masterfully control so they can achieve their ends. Anything they promote that weakens you strengthens them; their charity does not help you but hurts you. They amass power and control to your detriment; only they benefit. In the end you are expendable—all of us are—and both the guilty and innocent will suffer the consequences.

This is also spiritual warfare. God cannot be removed from society without disastrous results. When man removes God, the ideologies I've described replace Him. Who or what do you want on your side? God or man? Providence or humanity? The Creator or evolution? Wisdom or foolishness? Righteousness or wickedness? Love or hate? Peace or turmoil? Happiness or misery? Blessings or curses? The Way or the lost? Truth or lies? Life or death?

The serpent fooled Adam and Eve in the garden of Eden. The Devil first tricked Eve into eating the apple, then Adam foolishly followed her. The Devil is still playing tricks on human beings, and his biggest achievement is convincing them that neither he nor God exists. It is interesting how history repeats itself. As woman was fooled into eating the apple, woman has also been fooled into believing that murdering her unborn children leads to empowerment. As man heeded the voice of Eve, man has also foolishly followed the modern woman.

People who are spiritually strong reject foolishness and thus the "intellect" of the socialist-leaning liberal; however, if they are spiritually weak, they will gullibly accept any notion. So the intellectual war is reduced to that which is spiritual, for people will make their choices based on their spiritual beliefs and by whom they can be swayed. People are slaves to whatever controls them. "For by whom a person is overcome, by him also he is brought into bondage" (2 Peter 2:19). Therefore, people will ally with whatever pleases their desires; they will be bound by those in whom they trust. If the flesh rules their bodies, they will succumb to pleasures and iniquity. But if their souls are dominant, they will aspire to wisdom and righteousness. The question is, will we revere God and be spiritually strong, or will we exhibit spiritual weakness by worshipping the trinity comprising the environment, relativism, and man? Removing God from our culture does not cause Him to disappear like a waft of smoke. He is there, He is aware, He is monitoring our actions, and He will be victorious in the end.

An apple symbolizes disobedience to God in the garden of Eden. Interestingly, an apple is also the fruit used to signify education beginning in kindergarten, which is the German word translated "garden for children"? Monitor, be aware, be vigilant.

The next chapter is a brief, personal discussion about physical, mental, emotional, and spiritual strength, which is fundamental to the health and well-being of each person. It is also fundamental to a nation like ours, for a nation's vitality is invariably connected to that of individuals.

CHAPTER 8

A PERSONAL STORY

THIS STORY BEGINS in the fall of 1994 when I purchased a five-year-old used car. A year later the transmission failed and was replaced, costing about twelve hundred dollars. A few months later, the computer failed, resulting in an approximate nine-hundred-dollar replacement cost for a used component. Since my salary was only twenty-one thousand dollars per year, I paid for these repairs with a credit card, upon which I had already charged several smaller, affordable expenses.

Due to the increased balance caused by the car repairs, I could not afford the minimum credit card payment plus bills for rent, groceries, utilities, the car payment, gasoline, and student loan payments. I was spending more than my monthly paycheck, so I would have exhausted my meager checking account in just a few months. After evaluating my options in dealing with this crisis, I decided not to ask anyone for help or to demand government assistance; instead, I settled on either refinancing my three-year car loan or securing a second job.

My first strategy was to refinance my car loan and obtain a lower payment so I could pay all my bills. On a Saturday morning, I went to the bank and learned the lending institution had just changed ownership and its name, making me the first customer for the new customer service representative. After taking my information, she broke the disappointing news that my refinance request had been declined because my debt-to-income ratio was too high. After she compassionately shared this news, her last words to me were, "How do you eat?" Unbeknownst to her, I ate most meals at work for free, but I was still coming up short in paying my bills.

I was now forced to pursue my alternate option of acquiring a second job. Since my full-time job consumed forty to fifty hours per week, I wondered if I would be able to find employment compatible with my schedule. What type of job would I get? What kinds of jobs were available? What occupation would allow me to earn enough money to expeditiously pay off my credit card debt?

I was determined to solve this problem on my own, but after hearing about my plight, two loyal friends, a married couple, Mike and Dorislyn, lent me one thousand dollars without question, interest, or repayment timetable. Since I regularly visited with them, we pretty much shared everything that transpired in our lives. Their act of kindness allowed me to save on interest charges, but I was resolute to quickly repay them. It is rare that you find people who truly fulfill the definition of friendship.

I perused the classifieds and noticed an advertisement for pizza delivery drivers; it claimed that employees earned twelve to fourteen dollars per hour. I was ambivalent about the job and skeptical about the salary, but my dilemma was not solving itself, so I applied, completed training, and in spring 1996 became a pizza delivery driver—with a master's degree in hand.

With a local street map and a flashlight for reading the map at night, I soon discovered that the ad was true to its word; in fact, I made a higher hourly wage delivering pizza than I did working at my regular profession. On Friday, Saturday, and Sunday nights, I typically worked between twelve and twenty hours per weekend.

My hours increased along with my tenure, and occasionally I exceeded the twenty-hour mark. Once supervisors realized my dependability, my hours increased and included a rare Monday night during football season.

I delivered pizza for fourteen to fifteen months. During that time I purchased only necessities, deciding not to spend money on extra or conspicuous items. I didn't buy clothes or compact discs, go to the movies, go out to dinner, take a vacation, or buy other material possessions. I used every penny I earned at the pizza place to reduce my credit card debt and repay my friends. I kept a running record of how much money I earned in tips, added that to the hourly wage, and sent that amount to the credit card company monthly. Unfortunately, while paying off this liability, my vehicle required additional repairs—brakes, exhaust system, rotors, and so on—which resulted in more credit card debt. On one occasion I charged over one thousand dollars for repairs that were necessary for my vehicle to pass state inspection.

While laboring a minimum of fifty-two to seventy hours a week at two jobs, I never missed a day of work except one weekend (from delivering pizzas) to attend my grandmother's funeral. In addition, I worked out with weights six days a week for about ninety minutes a day and jogged two to three miles three days per week during the warm months of the year; as with work, I never missed a workout. Furthermore, I studied the Bible five days each week, thirty to sixty minutes per session. Here I exhibited the traits of persistence, dedication, sacrifice, determination, and reliability.

Here are four points to consider about my money management: First, as I already said, I spent my overall salary only on necessities—no luxuries or desires. Second, I used my secondary income solely to pay off my credit card debt. Third, I never missed a payment, asked for debt forgiveness, or requested help. Fourth, I claimed every penny I earned in tips on my W-2 form.

Let me explain the process for claiming tips. When an employee clocked out each night, the store manager asked how much he was claiming for tips. The typical response from most delivery drivers, if not from all of them, was something like "two dollars and fifty cents" or "four dollars and eight-two cents." Depending on the robustness of business and number of hours worked, a driver could make anywhere from twenty to over one hundred dollars in tips nightly. The base pay was minimum wage, and we easily earned twelve to fourteen dollars per hour, which translates to about eight to ten dollars per hour in tips. My response to the manager was always the exact amount I received from customers. I was determined to manage my finances the right way, to be honest, and to set an example for others. This attitude exemplifies moral strength—doing right when everyone else is compromising and trusting God's blessing as a result.

Instead of demonstrating attributes of strength in taking care of themselves, many today expect the government to do for them. Too often people miss payments, default on their loans, declare bankruptcy, fault their circumstances for various actions or inactions, and blame their more prosperous fellowmen. This attitude did not make America great; on the contrary, citizens practicing the characteristics listed above, among others, translated into greatness.

I also want to describe spiritual strength here. I worked forty to fifty hours a week at a full-time job and twelve to twenty-plus hours per week in part-time employment, exercised regularly, never missed a day of work, conscientiously saved money, carefully spent my salaries, and read my Bible at least five days per week. The last statement is the most essential. I could not have accomplished all my goals without spiritual strength, faith in God, and a budding relationship with Jesus Christ.

When I awoke in the morning, I thanked God for a new day, ability, health, and blessings. I prayed in Jesus' name for the strength, energy, wisdom, and ability to take on the day. Before lying down to rest at night, I gave God thanks for a successful day, repented of my transgressions, and prayed, again in Jesus' name, for a good night's sleep and the energy and ability to tackle tomorrow. I did not consume energy drinks, ingest a bunch of caffeine, or take legal or illegal supplements, such as steroids, creatine, protein shakes, or other pills available at nutrition outlets. The Bible teaches in 1 Corinthians 10:23, "All things are lawful for me, but not all things are helpful; all things are lawful for me, but not all things edify."

It was God's blessing, attention, and answer to my prayers that allowed me to complete the tasks expressed in this testimonial and to demonstrate mental, physical, emotional, and spiritual strength. God's Word, influence, and encouragement allowed me to do things well. Being single allowed me to devote my time in this way. Others maintain different lifestyles, experience different circumstances, and have different abilities, so their situation dictates what they can or cannot do. For example, if I had had children of my own, I may have spent less time exercising and more time with family. My story is not superior; it is simply an example of doing right, facing adversity, overcoming a dilemma, and becoming better through strength.

Many in our nation experience greater hardships, challenges, disabilities, conditions, and circumstances than I did. Countless others face their adversities without making excuses, whining, failing to fulfill obligations, or seeking a government program. We can lift up numerous people in our nation as examples of overcoming obstacles, struggles, and disadvantages. But the media continually portray the "helpless," those who refuse to help themselves or accept the consequences of their choices.

Life is about choices—about choosing to be strong or weak, about striving for improvement or deciding to wallow in one's circumstances. It's about either being resolute with encouragement from family, friends, and God or depending on the government. As stated previously, I am aware that some people cannot solve their own problems, but they are the exception. We must quit focusing on exceptions that expand the roles of the dependent and instead emphasize the possibility and importance of fighting to overcome our own hardships. Our nation must vacate the valley of exceptions.

Strength is always the harder choice, and in a society that has been comprehensively weakened in the four areas discussed in chapter 5, it should be no surprise that many follow the easy path. Such an inclination is part of human nature, but it becomes more frequent when a culture adopts a tendency toward weakness. Again, Plato's Greece parallels this condition. When people experience adversity, he stated, "we should take counsel about what has happened, and when the dice have been thrown order our affairs in the way which reason deems best; not, like children who have had a fall,…wasting time in setting up a howl, but always accustoming the soul forthwith to apply a remedy, raising up that which is sickly and fallen, banishing the cry of sorrow."[1]

I again quote Paul in 1 Corinthians 13:11. "When I was a child, I spoke as a child, I understood as a child, I thought as a child; but when I became a man, I put away childish things." In other words, quit lamenting, whining, and complaining. Step up, be strong, have faith, and take action to correct your problem. "I can do all things through Christ who strengthens me" (Phil. 4:13). "The God of Israel is He who gives strength and power to His people" (Ps. 68:35).

In the end, I paid off my credit card debt and repaid my friends. In the summer of 1997 I resigned from my second job and, again on a Saturday morning, went to the same bank that had rejected my loan refinance request. I had the pleasure of being assisted by the same customer service representative. She remembered me from about fifteen months earlier because I had been her first client. She said—I paraphrase—"I remember you. We rejected your loan request. That was a mistake. We should have given you that loan." My modest reply was, "That was the best thing that could have happened. I got a second job, I paid off my debt, I began investing in a 401(k) account through work, and here is six hundred dollars to open a savings account." The representative was dismayed and nearly speechless; fifteen or so months before, I had credit card debt up to several thousands of dollars, a car payment, student loan payments, rent, and other necessary expenses. Now I was opening a savings account.

The other benefits she did not realize was that I had paid off my car loan on time in the fall of 1997, allowing me to quit my job and enroll in college full time to pursue my bachelor's degree in teacher education. Without that initial rejection, my financial situation would have been much worse, possibly preventing my ability to return to school. Since I had started a 401(k) savings account, I was able to cash it in and pay tuition without incurring further debt through student loans. One never knows where a blessing is coming from; what originally seemed like a setback was actually a blessing in disguise.

If I can do this, anyone can. Support from friends, family, and coworkers; faith and prayer; sacrifice; discipline; perseverance; hard work; determination; and dedication were instrumental to my success. With these characteristics, you can succeed and achieve—morally, ethically, uprightly, and legally.

This is the American Dream. Anyone can experience this, as testified by the millions of immigrants who achieved this dream or their children, grandchildren, great-grandchildren, or great-great-grandchildren living today. You do not need the government, entitlements, or a welfare state. On the contrary, all you need are the Christian-based rights to "Life, Liberty, and the pursuit of Happiness" your God-fearing Founding Fathers wisely infused into their grand experiment of democracy. The United States of America is the greatest nation in the history of the world. Others should emulate it, not try to eradicate it. Only those of an evil nature would aspire to the latter. Matthew 20:15 says, "Or is your eye evil because I am good?"

What are you going to pursue with your freedom? The choice is yours. The consequences of your decisions are real and impact others in addition to yourself.

CHAPTER 9

AMERICA ON THE BRINK OF JUDGMENT

S CHOLARS WHO HAVE studied the Bible have observed that the United States is absent from its prophecies. Though it is true that the Bible does not mention America by name, biblical texts do describe the United States. The Bible refers to other nations by their current or former names; for example, Israel, Egypt, Magog (Russia), Persia (Iran), Cush (Sudan and Ethiopia), Beth-togarmah (Turkey, Armenia, and other Turkic-speaking peoples), both Sheba and Dedan (Saudi Arabia, Yemen, Oman, and the Gulf States).[1] The Bible includes the United States in a less direct manner. In essence, God's intended purpose for ancient Israel was also written to fulfill the destiny of the United States. I extensively quote the Bible in this chapter, and all verses come from the New King James Version.

LAND OF MILK AND HONEY

Many have referred to the United States as the "land of milk and honey," to which millions have immigrated. The U.S. offers lakes, rivers, mountains, valleys, bountiful crops, a plethora of natural resources, abundant wildlife, and vast mineral deposits.

The Bible illustrates such a place in a number of verses, including the following:

> So I have come to deliver them…and to bring them up from that land to a good and large land, to a land flowing with milk and honey.
>
> —Ex. 3:8

> Go up to a land flowing with milk and honey.
>
> —Ex. 33:3

> For the Lord your God is bringing you into a good land, a land of brooks of water, of fountains and springs, that flow out of valleys and hills; a land of wheat and barley, of vines and fig trees and pomegranates, a land of olive oil and honey; a land in which you will eat bread without scarcity, in which you will lack nothing; a land whose stones are iron and out of whose hills you can dig copper.
>
> —Deut. 8:7–9

> The land which you cross over to possess is a land of hills and valleys, which drinks water from the rain of heaven, a land for which the Lord your God cares; the eyes of the Lord your God are always on it, from the beginning of the year to the very end of the year.
>
> —Deut. 11:11–12

Just as God delivered the Israelites from their Egyptian slavery and led them into His Promised Land, Canaan, He brought the Gentiles into His second land of milk and honey. He guided their transport and settlement in a land of liberty, where they could worship God according to His Word as opposed to the misguided teachings of the aristocracy and religious oppression of monarchs. For the Jews, God made a covenant between Him and them, He as their God and they as His people. America's purpose is to model to the world the new covenant, which brings salvation through Jesus Christ for all people, Jews and Gentiles alike.

GOD'S PURPOSE FOR AMERICA

America is God's chosen land, a land of milk and honey, a second promised land, if you will—a land possessing the previously listed waters, crops, and resources. God raised up America to glorify Himself. God elevated America to use it as a launching point from which His works could shine and His name would become known throughout the world. God lifted up America to spread His promise of salvation to all peoples. Exodus 9:16 says, "But indeed for this purpose I have raised you up, that I may show My power in you, and that My name may be declared in all the earth." In addition, Exodus 34:10 says, "Before all your people I will do marvels such as have not been done in all the earth, nor in any nation; and all the people...shall see the work of the Lord. For it is an awesome thing that I will do with you." Through the United States, God has done wondrous things the world has never before seen.

The first settlers and colonizers of America announced this same purpose. The First Charter of Virginia in Jamestown stated, "We,... by the providence of Almighty God, hereafter tend to the glory of His Divine Majesty, in propagating of Christian religion to such people, as yet live in darkness and miserable ignorance of the true knowledge and worship of God."[2] In Plymouth, Massachusetts, the Pilgrims stated that their objective was an "advance of the Gospel of the kingdom of Christ in the remote parts of the world."[3] The Massachusetts Bay Colony considered itself a "city upon a hill," from which to spread salvation through Christ.[4]

Every colonial charter and state constitution expresses its dedication to God and Jesus Christ in some way. This standard was not limited to individual colonies. The New England Confederation

(1643), a union among New Plymouth, New Haven, Massachusetts, and Connecticut, declared its purpose "to advance the kingdom of our Lord Jesus Christ."[5] Isaiah 41:9 says, "You whom I have taken from the ends of the earth, and called from its farthest regions, and said to you, *You are My servant,* I have chosen you and have not cast you away'" (emphasis added).

Therefore, the United States is a land of plenty, God's chosen nation, whose purpose is to proclaim the good news of salvation through Christ. God spoke through Isaiah and said that a root from the line of Jesse would "stand as a banner to the people; for the Gentiles shall seek Him" (Isa. 11:10). Isaiah 42:1 also says, "Behold! My Servant whom I uphold, My Elect One in whom My soul delights! I have put My Spirit upon Him; He will bring forth justice to the Gentiles." But the United States mirrors ancient Israel to a greater degree than I have so far described.

THIRTEEN TRIBES AND COLONIES

Jacob (called Israel), the son of Isaac, the son Abraham, had twelve sons who led tribes and received allotments of land in Canaan: Reuben, Simeon, Levi, Judah, Dan, Naphtali, Gad, Asher, Issachar, Zebulun, Joseph, and Benjamin. The tribe of Joseph, however, was split into two and named after his sons, Manasseh and Ephraim. The Levites did not receive a portion of land because God consecrated them as His priests, whose inheritance was performing His work in His tabernacle. Therefore, the twelve tribes that received land were Reuben, Simeon, Judah, Dan, Naphtali, Gad, Asher, Issachar, Zebulun, Benjamin, Manasseh, and Ephraim. Including the priestly tribe of Levi, thirteen Israelite tribes were established in the Promised Land, called Israel.

Early America also had thirteen original colonies, including New Hampshire, Rhode Island, Connecticut, Massachusetts, New York, New Jersey, Pennsylvania, Delaware, Maryland, Virginia,

North Carolina, South Carolina, and Georgia. Between the time of the thirteen Israelite tribes and the thirteen American colonies, Jesus Christ, the High Priest, led twelve apostles. Together, they numbered thirteen.

Other Nations in the Land

Just as in Israel's time, various peoples inhabited the land the colonists entered to settle. God's directives concerning these nations included the following:

> You shall not bow down to their gods, nor serve them, nor do according to their works; but you shall utterly overthrow them and completely break down their sacred pillars.
>
> —Ex. 23:24

> Driving out from before you nations greater and mightier than you, to bring you in, to give you their land as an inheritance, as it is this day.
>
> —Deut. 4:38

> And you shall do what is right and good in the sight of the Lord, that it may be well with you, and that you may go in and possess the good land…to cast out all of your enemies from before you, as the Lord has spoken.
>
> —Deut. 6:18–19

> And the Lord your God will drive out these nations before you little by little; you will be unable to destroy them at once, lest the beasts of the field become too numerous for you. But the Lord your God will deliver them over to you, and you will inflict defeat upon them until they are destroyed.
>
> —Deut. 7:22–23

For if you carefully keep all these commandments...to love
the Lord your God, to walk in all His ways, and to hold fast to
Him—then the Lord will drive out all these nations from before
you, and you will dispossess greater and mightier nations than
yourselves.

—Deut. 11:22–23

SHARING THE GOSPEL

Slowly and gradually, settlers exited Europe and traveled
across the vast Atlantic (just as the Israelites traversed the immense desert), and Americans spread across the fruited plain and
gained possession of the land. Unlike ancient Israel, due to the
new covenant in which salvation in Christ was available to all,
the mission in America was to spread the gospel to the Indians
while not adopting their religious customs. The bottom line is
that the struggle between Americans and Indians was a spiritual
one—the Christian God and faith versus the Native American
gods and idols. The struggle was the same in ancient Israel's age,
when the Lord God was victorious over Baal, Chemosh, Molech,
Asherah, and other idols concocted of gold, silver, bronze, stone,
and wood.

In America those who worshipped the true God won the
battles and gained control of the land, converting as many as
possible to Christianity along the way. What is underreported in
education is that many Indian tribes faced an internal spiritual
struggle. Many tribes chose Christianity, some maintained their
faith, others were divided over religion, and history unfolded
according to God's plan. This is a fact for which to be grateful but
not to be proud. Our nation's destruction will come to fruition if
its citizens fail to revere God and continue to forsake Him who
made them preeminent.

DELIVERY FROM ENEMIES

Beyond those already residing on the continent were European powerhouses claiming their portions of land. Americans needed to dispossess those nations as well, and God allowed that to happen with and without American action. England, France, Spain, the Netherlands, and Russia all succumbed to American superiority or withdrew without conflict. These successes resulted from Americans' preference to do "what is right and good in the sight of the Lord" (Deut. 6:18).

Blessed be the Lord, who has delivered you out of the hand of the Egyptians and out of the hand of Pharaoh.

—Ex. 18:10

I will not drive them out from before you in one year, lest the land become desolate and the beasts of the field become too numerous for you. Little by little I will drive them out…until you have increased, and you inherit the land.

—Ex. 23:29–30

The Lord delighted only in your fathers, to love them; and He chose their descendants after them, you above all peoples, as it is to this day.

—Deut. 10:15

Every place on which the sole of your foot treads shall be yours: from the wilderness…from the river…even to the Western Sea [Mediterranean], shall be your territory.

—Deut. 11:24

If you diligently obey the voice of the Lord your God,…the Lord your God will set you high above all the nations of the earth.

—Deut. 28:1

You come to me with a sword, with a spear, with a javelin. But I come to you in the name of the Lord of hosts,…whom you have defied. This day the Lord will deliver you into my hand.…Then all this assembly shall know that the Lord does not save with sword and spear; for the battle is the Lord's, and He will give you into our hands [David speaking to Goliath, the Philistine].

—1 Sam. 17:45–47

Be of good courage, and let us be strong for our people and for the cities of our God. And may the Lord do what is good in His sight.

—2 Sam. 10:12

Israel Not Displaced by America

Though I contend that America is God's chosen land and its populace His chosen people, several clarifications must be made. First, Israel and the Jewish people continue to be God's primary chosen land and people, whom Americans have not supplanted. The United States is God's selected land to spread the good news of salvation through His Son, Jesus Christ; this is the new covenant between God and the peoples of the world, Jews and Gentiles alike. However, Americans are second in God's hierarchy. Although He has created the United States and raised it to preeminence, He still reserves in His heart a special place for Israel and the Jewish race. Second, God furnished America not to subordinate other nations to itself but to spread God's Word and plan for salvation; America was chosen because of the colonists' faith and devotion toward Him, and it would prosper as long it maintained that loyalty and exclusive worship. It would receive special blessings for fulfilling its role, but other nations would also be blessed for their reverence of God. Third, the Lord's hand will defeat those who reject Him. He uses the armies of nations that trust in Him to crush evil, including defeating superior enemies.

Peace and God's Favor

After defeating the British and King George III in the Revolutionary War, America, through God's watchful eye and blessing, experienced peace within, received protection from her enemies, and experienced success against them, gradually increasing her borders and gaining respect from other world powers.

> I will send My fear before you, I will cause confusion among all the people to whom you come, and will make all your enemies turn their backs to you.
>
> —Ex. 23:27

> I will give you peace in the land,…and none will make you afraid;…and the sword will not go through your land. You will chase your enemies, and they shall fall by the sword before you. Five of you shall chase a hundred, and a hundred of you shall put ten thousand to flight.
>
> —Lev. 26:6–8

> I will begin to put the dread and fear of you upon the nations under the whole heaven, who shall hear the report of you, and shall tremble and be in anguish because of you.
>
> —Deut. 2:25

> No man shall be able to stand against you; the Lord your God will put the dread of you and the fear of you upon all the land where you tread.
>
> —Deut. 11:25

> When you go out to battle against your enemies,…do not be afraid of them; for the Lord your God is with you….Do not let your heart faint, do not be afraid, and do not tremble or be terrified

because of them; for the Lord your God is He who goes with you, to fight for you against your enemies, to save you.

—Deut. 20:1, 3–4

Be strong and of good courage, do not fear nor be afraid of them; for the Lord your God, He is the One who goes with you. He will not leave you nor forsake you.

—Deut. 31:6

When the Most High divided their inheritance to the nations,... He set the boundaries of the peoples according to the numbers of the children.

—Deut. 32:8

One man of you shall chase a thousand, for the Lord your God is He who fights for you.

—Josh. 23:10

Were the Ethiopians and the Lubim not a huge army...? Yet, because you relied on the Lord, He delivered them into your hand. For the eyes of the Lord run to and fro throughout the whole earth, to show Himself strong on behalf of those whose heart is loyal to Him.

—2 Chron. 16:8–9

Be strong and courageous; do not be afraid nor dismayed....With us is the Lord our God, to help us and to fight our battles.

—2 Chron. 32:7–8

Wherever you hear the sound of the trumpet, rally to us there. Our God will fight for us.

—Neh. 4:20

THANKING GOD

Through the War of Independence, War of 1812, Mexican War, Civil War, and battles against the Indians, Americans maintained their gratefulness to God for His blessings. From colonial times to George Washington to Abraham Lincoln, the nation and its leaders expressed thanks to the Lord. On October 3, 1789, Mr. Washington issued a proclamation for public thanksgiving and prayer to almighty God. On that day, the entire Congress convened at St. Paul's Cathedral in New York to worship God and specifically thank Him for the U.S. Constitution.[6] Mr. Lincoln proclaimed the first National Day of Thanksgiving in 1863, stating, "They are the gracious gifts of the Most High God, who...hath nevertheless remembered mercy....They should be solemnly, reverently, and gratefully acknowledged as with one heart and one voice by the whole American People. I do therefore invite my fellow citizens... to...observe...a day of Thanksgiving and Praise to our beneficent Father who dwelleth in the Heavens. And...[we offer] humble penitence for our national perverseness and disobedience."[7]

Of course, the need for God's chosen nation to extend its appreciation to Him is also grounded in the Bible.

So you shall rejoice in every good thing which the Lord your God has given to you and your house....Look down from Your holy habitation, from heaven, and bless Your people Israel and the land which You have given us.
—Deut. 26:11, 15

Only fear the Lord, and serve Him in truth with all your heart; for consider what great things He has done for you.
—1 Sam. 12:24

Blessed be the Lord, who has given rest to His people Israel....May the Lord our God be with us, as He was with our fathers. May

He not leave us nor forsake us, that He may incline our hearts to Himself, to walk in all His ways, and to keep His commandments and His statutes and His judgments, which He commanded our fathers. And may these words of mine, with which I have made supplication before the Lord, be near the Lord our God day and night, that He may maintain the cause…of His people Israel,… that all the peoples of the earth may know that the Lord is God; there is no other. Let your heart therefore be loyal to the Lord our God.

—1 Kings 8:56–61

David…blessed the people in the name of the Lord….And he appointed some of the Levites…to commemorate, to thank, and to praise the Lord God of Israel….On that day David first delivered this psalm…to thank the Lord.

—1 Chron. 16:2, 4, 7

Blessings for Obedience

God instructed Israel that He would bless it in exchange for obedience to Him and warned that He would punish it if it disobeyed. The directive was simple: worship God alone and follow His commands, and He would be their God and they His people. These blessings are also applicable to the United States.

If you will indeed obey My voice and keep My covenant, then you shall be a special treasure to Me above all people; for all the earth is Mine. And you shall be to Me…a holy nation.

—Ex. 19:5–6

You shall not bow down to their gods, nor serve them….You shall serve the Lord your God, and He will bless your bread and your water. And I will take sickness away from the midst of you.

—Ex. 23:24–25

And you shall not walk in the statutes of the nation which I am casting out before you…."You shall inherit their land, and I will give it to you to possess, a land flowing with milk and honey."

—Lev. 20:23–24

So you shall observe My statutes and keep My judgments,…and you will dwell in the land in safety. Then the land will yield its fruit, and you will eat your fill, and dwell there in safety.

—Lev. 25:18–19

You shall therefore keep His statutes and His commandments… that it may go well with you and with your children after you, and that you may prolong your days in the land which the Lord your God is giving you for all time.

—Deut. 4:40

If you diligently obey the voice of the Lord your God, to observe carefully all His commandments…[,] the Lord your God will set you high above all nations of the earth. And all these blessings shall come upon you and overtake you….Blessed shall you be in the city, and…in the country. Blessed shall be the fruit of your body, the produce of your ground and the increase of your herds,…cattle[,] and…flocks. Blessed shall be your basket and your kneading bowl. Blessed shall you be when you come in, and…when you go out. The Lord will cause your enemies…to be defeated….The Lord will command the blessing on you in your storehouses and in all to which you set your hand, and He will bless you in the land.

—Deut. 28:1–8

That you may love the Lord your God, that you may obey His voice,…for He is your life and the length of your days.

—Deut. 30:20

Now if you walk before Me…in integrity of heart and in upright-ness, to do according to all that I have commanded you, and if you keep My statutes and My judgments, then I will establish… your kingdom…forever.

—1 Kings 9:4–5

Then you will prosper, if you take care to fulfill the statutes and judgments which the Lord charged Moses.

—1 Chron. 22:13

Lord God of Israel, there is no God in heaven or on earth like You, who keep Your covenant and mercy with Your servants who walk before You with all their hearts.

—2 Chron. 6:14; also see Deut. 5:33; 6:2–3, 25; 28:14; and Neh. 1:5

PROSPERITY

With obedience comes blessing, and with blessing comes prosperity. The United States is one of the most prosperous countries in the world with the natural beauty of the land, a variety of natural resources and minerals, technological advancements and inventions, comforts at home and in the workplace, a multitude of entertainment and leisure activities, and, of course, the liberty that allows ordinary people to realize extraordinary achievement.

You shall lend to many nations, but you shall not borrow; you shall reign over many nations, but they shall not reign over you.

—Deut. 15:6

The Lord will establish you as a holy people to Himself….Then all peoples of the earth shall see that you are called by the name of the Lord….And the Lord will grant you plenty of goods, in the fruit of your body, in the increase of your livestock, and in the produce of your ground....The Lord will open to you His good treasure, the heavens, to give the rain to your land in its season, and to bless all the work of your hand....You shall be above only, and not be beneath, if you heed the commandments of the Lord your God.

—Deut. 28:9–13

Both riches and honor come from You, and You reign over all. In Your hand is power and might; in Your hand it is to make great and to give strength to all.

—1 Chron. 29:12

As long as he sought the Lord, God made him prosper.

—2 Chron. 26:5

And in every work...in the service...of God,...he did it with all his heart. So he prospered.

—2 Chron. 31:21

The God of heaven Himself will prosper us.

—Neh. 2:20; also see Deut. 11:13–15; 28:1;
and 32:13–14

PRIDE IN SELF

Inevitably, people become proud of their accomplishments. As the occurrence of prosperous events becomes further separated from the time of original blessing, pride in self overwhelms remembrance of and thankfulness for the gifts that allowed such success and prosperity. Students fail to respect their teachers, children falter in honoring their parents, and people forget to recognize the blessings of God Almighty. Instead, they credit their own ability, desire, and intelligence; they begin to replace God with worthless idols and exterminate Him from their lives.

Beware that you do not forget the Lord your God...when you have eaten and are full, and have built beautiful houses and dwell in them; and when your herds and your flocks multiply, and your silver and your gold are multiplied, and all that you have is multiplied....Then you say in your heart, "My power and the might of my hand have gained me this wealth."...For it is He who gives you power to get wealth.

—Deut. 8:11–13, 17–18

When I have brought them to the land flowing with milk and honey...and they have eaten and filled themselves and grown fat, then they will turn to other gods and serve them.

—Deut. 31:20

Shall the ax boast itself against him who chops with it?

—Isa. 10:15

For shall the thing made say of him who made it, "He did not make me"? Or shall the thing formed say of him who formed it, "He has no understanding"?

—Isa. 29:16

REBELLION AGAINST GOD

Attached to pride is rebellion. Once people determine that they are the source of their own prosperity and ability, they reject God and turn to idols, including themselves. They cast away God's statutes as being outdated, constraining, and restrictive; in their place, they substitute their own principles. All ideas, thoughts, notions, and attitudes are equally relevant, though they completely exclude traditional norms, codes, morals, and ethics from this mindset. They forbid conventional ways of life and aggrandize new, "enlightened" beliefs; they justify their unethical, immoral, illegal, and deviant disposition.

In turn, they view God with animosity, derision, and hatred, so they exile Him from their society and prefer to worship idols of self, the creation, and relativism. They languish in their futile attempt to fill the resultant void left by God's banishment from their culture. The following quotes are reminiscent of the mentality that exploded with the 1960s hippie rebellion. Though I cannot say the rebellion began in this decade, it definitely accelerated during those years.

> They gathered together against Moses and Aaron, and said to them, "You take too much upon yourselves, for all the congregation is holy, every one of them, and the Lord is among them. Why then do you exalt yourselves above the assembly of the Lord?"
> —Num. 16:3

> This people will rise and play the harlot with the gods of the foreigners of the land,…and they will forsake Me and break My covenant which I have made with them. Then My anger shall be aroused against them…, and I will forsake them, and I will hide My face from them….And many evils and troubles shall befall them, so that they will say in that day, "Have not these evils come upon us because our God is not among us?" And I will surely hide My face in that day because of all the evil which they have done, in that they have turned to other gods.
> —Deut. 31:16–18

> I will hide My face from them,…for they are a perverse generation, children in whom is no faith.
> —Deut. 32:20

> Why do you transgress the commandments of the Lord, so that you cannot prosper? Because you have forsaken the Lord, He also has forsaken you.
> —2 Chron. 24:20

Woe to those who draw iniquity with cords of vanity...that say, "Let Him make speed and hasten His work, that we may see it."
—Isa. 5:18–19

You despise this word, and trust in oppression and perversity, and rely on them.
—Isa. 30:12

God is not mocked; for whatever a man sows, that he will also reap. For he who sows to his flesh will of the flesh reap corruption, but he who sows to the Spirit will of the Spirit reap everlasting life.
—Gal. 6:7–8

God's Wrath

Therefore, pride collaborates with rebellion, which produces punishment. This is not to say that culture portrayed a utopia-like, sinless existence before the sixties. Sin has always been present in the world; it is one thing to succumb to the appetites of the flesh and sin but quite another to engage in flagrant disobedience that condones and justifies transgression and immorality. Scripture repeatedly refers to punishment for forsaking God. In addition to what is written here, see Deuteronomy 11:16–17; 28:20–68; 2 Kings 18:12; 2 Chronicles 7:19–20; 24:20; and 34:24–25.

Do not defile yourselves with any of these things; for by all these the nations are defiled....For the land is defiled; therefore I visit the punishment of its iniquity upon it, and the land vomits out its inhabitants.
—Lev. 18:24–25

When he gives some of his descendants to Molech,...then I will set My face against that man and against his family.
—Lev. 20:4–5

But if you do not obey Me, and do not observe all these commandments,...or if your soul abhors My judgments,...I will even appoint terror over you, wasting disease and fever....And you shall sow your seed in vain, for your enemies shall eat it. I will set My face against you, and you shall be defeated by your enemies. Those who hate you shall reign over you....I will make your heavens like iron and your earth like bronze....Your land shall not yield its produce, nor shall the trees...yield their fruit....I will also send wild beasts among you,...and your highways shall be desolate....I will send pestilence among you....You shall eat the flesh of your sons, and...your daughters.
> —Lev. 26:14–17, 19–20, 22, 25, 29

When you beget children and grandchildren and have grown old in the land, and act corruptly...and do evil in the sight of the Lord your God...[,] you will soon utterly perish from the land.
> —Deut. 4:25–26

If you by any means forget the Lord your God, and follow other gods, and serve them and worship them,...you shall surely perish. As the nations which the Lord destroys before you, so you shall perish, because you would not be obedient to the voice of the Lord your God.
> —Deut. 8:19–20

If you do not obey the voice of the Lord your God, to observe carefully all His commandments and His statutes...[,] cursed shall you be in the city, and...in the country. Cursed shall be your baskets and your kneading bowl. Cursed shall be the fruit of your body and the produce of your land,...your cattle and...your flocks. Cursed shall you be when you come in, and...when you go out. The Lord shall send on you cursing, confusion, and rebuke in all that you set your hand to do....The Lord will make the plague cling to you....strike you with consumption, with fever, with inflammation, with severe burning fever, with the sword, with scorching, and with mildew….Your heavens…shall be bronze, and the earth…shall be iron.

—Deut. 28:15–23

The Lord will cause you to be defeated before your enemies…. The Lord will strike you with the boils of Egypt, with tumors, with the scab, and with the itch, from which you cannot be healed….with madness and blindness and confusion of heart…. You shall not prosper in your ways; you shall be only oppressed and plundered continually.

—Deut. 28:25, 27–29

You shall betroth a wife, but another man shall lie with her; you shall build a house, but you shall not dwell in it; you shall plant a vineyard, but shall not gather its grapes. Your ox shall be slaughtered…, but you shall not eat of it….So you shall be driven mad because of the sight which your eyes see. The Lord will strike you…from the sole of your foot to the top of your head.

—Deut. 28:30–31, 34–35

The alien who is among you shall rise higher and higher….He shall lend to you, but you shall not lend to him….You shall serve your enemies….The Lord will bring a nation against you from afar,…whose language you will not understand….You shall eat… the flesh of your sons and your daughters.

—Deut. 28:43–44, 48–49, 53

He will bring back on you….every sickness and every plague, which is not written in the Book of the Law….a trembling heart, failing eyes, and anguish of soul….You shall…have no assurance of life.

—Deut. 28:60–61, 65–66

But if your heart turns away so that you…worship other gods and serve them,…you shall surely perish.

—Deut. 30:17–18

Their foot shall slip in due time; for the day of their calamity is at hand, and the things to come hasten upon them….I will render vengeance to My enemies, and repay those who hate Me.

—Deut. 32:35, 41

All the good things have come upon you which the Lord your God promised you….When you have transgressed the covenant of the Lord your God,…and have gone and served other gods,… then the anger of the Lord will burn against you, and you shall perish quickly.

—Josh. 23:15–16

Go, inquire of the Lord…for great is the wrath of the Lord that is aroused against us, because our fathers have not obeyed the words of this book.

—2 Kings 22:13

You have forsaken Me, and therefore I also have left you in the hand of Shishak [king of Egypt].

—2 Chron. 12:5

Do not fight against the Lord God of your fathers, for you shall not prosper!

—2 Chron. 13:12

For the army of the Syrians came with a small company of men; but the Lord delivered a very great army into their hand, because they had forsaken the Lord God of their fathers.

—2 Chron. 24:24

REALITIES FOR AMERICA

Several evident themes are repeated throughout these passages and others not listed here. Obedience to God and His commandments is a priority. The charge is simple—obey God and be blessed; disobey and face reprisal. Worshipping or serving idols is the second-most common theme. The first commandment states, "You shall have no other gods before me," and the second commandment says, "You shall not make for yourself a carved image" (Ex. 20:3–4; also see Deut. 4:7–8). Perishing from the land for committing evil and iniquity is also a common theme of these admonishments. God specifically enumerates the punishments that result for these transgressions. Finally, being defeated by a foreign enemy is clearly stipulated. Being challenged by a smaller, inferior army and facing "a nation against you from afar,…whose language you will not understand" (Deut. 28:49) must reverberate with the American public.

Recall an earlier part of this discussion. Part of God's blessings for obedience includes no fear from enemies; however, He reversed this promise if His people chose to disobey and revere idols. When one examines the Old Testament, he sees that Israel conquered several armies due to its obedience, and King David's conquests are explained in detail. On the other hand, Israel and Judah's might became impotent when the populace chose to turn its back on its God and serve other gods.

Modern America needs to heed this fact. At its inception, the United States twice defeated the superior British military and later routed the renowned Mexican army. Other nations such as France, Spain, and Russia willingly withdrew their claims to American soil. In recent history America struggled during the Vietnam War and currently faces a severe challenge and threat in the war on terror against the axis of evil.

The solution is simple: return to honoring, worshipping, and revering God, and He will help us defeat this enemy. He continues to guide America, but He will withdraw this assistance unless the nation returns to worshipping Him alone (I must reiterate that citizens must *not* be forced to worship Christianity; rather, America must honor her Christian foundation while upholding the precept of religious freedom). God was patient and forgiving with the Israelites; He gave them multiple opportunities and approximately seven hundred years to correct the error of their ways, but He eventually rendered His punishment. The same holds true for the United States today. How long will God be patient? Only He knows His timetable. "It is not for you to know times or seasons which the Father has put in His own authority" (Acts 1:7). "But of that day and hour no one knows, not even the angels of heaven, but My Father only....Watch therefore, for you do not know what hour your Lord is coming....Be ready, for the Son of Man is coming at an hour you do not expect" (Matt. 24:36, 42, 44).

GOD'S MERCY

Some consequences described in God's Word have been occurring in the world for centuries, but if a nation is truly dedicated to the Lord God, He will protect it from such calamities. The key is to be devoted to God and His declarations. Since sin entered the world during the lives of Adam and Eve, a variety of infirmities have plagued sinful mankind; this is part of the fall of man. Despite that reality, God clearly states that He blesses those who serve and obey Him, while He turns His face away from and punishes those who choose not to do so. Although we experience illness, drought, famine, earthquakes, and other natural disasters, these misfortunes are not a complete demonstration of God's anger. He is a kind, patient, loving, forgiving, and merciful God, who is slow to anger. But He will eventually punish His chosen nation, even if it is secondary in value to the nation of Israel, which has already faced God's retribution.

> For the Lord is good; His mercy is everlasting.
>
> —Ps. 100:5

> The Lord is merciful and gracious, slow to anger, and abounding in mercy....He has not dealt with us according to our sins, nor punished us according to our iniquities.
>
> —Ps. 103:8, 10

> For the Lord is a God of justice; blessed are all those who wait for Him.
>
> —Isa. 30:18

> To the Lord our God belong mercy and forgiveness, though we have rebelled against Him.
>
> —Dan. 9:9

> But God, who is rich in mercy, because of His great love with which He loved us.
>
> —Eph. 2:4

Studying the Old Testament provides an understanding of God's patience, benevolence, and forgiveness; He tolerated an overabundance of sinful behaviors, idolatry, and evil kings. The Old Testament also clearly illustrates that punishment cannot be averted in perpetuity. We need to be thankful for God's character traits and recognize that our nation, the United States of America, is in the same predicament almost three thousand years later. God told the Israelites, "'I have held My peace a long time, I have been still and restrained Myself....I will lay waste the mountains and hills, and dry up all their vegetation; I will make the rivers coastlands'....Therefore He has poured on him the fury of His anger" (Isa. 42:14–15, 25).

FALSE TEACHERS

It is important to note that failing to abide by God's Word also applies to its teachers. We cannot refute that many have rejected Christianity due to the hypocritical behavior some of its practitioners have exhibited. Certainly, false teachers use the name of God and Christ to con faithful followers; at the same time, pastors, priests, ministers, and evangelists have misrepresented God's Word, added to it, subtracted from it, amended its meaning, and egregiously misinterpreted it. Jesus warned, "Beware of false prophets, who come to you in sheep's clothing, but inwardly they are ravenous wolves" (Matt. 7:15). The apostle John cautioned in 1 John 4:1, "Beloved, do not believe every spirit, but test the spirits, whether they are of God; because many prophets have gone out into the world."

Some false teachers twist God's Word for their own interests to endorse behavior such as same-sex marriage and abortion. They are similar to the elders and Pharisees in Jesus' time, who, though "experts" in the law, failed to recognize Christ's glory due to their own corruption. They share in the responsibility for God's anger and wrath. The prophet Isaiah wrote, "For the leaders of this people cause them to err" (9:16).

This truth does not provide forbearance to mayors, governors, congressmen, presidents, and others in leadership positions for their guilt in misleading the people through corruption, greed, injustice, fraud, and abuse of power—and some of them doing so in Jesus' name. A brief examination of a handful of President Barack Obama's forty-three or more czars provides an illustration of errant leadership caused by a misguided worldview. John Holden, the science czar, believes in forced abortion, family-size restrictions, government seizure of illegitimate children, and a water supply containing sterilants. Kevin Jennings, the school safety czar, supports the gay agenda and promotes teaching homosexuality at the elementary school level. Cass Sunstein, the regulatory czar, advances a ban on hunting and promotes enforced organ donation and the right of animals to sue for animal cruelty. Kenneth Feinberg, the pay czar, forced the Bank of America CEO to surrender all his compensation and benefits. Mark Lloyd, the FCC diversity czar, reveres socialist Venezuelan dictator Hugo Chavez and favors discrimination by removing certain media personnel in exchange for gays, people of color, and others.[8]

This small sampling of Mr. Obama's forty-three or more czars does not include fifteen cabinet members, liberal members of Congress and the Supreme Court, or other consultants such as the Reverend Jeremiah Wright. Such leaders exude haughtiness and mock God, believing in their hearts that "when the overflowing scourge passes through, it will not come to us, for we have made lies our refuge, and under falsehood we have hidden ourselves" (Isa. 28:15).

Citizens who choose to blindly follow such leaders due to their own ignorance and laziness are also held accountable by God. I again quote from Isaiah 9:16: "And those who are led by them are destroyed." Moreover, all are sinners and fall short of God's glory, which is why Jesus died for the sins of the world. No matter whom people are, they cannot gain salvation on their own accord; it is impossible for man to keep all God's laws without ever committing an offense against them. Romans 3:20 says, "Therefore by the deeds of the law no flesh will be justified in His sight, for by the law is the knowledge of sin." Furthermore, in a corrupt culture, association contaminates all. "There is none righteous, no, not one....They have all turned aside;...there is none who does good, no, not one" (Rom. 3:10, 12). "The Lord looks down from heaven upon the children of men....They have all turned aside, they have together become corrupt; there is none who does good, no, not one" (Ps. 14:2–3).

TAINTED BY SIN

Just as we cannot swim in a pool without being exposed to chlorine, we are unable to exist in a sinful society without being tainted. The more corrupt the society is, the more damaged are those who live in it. Based on the evolution of American culture and that of the world's, we see that sin we face today is far more extensive than that of our country at the time of its founding. That is not to say that the sin we face today did not exist in the eighteenth century or any other, but sinful behavior has dramatically accelerated at exponential proportions since the rebellious '60s generation.

ISRAEL–U.S. PARALLELS

After the schism that divided Israel and Judah, the nations swung pendulum-like between various degrees of righteousness and evil. Israel's division occurred in 930 BC with the split being mostly a north-south fissure—Judah to the south and west, and tribes comprising Israel to the north and east. God eventually exiled and later returned them to Jerusalem. The United States experienced a similar, though temporary, division during the Civil War (1861–1865). Thankfully, Americans were not cast from their country. Nevertheless, about five centuries after Israel was reestablished, Jesus Christ was born into God's chosen nation to sacrifice Himself once and for all for the sins of the world. "So Christ was offered once to bear the sins of many" (Heb. 9:28).

The United States is also God's chosen nation—His second chosen people, if you will—whose mission is to spread throughout the earth the good news of Christ's birth, death, resurrection, ascension, and salvation. Jesus will again come into the world, this time to judge each person according to his faith and deeds, and to grant eternal life or everlasting suffering to each. "And behold, I am coming quickly, and My reward is with Me, to give to every one according to his work" (Rev. 22:12). "To those who eagerly wait for Him He will appear a second time, apart from sin, for salvation" (Heb. 9:28).

Let us review the parallels between ancient Israel and the United States.

- Ancient Israel comprised thirteen tribes, twelve of which received land and one that did not. America was established with thirteen original colonies and states.
- Both the Israelites and American settlers entered a land flowing with milk and honey.
- The Israelites escaped brutal slavery and crossed a vast desert to reach their Promised Land; those who settled the United States escaped tyranny, including religious persecution, and traversed an immense ocean to enter their inheritance.
- God commissioned Israel with the task of destroying the nations that possessed the land of their inheritance; the goal of America's settlers as they spread across the continent was to convert Indians to Christianity.
- The Israelites faced a spiritual battle between their God and other nations' idols, and God won. Americans undertook such a conflict between their God and the gods of the Native Americans; God also won.
- Israel spread slowly throughout the land so wild beasts and forests would not overrun it. The United States gradually expanded across the fruited plain to its boundaries for the same reason.
- God blessed Israel because the people devoted themselves to Him, His covenant, and His commandments. Likewise, God blessed the United States as its settlers strived to abide by

God's decrees and extended the new covenant of salvation through Christ to all peoples.

- The Israelites became rebellious, cast aside God's regulations, invited God's anger, and lost His blessings. Americans have followed that example, regressing from their Christian foundation and expelling God from their institutions. Our country is experiencing God's disfavor and is on the verge of receiving His wrath.

- Israel rejected God and served various gods in the region, while the United States has expunged God from its life in favor of worshipping a pantheon of the world's idols and self. Environmental and relativistic ideals have opened a Pandora's jar of iniquities into our culture.

- In Israel, Christ was born in Bethlehem to carry the sins of mankind, dispose of them by dying on the cross, free mankind from the law, and provide salvation through faith in the Son of the Father. For America and every nation, Christ will again enter the world to justly judge its nations and peoples, both Jews and Gentiles. He will reward those who have faith in the Son, while punishing those who practice idolatry and infidelity toward the Father.

The parallels are undeniable. What the future holds is still a mystery, though the book of Revelation and books by Old Testament prophets provide hints of God's plan. When God brought the Israelites out of Egypt, He performed a series of miraculous signs and plagues against Pharaoh and his subjects. During the final plague, known as the Passover, God killed the firstborn of every man and animal in Egypt but passed over the firstborn of the Israelites. But God's vengeance was directed not only toward the Egyptians, for God declared, "Against all the gods of Egypt I will execute judgment" (Ex. 12:12).

Christ's Judgment

When Christ returns to judge the nations, He will mightily shake and destroy heaven and earth, establishing new ones in their place. John wrote in Revelation 21:1, "Now I saw a new heaven and a new earth, for the first heaven and the first earth had passed away. Also there was no more sea." Jesus declares in Matthew 24:35, "Heaven and earth will pass away, but My words will by no means pass away." Just as God exacted judgment on the gods of Egypt, He will pour out His wrath against the god of our day—the earth.

Christ's Salvation

As God chose the Israelites to be His people and Him their God, He now accepts any people who put their faith in His Son, Jesus Christ. "Behold, the tabernacle of God is with men, and He will dwell with them, and they shall be His people. God Himself will be with them and be their God" (Rev. 21:3). "I, the Lord, have called You [Jesus] in righteousness, and will hold Your hand; I will keep You and give You as a covenant to the people, as a light to the Gentiles" (Isa. 42:6). "God our Savior…desires all men to be saved and to come to the knowledge of the truth….[through] the Man Christ Jesus, who gave Himself a ransom for all" (1 Tim. 2:3–6).

Separation of Church and State Invalid

Since we live in a country that has modeled the concept of religious freedom to the world, I should state that I fervently support that great American precept. My purpose is to defend and proclaim our Christian heritage, which was necessary to our becoming the greatest nation in the history of the world. Without our Christian faith and foundation, God would not have chosen and bolstered the United States to fulfill His purpose. Therefore, America is first a Christian nation, but it also accepts and tolerates other faiths.

It is wrong for anyone to contend that "separation of church and state" is a viable concept. Regardless of what we choose, everyone follows a faith, be it Christianity, Judaism, Hinduism, atheism, or relativism. In the end faith guides our nation. Will we follow the false gods described in this book, or will we follow God? Will we foolishly allow secularists, relativists, and atheists to lead us? Or will God-fearing leaders wisely guide us? Will we aspire to be gods ourselves in our feeble attempts to control every aspect of the world, including temperature? Or will we abide by our Christian principles and lead the world by example according to the God-granted rights of life, liberty, and the pursuit of happiness, which our Founding Fathers so aptly identified and implemented?

CONCLUSION

I did not choose my country, but I have been blessed by it; therefore, it is my duty to fight for its survival, to help maintain its greatness at the divine author's discretion, and to uphold its hope for the peoples of the world. Witnessing the destruction being wrought on our nation is heart wrenching. We are killing the greatest nation in the history of the earth; yes, this is premeditated homicide. As a rule, the general public is the victim through intentional deception, abuse of power, and seizure of authority by socialist-leaning, tyrannical idolaters. Those who blindly, ignorantly, selfishly, lazily, and gladly abide by this counsel and leaders who guide or allow the United States to be led toward this demise will receive their just recompense. God is watching, Jesus is preparing, and He will act against His nation—America the Beautiful, one nation under God!

People can choose to disagree with this assertion, but consequences are inseparable from their choices. They can continue to worship relativistic notions, the environment, and self—and thus continue to struggle and experience Pandora's jar of reprisals. Or they can abide by the Christian precepts that made our country the foremost nation in the world. Solomon correctly wrote, "That which has been is what will be, that which is done is what will be done, and there is nothing new under the sun" (Eccl. 1:9).

History will be repeated, and we will face the wrath of God the Father, the Lord of Hosts, the Holy One of Israel. Jesus will return to earth with power and great glory. When Jesus walked in Israel, He admonished the "experts" who mocked His teachings, "You know how to discern the face of the sky, but you cannot discern the signs of the times" (Matt. 16:3). As a nation, we must preserve our Christian heritage to reap God's blessings; other countries can emulate our example or not, but specific consequences follow either decision.

Oh, that you had heeded My commandments!
Then your peace would have been like a river,
And your righteousness like the waves of the sea.
Your descendants also would have been like the sand,
And the offspring of your body like the grains of sand;
His name would not have been cut off
Nor destroyed from before Me.
(Isa. 48:18–19)

Who among you fears the Lord?
Who obeys the voice of His Servant?
Who walks in darkness
And has no light?
Let him trust in the name of the Lord
And rely upon his God.
Look, all you who kindle a fire,
Who encircle yourselves with sparks:
Walk in the light of your fire and in the sparks you have kindled—
This you shall have from My hand:
You shall lie down in torment.
(Isa. 50:10–11)

Seek the Lord while He may be found,
Call upon Him while He is near.
Let the wicked forsake his way,
And the unrighteous man his thoughts;
Let him return to the Lord,
And He will have mercy on him;
And to our God,
For He will abundantly pardon.
(Isa. 55:6–7)

ENDNOTES

Introduction

1. Mark R. Levin, *Men in Black* (Washington, DC: Regnery, 2005), 18–19.
2. Ibid., 19–20.
3. Ibid., 21.

Chapter 1

1. Gary Cass, "America's Tolerance Showdown," *Enjoying Everyday Life*, April 2008, 14.
2. Larry Schweikart and Michael Allen, *A Patriot's History of the United States: From Columbus's Great Discovery to the War on Terror* (New York: Penguin Group, 2004), 16.
3. U.S. Const. art. VII.
4. U.S. Const. art. I, sec. 7, no. 2.
5. Marvin Olasky, "Opportunity Knocks Twice: Christians Can Help Shape the Next Great Era of American Journalism," *World Magazine*, October 24, 2009, 76.

6. Dave Meyer, "God's Hand on Inauguration Day," *Enjoying Everyday Life*, December 2008/January 2009, 14.

7. Thomas A. Bailey, David M. Kennedy, and Lizabeth Cohen, *The American Pageant* (Boston: Houghton Mifflin, 1998), 73.

8. Ibid., 589.

9. Betzaida Tejada-Vera and Paul D. Sutton, "Births, Marriages, Divorces, and Deaths: Provisional Data for 2008," *National Vital Statistics Reports*, vol. 57, no. 19 (Hyattsville, MD: National Center for Health Statistics), 5, last modified July 29, 2009, http://www.cdc.gov/NCHS/data/nvsr/nvsr57/nvsr57_19.pdf.

10. "No. HS-14. Births to Teenagers and to Unmarried Women: 1940 to 2002," United States Census Bureau, *Statistical Abstract of the United States: 2003*, accessed December 14, 2009, http://www.census.gov/statab/hist/HS-14.pdf.

11. Ibid.

12. "America's Forests, Liquidated," *Forest Voice*, Winter 2000, 12.

13. Schweikart and Allen, *A Patriot's History*, 28.

14. Levin, *Men in Black*, 135–137.

15. Ibid., 41.

16. Ibid., 57.

17. Ibid., 58–59.

18. Ibid., 60.

19. Ibid., 67.

20. Ibid., 122.

21. David Barton, *Original Intent: The Courts, the Constitution, and Religion* (Aledo, TX: Wall Builder Press, 2002), 218.

22. Ibid.

Chapter 2

1. "Miller: New Report Shows Too Many States Weakening Education Standards," Committee on Education and Labor, last modified October 29, 2009, http://democrats.edworkforce.

house.gov/newsroom/2009/10/miller-new-report-shows-too-ma.shtml.

2. "School Report Card: Accountability Guide, 2010-11," Virginia Department of Education, accessed March 24, 2011, http://www.doe.virginia.gov/statistics_reports/school_report_card/accountability_guide.shtml#content.

3. "Local School Division Policies for Changing Students' Course Schedules," Superintendents Memo No. 52, Virginia Department of Education, last modified March 7, 2008, http://www.doe.virginia.gov/administrators/superintendents_memos/2008/inf052.html.

4. "High Schools Skip Over Basics in Rush to College Classes," *USA Today*, last modified February 26, 2004, accessed November 6, 2009, http://www.usatoday.com/news/opinion/editorials/2004-02-26-our-view_x.htm.

5. David Bahnsen, "Budget Buster: The High Cost of Education is Behind California Crisis," *World Magazine*, August 15, 2009, 41.

6. Lynn Vincent, "Reforming School Reform: Analysts and Lawmakers Try to Rescue No Child Left Behind," *World Magazine*, March 3, 2007, 28.

7. "Mapping State Proficiency Standards Onto NAEP Scales: 2005–2007," National Center for Educational Statistics, last modified October 2009, http://nces.ed.gov/nationsreportcard/pdf/studies/2010456.pdf.

8. Martin Luther King Jr., *Why We Can't Wait* (New York: Penguin Group, 1964), 43.

9. Joel Schectman and Rachel Monahan, "CUNY's Got Math Problem: Report Shows Many Freshmen from City HS Fail at Basic Algebra," *New York Daily News*, last modified November 12, 2009, http://www.nydailynews.com/ny_local/education/2009/11/12/2009-11-12_cunys_got_math_problem_many_freshmen_from_city_hs_fail_at_basic_algebra.html.

10. Shane R. Jimerson, "Meta-Analysis of Grade Retention Research: Implications for Practice in the 21st Century," *School Psychology Review*, 2001, vol. 30, no. 3, 422, accessed March 1, 2011, http://education.ucsb.edu/jimerson/NEW%20retention/Publications/MetaAnalysis.SPR01.pdf.

11. Ibid.

12. Ibid., 433.

13. "High School Dropouts in America," Alliance for Excellent Education, last modified February 2009, http://www.all4ed.org/files/GraduationRates_FactSheet.pdf.

14. Robert McGarvey, "America's Brainchild," *The American Legion*, September 2002, 50.

Chapter 3

1. William F.B. Vodrey, "George Washington: Hero of the Confederacy?" *American History*, October 2004, 61.

2. M. L. West, *Hesiod: Theogony and Works and Days* (New York: Oxford University Press, 1988), 38–40.

3. "National School Breakfast Week, March 2–6, 2009, and National Nutrition Month, March 2009," Patricia I. Wright, Superintendents Memo *#034-09*, Virginia Department of Education, last modified February 13, 2009, http://www.doe.virginia.gov/administrators/superintendents_memos/2009/034-09.shtml.

4. Ibid.

5. Rush Limbaugh, "Sebelius: Send Kids to School Despite Swine Flu or They'll Starve," last modified October 27, 2009, http://www.rushlimbaugh.com/home/daily/site_102709/content/01125114.guest.html.

6. Ann Landers, "In 1872, Teachers Had to Rough It," *Daytona Beach News-Journal*, November 11, 1989, 8B, http://news.google.com/newspapers?nid=1901&dat=19891111&id=SocfA

AAAIBAJ&sjid=d9IEAAAAIBAJ&pg=1239,2901701. Attributed to the Piedra Valley Parent-Teachers Association at San Mateo, NM, by the Alamosa (CO) *Valley Courier*.

Chapter 4

1. Levin, *Men in Black*, 42.
2. Barton, *Original Intent*, 189.
3. Ibid., 177.
4. Ibid., 164.
5. Ibid., 165.
6. Ibid., 29.
7. Richard G. Lee, *The American Patriot's Bible* (Nashville: Thomas Nelson, 2009), I–11.
8. "Issues to Watch," *World Magazine*, January 16, 2010, 49.
9. Dixy Lee Ray and Louis R. Guzzo, *Environmental Overkill: Whatever Happened to Common Sense?* (Washington, DC: Regnery Gateway, 1993), 32, 37.
10. "What is Glaciation? What Causes It?", NOAA Paleoclimatology, last modified January 28, 2003, http://www.ncdc.noaa.gov/paleo/glaciation.html.
11. "Global Climate Cooling Facts: The Global Climate Change Debate: The Facts," Climate Cooling, last modified July 2010, http://climatecooling.org.
12. "Sunspots and Climate Change: Is There a Connection Between Sunspot Activity and Global Cooling," Dennis Holley, *Suite101.com*, last modified July 22, 2009, http://www.suite101.com/content/sunspots-and-climate-change-a133866.
13. "As of 12/31, 2009: 11-Year U.S. Cooling Trend is Now -10.03°F Per Century," *C3 Headlines*, last modified January 2010, http://www.c3headlines.com/2010/01/as-of-december-31-2009-12-year-cooling-trend-is-now-1103f-per-century.html.

14. "Global Warming: Is It Actually 'Global'? Temperature Maps Say 'No' and BTW, Cooling Rules," *C3 Headlines*, accessed January 2010, http://www.c3headlines.com/global-cooling-dataevidencetrends.

15 "4000+ Years—Earth's Major Warming and Cooling Periods," *C3 Headlines*, last modified January 2010, http://c3headlines.typepad.com/.a/6a010536b58035970c0120a62f87f3970c-pi.

16. "The Global Climate Change Debate: The Facts."

17. "The Missing Sunspots: Is This the Big Chill?" David Whitehouse, *The Independent*, last modified April 27, 2009, http://www.independent.co.uk/news/science/the-missing-sunspots-is-this-the-big-chill-1674630.html.

18. "Must-See Global Warming TV," Steven Milloy, *FOX News*, last modified March 15, 2007, http://www.foxnews.com/printer_friendly_story/0,3566,258993,00.html.

19. "The Global Climate Change Debate: The Facts."

20. Ibid.

21. Holley, "Sunspots and Climate Change."

22. "Harvard Astrophysicist: Sunspot Activity Correlates to Global Climate Change," Rick C. Hodgin, *TG Daily*, last modified April 10, 2009, http://www.tgdaily.com/general-sciences-features/42006-harvard-astrophysicist-sunspot-activity-correlates-to-global-climate.

23. Dr. Kelvin Kemm, "Evidence of Sunspot Involvement in Climate Change Compelling," *An Honest Climate Debate* (blog), last modified October 31, 2008, http://anhonestclimatedebate.wordpress.com/2008/10/31/evidence-of-sunspot-involvement-in-climate-change-compelling/.

24. Holley, "Sunspots and Climate Change."

25. Hodgin, "Harvard Astrophysicist."

26. "The Global Climate Change Debate: The Facts."

27. "Coconuts in Wyoming," Steven Milloy, *FOX News*, last modified June 17, 2004, http://www.foxnews.com/printer_friendly_story/0,3566,123013,00.html
28. "The Sunspot Cycle," David H. Hathaway, National Aeronautics and Space Administration, last modified November 2, 2009, http://solarscience.msfc.nasa.gov/SunspotCycle.shtml.
29. Ibid.
30. Holley, "Sunspots and Climate Change."
31. Hathaway, "The Sunspot Cycle."
32. Holley, "Sunspots and Climate Change."
33. Whitehouse, "The Missing Sunspots."
34. Rush Limbaugh, "Martian Chronicles," *The Limbaugh Letter*, October 2005, 4.
35. Plato, *The Republic: The Complete and Unabridged Jowett Translation* (New York: Vintage Books, 1991), 124.
36. Ibid., 287.
37. Marvin Olasky, "Edwards and Adams," *World Magazine*, June 6, 2009, 22.
38. Rush Limbaugh, "Bulb Bull," *The Limbaugh Letter*, August 2008, 5.
39. "Cleaner-Burning Gasoline Without MTBE – October 3, 2000," California Environmental Protection Agency, Air Resources Board, last modified October 3, 2000, http://www.arb.ca.gov/fuels/gasoline/cbgmtbe.htm.
40. Rush Limbaugh, "What's That Smelt?" *The Limbaugh Letter*, January 2007, 5.
41. Rush Limbaugh, "When the Bat Hits the Fan," *The Limbaugh Letter*, May 2009, 4.
42. Rush Limbaugh, "Breaking Wind," *The Limbaugh Letter*, June 2009, 5.
43. Bailey, Kennedy, and Cohen, *The American Pageant*, 96.
44. Lee, *The American Patriot's Bible*, I–22.
45. Ibid.

46. Ibid., I–23.

47. Ibid., I–24.

48. Ibid., I–24.

49. Jamie Dean, "Catch and Release: Across the Country, Public School Students Are Going to Bible Studies—and It's Entirely Legal," *World Magazine*, November 21, 2009, 60, 62.

50. Ibid., 63.

Chapter 5

1   Marvin Olasky, "Political Catastrophe: Disaster Spending Surges in Election Years and Turn Citizens into Subjects," *World Magazine*, July 22, 2006, 40.

2. "Declared Disasters by Year or State," Federal Emergency Management Agency, last modified April 8, 2011, http://www.fema.gov/news/disaster_totals_annual.fema.

3. Plato, *Republic*, 395.

4. Ibid., 137.

5. Ibid., 111.

6. Ibid., 114.

7. "Fortune 500: Our annual ranking of America's largest corporations," *CNN Money*, last modified May 4, 2009, http://money.cnn.com/magazines/fortune/fortune500/2009/industries/21/index.html.

8. "Outrageous Fortune: How the Drug Industry Profits from Pills, A Report by the Alliance for Retired Americans Educational Fund," Dianna M. Porter, Alliance for Retired Americans Educational Fund, last modified August 2007, 21, http://www.retiredamericansfund.org/system/storage/78/de/9/21/outrageous_fortune.pdf.

9. "The Truth About Drug Companies," Peter Meredith, *Mother Jones*, last modified September 6, 2004, http://motherjones.com/politics/2004/09/truth-about-drug-companies.

10. "LA City Council Moves to Close Pot Dispensaries," Greg Risling, *Associated Press*, accessed January 20, 2010, http://www.newsmax.com/US/US-Medical-Marijuana-Los/2010/01/20/id/347412.

11. Jamie Dean and Edward Lee Pitts, "Abbey's Road," *World Magazine*, November 7, 2009, 34.

12. America's Affordable Health Choices Act of 2009, H.R. 3200, 111th Cong., Title IX, Section 1904, Subpart 3, Section 440 [2009], accessed March 1, 2011, http://www.opencongress.org/bill/111-h3200/text.

13. Ibid.

14. Ibid.

15. Ibid.

16. Ibid.

17. Ibid.

18. "Obama Signs SCHIP Legislation, Says Bill is 'First Step' Toward Universal Health Coverage," *Medical News Today*, last modified February 6, 2009, http://www.medicalnewstoday.com/articles/138122.php.

19. "Census 2000 Demographic Profile Highlights," United States Census Bureau, accessed February 28, 2010, http://factfinder.census.gov/servlet/SAFFFacts.

20. "The 2009 HHS Poverty Guidelines: One Version of the [U.S.] Federal Poverty Measure," US Department of Health and Human Services, last modified February 3, 2011, http://aspe.hhs.gov/poverty/09poverty.shtml.

21. America's Affordable Health Choices Act of 2009.

Chapter 6

1. Plato, *Republic*, 285.

2. Ibid., 286.

3. Ibid., 289.

4. Ibid., 289.
5. Ibid., 123–126, 159.
6. Ibid., 284.
7. Ibid., 87.
8. Ibid.,147, 160.
9. Ibid., 125, 149.
10. Plato, *Republic*, 205.
11. Ibid., 72.
12. Ibid., 358.
13. Ibid., 134.
14. Ibid., 130.
15. Ibid., 125.
16. Ibid., 113.
17. Ibid., 114.
18. Ibid., 117.
19. Ibid., 133.
20. Ibid., 185.
21. Ibid., 202.
22. Ibid., 202.
23. Ibid., 201.
24. Ibid., 332.
25. Ibid., 358.
26. *The NeverEnding Story*, directed by Wolfgang Peterson (Munich, Germany: Warner Brothers, 1984), DVD.
27. Plato, *Republic*, 201.
28. Ibid., 202.
29. Ibid., 290.
30. Ibid., 227.
31. "High School Dropout: A Quick Stats Fact Sheet," Maggie Monrad, National High School Center, last modified September 2007, 3, http://www.betterhighschools.org/docs/NHSC_DropoutFactSheet.pdf.
32. Ibid.

33. "Did Plato write 'Only the dead have seen the end of war'?", Bernard Suzanne, Plato and His Dialogues, last modified August 31, 2002, http://plato-dialogues.org/faq/faq008.htm. Attributed to Plato in the movie *Black Hawk Down* and on the wall of the Imperial War Museum in London. However, this phrase has not been located in any of Plato's writings. It is cited in George Santayana's "Soliloquies in England," Soliloquy #25, "Tipperary."

Chapter 7

1. Bailey, Kennedy, and Cohen, *The American Pageant,* 125–26.
2. Dave Meyer, "233 Years Young: Freedom Never Gets Old," *Enjoying Everyday Life,* June/July 2009, 27.
3. Plato, *Republic,* 261.
4. Meyer, "God's Hand," 13.
5. Peter Marshall and David Manuel, *Sounding Forth the Trumpet* (Grand Rapids, MI: Fleming H. Revell, 1997), 137.
6. Clinton Rossiter, *The Federalist Papers* (New York: Penguin Group, 1961), 50.
7. Ibid., 52.
8. Ibid., 50–53.
9. Bailey, Kennedy, and Cohen, *The American Pageant,* 451.
10. James M. McPherson, *Ordeal by Fire: The Civil War and Reconstruction* (New York: Alfred A. Knopf, 1982), 216.
11. Plato, *Republic,* 325.
12. Ibid., 321.
13. Ibid., 311; for conditions that permit the rise of a tyrant, see pp. 323–327, 336.
14. Ibid., 329.
15. Ibid., 331.
16. Ibid., 319.
17. Ibid., 318.

18. Ibid., 319.
19. Ibid., 320.
20. Ibid., 320.
21. Ibid., 323.
22. Ibid., 351–352.
23. Ibid., 317.
24. Ibid., 377.
25. Lee, *The American Patriot's Bible*, I–48.
26. Dave Meyer, "Imparting a Legacy of Liberty," *Enjoying Everyday Life*, November 2007, 12.

Chapter 8

1. Plato, *Republic*, 374–375.

Chapter 9

1. Joel C. Rosenberg, *Epicenter: Why the Current Rumblings in the Middle East Will Change Your Future* (Carol Stream, IL: Tyndale House, 2006), 132.
2. Lee, *The American Patriot's Bible*, I–5.
3. Ibid., I–6.
4. Ibid., I–6.
5. Ibid., I–7.
6. Paul Schenck and Rob Schenck, "Restoring America's Spiritual Health," *Enjoying Everyday Life*, March 2007, 10.
7. Lee, *The American Patriot's Bible*, 1058.
8. Rush Limbaugh, "Obama's Czars—Worst of the Worst," *The Limbaugh Letter*, November 2009, 13–15.

BIBLIOGRAPHY

"America's Forests, Liquidated." *Forest Voice*, Winter 2000.

Bahnsen, David. "Budget Buster: The High Cost of Education is Behind California Crisis." *World Magazine*, August 15, 2009.

Bailey, Thomas A., David M. Kennedy, and Lizabeth Cohen. *The American Pageant*. Boston: Houghton Mifflin, 1998.

Barton, David. *Original Intent: The Courts, the Constitution, and Religion*. Aledo, TX: Wall Builder Press, 2002.

Cass, Gary. "America's Tolerance Showdown." *Enjoying Everyday Life*, April 2008.

Dean, Jamie. "Catch and Release: Across the Country, Public School Students Are Going to Bible Studies--and It's Entirely Legal." *World Magazine*, November 21, 2009.

Dean, Jamie, and Edward Lee Pitts. "Abbey's Road." *World Magazine*, November 7, 2009.

"Issues to Watch." *World Magazine*, January 16, 2010.

King Jr., Martin Luther. *Why We Can't Wait*. New York: Penguin Group, 1964.

Lee, Richard G. *The American Patriot's Bible*. Nashville: Thomas Nelson, 2009.

Levin, Mark R. *Men in Black*. Washington, DC: Regnery, 2005.

Limbaugh, Rush. "Breaking Wind." *The Limbaugh Letter*, June 2009.

———. "Bulb Bull." *The Limbaugh Letter*, August 2008.

———. "Martian Chronicles." *The Limbaugh Letter*, October 2005.

———. "Obama's Czars—Worst of the Worst." *The Limbaugh Letter*, November 2009.

———. "Sebelius: Send Kids to School Despite Swine Flu or They'll Starve." *RushLimbaugh.com*, October 27, 2009.

———. "What's That Smelt?" *The Limbaugh Letter*, January 2007.

———. "When the Bat Hits the Fan." *The Limbaugh Letter*, May 2009.

Lincoln, Abraham. *Gettysburg Address*. November 19, 1863.

"Local School Division Policies for Changing Students' Course Schedules." Superintendents Memo, Number 52. Richmond, VA: Virginia Department of Education, March 7, 2008.

Marshall, Peter, and David Manuel. *Sounding Forth the Trumpet*. Grand Rapids, MI: Fleming H. Revell, 1997.

McGarvey, Robert. "America's Brainchild." *The American Legion*, September 2002.

McPherson, James M. *Ordeal by Fire: The Civil War and Reconstruction*. New York: Alfred A. Knopf, 1982.

Meyer, Dave. "God's Hand on Inauguration Day." *Enjoying Everyday Life*, December 2008/January 2009.

———. "Imparting a Legacy of Liberty." *Enjoying Everyday Life*, November 2007.

———. "233 Years Young: Freedom Never Gets Old." *Enjoying Everyday Life*, June/July 2009.

The NeverEnding Story. DVD. Directed by Wolfgang Peterson. Munich, Germany: Warner Brothers, 1984.

Olasky, Marvin. "Edwards and Adams." *World Magazine*, June 6, 2009.

———. "Opportunity Knocks Twice: Christians Can Help Shape the Next Great Era of American Journalism." *World Magazine*, October 24, 2009.

———. "Political Catastrophe: Disaster Spending Surges in Election Years and Turn Citizens into Subjects." *World Magazine*, July 22, 2006.

Plato. *The Republic: The Complete and Unabridged Jowett Translation.* New York: Vintage Books, 1991.

Ray, Dixy Lee, and Louis R. Guzzo. *Environmental Overkill: Whatever Happened to Common Sense?* Washington, DC: Regnery Gateway, 1993.

Rosenberg, Joel C. *Epicenter: Why the Current Rumblings in the Middle East Will Change Your Future.* Carol Stream, IL: Tyndale House, 2006.

Rossiter, Clinton. *The Federalist Papers.* New York: Penguin Group, 1961.

Schenck, Paul, and Rob Schenck. "Restoring America's Spiritual Health." *Enjoying Everyday Life*, March 2007.

Schweikart, Larry and Michael Allen. *A Patriot's History of the United States: From Columbus's Great Discovery to the War on Terror.* New York: Penguin Group, 2004.

Vincent, Lynn. "Reforming School Reform: Analysts and Lawmakers Try to Rescue No Child Left Behind." *World Magazine*, March 3, 2007.

Vodrey, William F. B. "George Washington: Hero of the Confederacy?" *American History*, October 2004.

West, M. L. *Hesiod: Theogony and Works and Days.* New York: Oxford University Press, 1988.

Wright, Patricia I. "National School Breakfast Week, March 2–6, 2009, and National Nutrition Month, March 2009." Superintendents Memo #034-09. Richmond, VA: Virginia Department of Education, February 13, 2009.

WinePressPublishing
Great Books, Defined.

CPSIA information can be obtained at www.ICGtesting.com
Printed in the USA
LVOW100429300312

275408LV00003B/37/P

9 781414 120324